The Harem Conspiracy

The HAREM CONSPIRACY
The Murder of Ramesses III

Susan Redford

*With an Historical Overview
by Donald B. Redford*

NORTHERN ILLINOIS UNIVERSITY PRESS / DEKALB

© 2002 by Northern Illinois University Press

Published by the Northern Illinois University Press, DeKalb, Illinois 60115

Manufactured in the United States using acid-free paper

All Rights Reserved

Design by Julia Fauci

Library of Congress Cataloging-in-Publication Data

Redford, Susan

The harem conspiracy : the murder of Ramesses III / Susan Redford.

   p.   cm.

Includes bibliographical references and index.

ISBN 0-87580-29508 (alk. paper)

1. Ramses III, King of Egypt—Death and burial. 2. Egypt—Politics and government—
To 332 B.C. 3. Harem—Egypt. I. Title.

DT88.8 .R44 2002

932'.014'092—dc21

[B]   200105140

For my sons ~ A.J. and Aksel

Contents

List of Illustrations and Tables   ix

Acknowledgments   xi

Egypt's Imperial Age: An Historical Overview *by Donald B. Redford*   xiii

INTRODUCTION   Evidence of a Conspiracy   3

1   Murder at Court   7

2   A House Divided   26

3   The Royal Harem   49

4   All the King's Men   72

5   Mansion of Millions of Years   89

6   "The Hawk Has Flown to Heaven"   105

7   "United with Eternity"   117

EPILOGUE   "Of Whom Is Pharaoh Still Master?"   133

Appendix A: Dramatis Personae   143

Appendix B: The Calendar   147

Notes   149

Bibliography   159

Index   169

Illustrations and Tables

ILLUSTRATIONS

1   Egypt in the Age of Ramesses III   2

2   Facsimile of Papyrus Rollin   4

3   Pharaoh Ramesses III Offers to Osiris   12

4   "The Mistress of the Two Lands, Ese"   33

5   The Valley of the Queens   36

6   Procession of Princes at the Ramesseum   39

7   Prince Amanakhopshaf   41

8   Titles of the Rival Heirs Apparent   42

9   An Unidentified Prince, Most Likely Pentawere   43

10   An Adolescent Prince Khaemwese   45

11   Women of the Royal Harem Serving the King   47

12   Daughters of Foreign Chieftains in the Harem of Amenhotep III   55

13   Queen Hatshepsut at Deir el Bahari   66

14   Court Official Censing before the King   82

15   View of Ramesses III's Temple Complex   95

16   The Eastern High-gate   96

17   Women of the Royal Harem Playing a Game with Ramesses III   97

18   The Window from Which the King Addressed His Court   101

19   Ground Plan of the Royal Palace   102

20   The Palace Audience Hall in the Days of Ramesses III   102

21   The Face of Ramesses III   108

22   Ruins of the Workers' Village at Deir el Medineh   109

23   The Sacred Bark Carried on the Shoulders of Priests   123

24   Temple Altar for Burnt Offerings at Karnak   125

25   Unidentified Mummy at Deir el Bahari   131

26   Inscription of the Name of Ramesses IV   135

27   Ramesses IX at Karnak Rewarding His High Priest   140

TABLES

1   Docket of the Accused   23

2   Ramesses' Family and the Line of Succession   48

Acknowledgmets

I owe thanks to several colleagues who offered valuable comments during the course of researching this book, in particular: Dr. Gay Robins, the late Mr. Charles Shute, Dr. Lynn Green, Dr. Richard Wilkinson, and Mr. Ted Brock. The director of antiquities on the west bank at Luxor, Dr. Mohammed el-Baily kindly granted me access to the harem rooms at Medinet Habu and tombs in the Valley of the Kings with permission to photograph. I am grateful to him and also to my friend and colleague, Inspector Yasser Youssef Achmed, who accompanied me to these sites and facilitated my work. Dr. Christian LeBlanc was most generous in allowing me to reproduce photographs of his work in the Valley of the Queens; likewise the Oriental Institute, the University of Chicago permitted me use of facsimile drawings and photographs for which I am very appreciative. I would also like to express my gratitude to Kevin Butterfield for his thorough copy editing and to Martin Johnson, my editor, for seeing my manuscript through to publication. Finally, above all, I am deeply indebted to my husband, Donald, who gave me the benefit of his invaluable insights and unfailing support. I have, nevertheless, sometimes overridden his sound advise and have presented interpretations here that are entirely my own; nor are they necessarily subscribed to by those mentioned above.

Egypt's Imperial Age

An Historical Overview

DONALD B. REDFORD

Ramesses III came to the throne as heir to four centuries of what we to-day would brand unabashed imperialism. This new age had begun for Egypt in the middle of the sixteenth century B.C. From approximately 1660 to 1550 B.C. Egypt suffered the indignity of a foreign regime that had established itself in the Nile Delta and exercised sovereignty over the Nile Valley as far south as Middle Egypt, about 300 miles south of the Mediterranean. The foreigners came from Canaan and spoke a language ancestral to later Phoenician and Hebrew. Although their leaders eventually displayed a veneer of Egyptian culture, they largely refused to assimilate. They introduced Asiatic forms of architecture, costume, and religion in the Nile Valley, and their general contempt for native ways coupled with heavy taxation made them odious to the Egyptians.

Eventually, in the middle of the sixteenth century B.C., a national movement took shape in Upper Egypt, bent on liberating the land. With the city of Thebes at the head, the Egyptians rose up and, over a period of about 15 years, succeeded in ridding the land of the hated Asiatics. By 1545 B.C. the land was free, independent, and about to embark on one of the most exciting experiments in empire the world had yet seen.

The Empire of the Eighteenth Dynasty

The family that led the movement of liberation, called by historians the Eighteenth Dynasty, donned the pharaonic accoutrements and pre-pared to secure Egypt's position in this brave new world. Apprehensive lest the Asiatics might reinvade or the kingdom of the Sudan might ex-pand northward, the Egyptian kings determined on a general strategy of preemptive strikes. Military campaigns were mounted on a regular basis up the Nile into Nubia and the Sudan, and by 1500 B.C. the Sudanese kingdom had been drastically weakened and much reduced in size. A generation later it had ceased to exist. Asia posed a more complex prob-lem for the pharaohs, and their steps were at first halting and tentative.

Western Asia at the close of the sixteenth century B.C. comprised a number of sophisticated and warlike metropolitan states. Those dotting the great arc known as the Fertile Crescent exercised a quasi-feudal authority over their areas. Most of them spoke a language loosely (and improperly) designated as Amorite and were culturally directly related to the conquerors of Egypt in the preceding century. Beyond the Euphrates River, in the fertile lands between the upper Tigris and Euphrates, there flourished an ancient community belonging to a different and non-Afro-Asiatic language group, the nation of the Hurri-warriors. These people had struck up a symbiotic relationship with a small elite group of chariot-owning Mitannians, who spoke an Indo-European language and had recently appeared in the area. The resultant amalgam created a vibrant, imaginative, and belligerent community, clearly destined for a major confrontation in the Middle East, for the Kingdom of Mitanni that resulted from the union conceived of its geopolitical role in terms of a thrust westward across the Euphrates to the Mediterranean and southeastern Anatolia, and southward into central Syria. It was the attempt to realize this "manifest destiny" that brought Mitanni and its Hurri-warriors into sharp conflict with Egypt.

As early as ca. 1520 B.C., Egypt had experienced a brush with Mitanni, but not until 1485 B.C. did the two powers become enmeshed in an escalating confrontation. In the following 50 years Mitanni's hand can be discerned behind the scenes, moving its "pawns" to the detriment of Egypt. In 1484 B.C., a coalition of Canaanite towns under the leadership of the king of Kadesh (a city on the Orontes River in central Syria) convened a military mustering at Megiddo, the fortress guarding the all-important pass through the Carmel Range in modern Israel. Since mastery of the pass meant a clean and speedy descent upon the Nile Delta, the gathering of these hostile forces was tantamount to a casus belli. A pharaoh of extraordinary military prowess named Thutmose III, who had just ascended the throne, struck quickly and at the battle of Megiddo, the biblical Armageddon, routed the Kadesh coalition. Over the subsequent 20 years Thutmose struck repeatedly, ever deeper into Syria, defeating Mitanni's proteges on the Phoenician coast and inland at Kadesh itself. In 1471 and 1469 Thutmose and his army fought their way to the banks of the Euphrates and, with the help of prefabricated assault craft that Thutmose had had the foresight to assemble, pursued the retreating Mitannians into Mesopotamia itself.

The result was hegemony. A war of liberation had become a military struggle for imperial expansion. Now the Egyptian frontier stood 700 miles from home, and never again would an Asiatic army descend with ease upon the Nile Valley. The Egyptian army, a militia of citizen conscripts during the war of liberation, had by the end of Thutmose III's reign achieved a professional standard capable of victory over Mitanni or any other power.

Perhaps it was the realization of the growing military strength of Egypt that caused Mitanni to change its policy. By 1420 the two monarchs had entered into negotiations, which led shortly to a peace treaty, a mutually recognized border, and a diplomatic marriage between a daughter of the Mitannian king and the king of Egypt. The result was half a century of peace.

By the middle of the fifteenth century an empire had taken shape extending from the fifth cataract on the Nile, scarcely 300 miles north of modern Khartoum, to the foothills of Anatolia in Asia, a tract of land today occupied in part by seven nation-states. The Egyptian empire remained remarkably durable, surviving for nearly 400 years. After its eventual demise, the communities of the ancient world could not shake the memory of Egypt's military and commercial might, and the myth of its invincibility lived on long after the reality had vanished.

The Administration of an Imperial Power

The Eighteenth Dynasty represents a return to the highly centralized and efficient state and society that all Egyptians in ancient times seemed to have yearned for. The "age of the pyramids," which was always considered as a model, utopian epoch, lay a thousand years in the past, its memorials, the pyramids and sphinx, already hoary tourist attractions. With the shadow of these monumental achievements ever in their gaze, the pharaohs created a civil service and a society proverbial for power, efficiency, and wealth.

Egypt now sat atop the world, with Pharaoh responsible for the hierarchical governance of mankind. In the Eighteenth Dynasty, that governance posed new responsibilities that Egypt had never encountered before and that evoked novel responses of organization. The two "provinces" of its great empire—now nearly 2,000 miles long—were organized on ad hoc lines. In the south the conquered Sudan received an administration cloned from that of Egypt. A viceroy, responsible to Pharaoh alone, presided over a civil administration that, like Egypt's, was divided into two territories, Wawat and Kush, occupying what today is the southernmost part of Egypt and the northern Sudan. Like the central administration, the Sudan had a treasury, department of agriculture, department of livestock, and a garrison. An annual tax was forwarded to Egypt, consisting of gold, gems, cattle, sub-Saharan produce, and a work force. In the north, by contrast, Pharaoh refrained from imposing a Egyptian system, preferring to allow the Canaanite and Syrian mayors and headmen to run their own towns, as they had done from time immemorial. Egypt required a few significant sacrifices: the dispatch of the mayors' sons to the Egyptian court, an oath in Pharaoh's name, and the payment of whatever taxes the itinerant Egyptian commissioners might assess. Occasionally Egyptian garrisons might be placed in towns deemed strategically important, especially those along major transit corridors; a few towns might be taken over completely as headquarters for Egyptian administrators. As in the Sudan, priority was given to produce and the labor force from the conquered territories, both of which were brought into Egypt in quantity.

Beyond the boundaries of empire Egypt's fiat was scarcely impaired. A sphere of influence stretched eastward into Iran, northward to the Black Sea, and westward to the Aegean and Greece. Merchants from these regions flocked to Egypt, paying substantial front money to Pharaoh to be allowed to trade. So rich had Egypt become that it began to dispense foreign aid, in the form of diplomatic gifts. Diplomatic marriages, of the sort contracted with Mitanni, now targeted Babylon, states in Anatolia, and North Syrian principalities, creating a network of mutual obligations by which the king of Egypt came to dominate the known world through peaceful means.

Ideology and Belief Systems: The Grand Experiment

At the height of its imperial power Egypt was shaken by an aberrant program of reform that threatened to bring the country to its knees. It is a measure of the strength of the imperial system that the monarchy survived. The actual effects of this near disaster are difficult to assess today, but one seems to be the strengthening of the imperial army.

Amenhotep III (1412–1375 B.C.) ruled an Egypt at the height of its power. "In Egypt gold is (as plentiful) as dust" ran the proverb of a reign in which monumental construction and sophistication in art were the hallmarks. With the increasing power of the empire, solar symbols and a sun-worshipping cult began to ascend as outward signs of celestial approbation. Sensitive to the sun's role in all things imperial, Amenhotep III dubbed himself "the Dazzling Sun-disk" and, by a lavish outlay of wealth, sought to live up to the role of the sun's earthly representation. By the time he died Egypt's entire belief system seemed fixated on solar imagery.

Amenhotep III's son and successor, Akhenaten, indulged in the drastic modification of Egypt's belief system by denying the existence of all gods but one, the Sun-disk; and to this sole deity he dedicated a number of large, open sun temples, decorated in a new, vibrant art style. Although his monotheism lasted scarcely twenty years and was anathematized by later generations, Akhenaten lived on in folk memory, and his art, though repudiated, exerted a subtle effect on future generations.

But Akhenaten left the country teetering on the brink of disaster. Temples had been abandoned, their endowments curtailed and their staffs disbanded. The army had become a law unto itself, high-handedly extracting goods and services from the peasantry while the tax department gouged imposts from the population at an unconscionable rate. At the same time a new power from central Anatolia, the Hittite kingdom, had begun to pursue an expansionist policy in North Syria, and Egypt proved powerless to stop them. Egypt's ally, Mitanni, was overwhelmed by the Hittites, who seemed poised to attack Egyptian territory.

In Egypt a discredited Eighteenth Dynasty passed into oblivion and was replaced by the army. Three generals in succession occupied the throne, the second of whom, Horemheb, effectually ended the Amarna period by dismantling the temples Akhenaten had erected and restoring the status quo ante. Not apparently having offspring himself, he appointed as his heir apparent a comrade-in-arms, the general Pa-Ramesses, who later suppressed the first element of his name and was thenceforward referred to as Ramesses.

The Age of the Ramessides

Under Ramesses, the upheaval of the religious revolution of Akhenaten gave way to a return to normalcy. Although his advanced age on the death of Horemheb did not allow a long reign, General Ramesses purposed to restore the dynastic principle, and he appointed his son, Sety, as his successor. With the resultant Nineteenth Dynasty, the era of the Ramessides had begun.

Sety and his son Ramesses II actively pursued a war with the Hittites over a period of 30 years. Although Ramesses once fell into an ambush at the abortive seige of Kadesh, he successfully extricated himself and, by dint of effort, eventually turned the tide in Egypt's favor. Nonetheless, as Ramesses' twentieth year approached, a stalemate had developed. Try as they might, the Hittites could not prevent the Egyptian forces from penetrating the Syrian hinterland; and, for their part, the Egyptians could never hope to bring war to the Hittite homeland in the mountains of Anatolia. To compound the problem, civil war had broken out among members of the Hittite royal family, and a rising power on the upper Tigris, the Assyrians, were looking avidly westward to expand into the territory of the weakened Hittite regime. Facing the prospect of a two-front war, the Hittite king Hattusilis opened peace negotiations with Ramesses II.

On the twenty-first day of the first winter month in the twenty-first year of Ramesses II, plenipotentiaries of Hattusilis arrived at the new capital city, Pi-Ramesses, which the king had built in the Delta. They came with the completed draft of a mutual nonaggression pact (surviving today in Akkadian copies and an Egyptian translation) that bound the signatories to a renunciation of hostilities and mutual assistance in the case of future wars involving third parties. The former boundaries between the two empires were reaffirmed, and special clauses ensured the extradition and proper treatment of fugitives. One paragraph bound Ramesses to act as the guarantor for Hattusilis's son and successor upon the Hittite throne, although Hattusilis was not obliged to reciprocate on behalf of Ramesses' heir. Copies of the treaty on clay tablets were exchanged by the two kings and solemnly deposited, with the appropriate royal seals, in the temples of the chief gods of the two lands.

This pact, which apparently was never abrogated as long as the Hittite Empire existed, opened a new era of good relations throughout the ancient world. The Akkadian and Hittite letters recovered by the German excavations at the Hittite capital Hattusas (Boghaz Keui in modern Turkey) help to delineate the colorful picture of postwar relations between Egypt and the Hittites, incidentally providing an intimate glimpse of the Egyptian pharaoh, Ramesses II, for a lively correspondence soon sprang up between the former enemies as well as several members of their families.

In the letters Ramesses appears an honest if humorless man, with a tendency to be impatient and to adopt a superior attitude. He regarded the oath with which he had sealed the treaty as permanently binding and in his letters constantly reminds the Hittite king of his adherence to the text:

> I have not broken the oath, I have kept the oath! Behold the tablet of the oath which I have made for you lies before the sun god of Arinna and before the great gods of the Khatte-land; they are the witnesses to the words of the oath that I have made you. And behold! The tablet of the oath that you made for me lies before the sun god of Heliopolis, and before the great gods of the land of Egypt; they are the witnesses to the words of the oath that you have made me.

In replying to a complaint by the son and successor of Hattusilis, Ramesses dictated the following petulant letter:

I have just heard all the words that my brother [the Hittite king, the recipient] wrote to me saying "Why did you, my brother, write to me as though I were a servant of yours?" Now [as for] what you wrote saying "As though I were a subject of yours . . ." I resent this word that my brother wrote to me. I am looking at you, and great things you have accomplished in all countries. Surely you are the great king of the countries of the Hittites, and the Sun god and the Storm god have allowed you to be seated in the place of your grandfather in the Hittite land. Why should I write to you as though to a subject? That I am your brother you must keep in mind. You should speak a word that makes a man happy. . . . Instead you write these meaningless words, not fit to serve for a message! I am your father's brother! Thus I have spoken!

Diplomatic niceties revolved around deeply felt considerations of respect for power, face-saving, and the honor of peer acceptance. Uncouth form in communication was always felt to indicate weakness and lack of success.

Thirteen years after the treaty was signed Ramesses married a Hittite princess. He had already acquired several foreign princesses in marriage, including a daughter of the king of Babylon, but his union with the Hittite royal house was deemed a striking diplomatic success. It is uncertain which of the two kings took the initiative in opening negotiations concerning the marriage, but once mooted the proposed nuptials had the enthusiastic support of Hattusilis. "Behold!" he wrote Ramesses, "as for the daughter that I shall give you, her dowry shall be greater than that of the daughter of the king of Babylon, or the daughter of the king of Barga. . . . Behold! I shall give my daughter attendants, cattle, sheep, and horses, and in this year I shall send them off. . . !" After some haggling over the bride-price and the spiteful detention of envoys (a common diplomatic insult in the ancient world), the princess and her entourage were dispatched to Egypt. Her mother, the Hittite queen, wrote a letter of remonstrance and well-wishing to Ramesses:

It is my patron deity as well as the sun goddess of Arinna, Teshup, Hepat, and Ishtar that have made me queen and united me with your brother in marriage; and I have produced both sons and daughters so that the Hittites speak of my exceptional fertility. . . . As for the daughter whom I am sending to my brother, may she likewise be endowed with an exceptional queenly fertility!

The fifty years following the Egypto-Hittite peace treaty witnessed a prosperity in Egypt that had rarely been seen before and set a social standard of organization that was to remain a pattern for centuries to come. At the summit of the pyramidal society of the time sat the figure of Pharaoh, son of the sun god Re, divinely "chosen" by the god to rule. It was very important that he conform, not only to the expectation of a being imbued with supernatural intelligence that overrode the caution advised by his counselors, but also to the model of a physically strong and handsome individual. As central pivot of the state, he must be a sportsman and a strong warrior, a virile man who can save Egypt on the battlefield. His queen and concubines occupied lesser positions but still enjoyed their own households and harems. Each of the royal children had a small entourage of four or five attendants assigned for their protection and education, which, in the case of the royal sons, usually involved extensive military training.

At Thebes, Memphis, and Pi-Ramesses large cities arose to house the hundreds of officials, craftsmen, clerks, domestics, and unskilled laborers required to operate the machinery of an imperial state. The best scions of many an old family of provincial noblemen gravitated from the countryside, so that the residence of the king became a veritable Versailles beside the Nile. At Thebes and Memphis huge necropolises gradually blossomed in the vicinity of the towns. The biographical inscriptions in many of these tombs are a major source of information for the religion and society of the empire.

Socioeconomic power depended on being a member of the king's immediate entourage. These grandees were drawn in the main from "children of the nursery," the king's own peer group that had grown up with him in the palace from childhood. Most of them bore the title "king's scribe" and constituted a sort of cabinet of the heads of departments of government. These included the vizierate, the treasury, the granaries, the stewardship of royal estates, the army, the priesthood, the viceroyalty of Kush, and the mayoralty of Memphis and Thebes. Constantly in receipt of royal rewards for good service, these noblemen possessed large landed estates and, occasionally, were allowed to engage in external trade and to correspond with their counterparts in foreign lands.

Beneath the nobility and providing the single most important mechanism for the running of the government was the secretariat. The scribal class was divided into civil and military cadres, both products of the writing schools founded long ago in the major cities of Egypt to supply the bureaucracy with scribes. Because of the indispensable function they performed, scribes enjoyed a certain degree of independence within the civil service. They never lacked a job and received a remuneration that enabled them to maintain a comfortable lifestyle.

Beginning in the second half of the Eighteenth Dynasty the priesthood of Egypt had become professional, involving within its structure whole families that monopolized posts for generations. "Ye shall bequeath your offices," said one high priest to his fellow priests, "to your descendants from father to son, in [the god's] house for ever!" The clergy had turned itself into a "closed shop," which provided the security of regular income and personal fulfillment to a limited segment of the population. The size of the clerical establishment was substantial, and temple estates accounted for a quarter of all the arable land in Egypt. Of this amount fully three-quarters was owned by the great temple of Amun at Thebes, which through Amun's role as national guarantor of the empire had become the repository for vast amounts of booty from foreign wars. Amun disposed of more than 86,000 chattels, owned half a million head of cattle, 433 orchards, 56 Egyptian towns, 9 Syrian towns, and maintained a merchant fleet of 83 ships on the Mediterranean.

For many young men, disinclined to wear the cloth, the romance of the soldier's life beckoned. Egypt now had a professional, standing army, centered upon its three elite corps of infantry, chariotry, and archers. If the military looked glamorous, however, the reality was something different. Recruits were pressed into the service at a young age, and the barracks training was tough if not brutal. Garrison duty abroad could mean isolation in a foreign country from four to six years at a time. In peacetime the professional soldier was given a small farm to support himself and his family; when war threatened, the ranks were filled out by taking one-in-ten of the unskilled labor of temple estates.

Powerful and well organized Pharaoh's administration might have been, but the land itself and its riches made up the basic wealth on which the imperial superstructure was built. Under the empire, landholding was all important. As in the Old Kingdom the dogma of kingship asserted that Egypt belonged in toto to the king. Such a tenet must have been difficult to infuse with meaning in a weakened Egypt, as it had been especially from 1660 to 1550 B.C., when the northern half of the country was occupied by an Asiatic regime, known commonly as the Hyksos. Upon expulsion of the Hyksos, the divine power of the king again became a reality. When the Delta and Middle Egypt fell to the conquering Thebans, much of it probably came into the hands of the royal family. Some of this was subsequently bestowed in the form of land grants upon temples and favored courtiers during the Eighteenth Dynasty, but a good deal was undoubtedly retained by the monarch. Thus the picture that emerges for us around 1200 B.C. is one of the king as a landowner, sharing most of the arable land in Egypt with the temples.

The Great Harris Papyrus, a record of Ramesses III's donations to the temples, and the Wilbour Papyrus, a tax assessor's journal from Middle Egypt, are the chief sources for land tenure and taxation in the period of the empire. Most of the arable land in Egypt during the twelfth century B.C. was the private preserve of a relatively small number of powerful institutions. Chief among these were the wealthy temple estates, of which the temple of Amun owned more land than all the others combined. Perhaps an equal amount of land comprised the landed estates of the king, "the fields of Pharaoh." Other royal land was divided into two types, *khato* and *mine* (perhaps land that for one reason or another had been abandoned or lacked an owner), and was administered either by controllers and stewards sent out by the king or by local mayors. The "House of the Queen" was a landowning institution of only slightly less importance, and the concubines and the royal harems scattered about the kingdom could also own land in their own right. The remainder of the cultivable land was held by private individuals, "freemen of Pharaoh's land," whose lot was often far worse than that of medieval serfs. The vast mass of cultivators at the bottom of the social pyramid, who worked the land on the great estates, comprised sharecroppers, prisoners of war, and convicted felons.

The theory of taxation in ancient Egypt lay in the moral obligation of every Egyptian to present some, if not all, the products of his labor to his lord. Guilds of artisans, workshops, harems, settlements of foreigners, cultivators on a farm—all were assessed collectively in a portion of their respective forms of labor, and this constituted their "tax quota." Theoretically the tax was due the king. In fact, however, it went to those many institutions dependent on the king, and they were empowered to collect it. For example, in a single fiscal year a temple might require 365 oxen for sacrifice, one victim being offered per day, together with quantities of vegetables and other edibles. The exact requirements of the shrine, correctly assessed for the coming year, made up the tax burden of the towns and fields attached to the temple, and all the artisans, farmers, and other collective units of production resident therein would have each to supply one or more oxen and a portion of the edibles for the year in question. Similarly, the supplying of quarrymen or foreign expeditions with food and necessities would be imposed as a tax quota upon selected districts at the behest of the king.

The tax quota, or levy, was not only exacted from the working class but from administrative officials of varying grades. There were also dues levied collectively on temple priesthoods. These were assessed in weights of copper, but could probably be paid in the equivalent perishables. A special tax of man hours of labor was the special burden of mayors and high priests who had to supply men for state construction projects.

All cultivable land, royal, ecclesiastical, or private, was obliged to pay a levy in grain. Records were kept of the height of the annual flooding according to the measurements of the nilometers, or graduated scales on vertical rock surfaces in the cataract regions of the Nile and elsewhere. Low water levels on the Nile were compensated for by lower taxes, and land closer to the river and therefore better irrigated was taxed more heavily than land bordering the desert. By consulting the height of the annual flood and the records of the arable land in each township, the scribes of the grain count could accurately estimate the amount of harvest due from every plot of ground in the country.

None of the prosperity latent in the rich soil of the Nile Valley could have been realized without the hard manual labor of the mass of the population, the rural peasantry. Augmented during the years of the empire by large numbers of captives from the wars in Asia, the farming population of Egypt acted by and large as sharecroppers working the fields for the large landowning institutions. Their lot was hard, their remuneration meager, yet it was their work that turned Egypt into the breadbasket of the ancient world.

The Close of the Nineteenth Dynasty

The accomplishments of the long-lived Ramesses II, "The Great," caused his memory to endure and his legend to thrive for hundreds of years. His immediate successors, by contrast, proved to be ineffectual and, at times, quite incompetent. Ramesses outlived his first twelve sons and was succeeded in about 1236 B.C. by his thirteenth, Merenptah, already a decrepit old man. Tragically, it was upon Merenptah that the blow fell. The Libyan tribes of the Labu and Meshwesh, in concert with certain piratical "Peoples of the Sea," at home in the Aegean, descended in force upon the western fringe of the Delta. Afflicted by a host of infirmities the aged Merenptah was scarcely able to rise from his bed, and the invaders were barely repelled by a supreme effort on the part of the military. Uncertainty as to the capabilities of the head of state gave rise to a spate of palace cabals, and when Merenptah passed away in 1225 B.C. the throne was seized by one Amenmesse who was himself swept away within months by a son(?) of Merenptah, Sety (II). Sety showed great energy in administration, both domestic and foreign, but he expired unexpectedly after a short reign of six years.

At this point there emerged from the ranks of the courtiers a chancellor named Beya, a Canaanite in origin who had worked his way up the administrative ladder. Perhaps in collusion with others of his ethnic community as well as a princess named Tawosret, Beya placed on the throne a certain Siptah, possibly a child of Sety. Examination of his mummy proves that Siptah had suffered from an attack of poliomyelitis. Throughout his brief reign he remained a figurehead only, and the Beya-Tawosret alliance ran the affairs of state to their own benefit. Beya even took it upon himself to correspond with foreign potentates and, when Siptah died, to elevate Tawosret to the throne as queen.

Many of the acts of the protagonists of this sorry period would have registered with Egyptians as gross breaches of tradition and etiquette. As the century drew to a close the prospect of a continued descent into in-competent administration by unacceptable scions of a once-great house forced "responsible" Egyptians to take action. Sethnakhte, of uncertain family but possibly a distant relative of the Ramessids through a cadet branch of the house, organized a counterrevolt. The details are un-known, but the outcome was certain. Here, with all the cryptic allusions and ambiguous remarks, is Sethnakhte's own statement:

> Since this land was in desolation and Egypt had drifted away from trusting in god, [this great god(?)] extended his hand, and chose [Sethnakhte] out of myriads, passing over hundreds of thousands ahead of him. . . . Now [he] was like his father Seth, [one who flexed] his arms in order to snatch Egypt from [him that had vio]lated her; his might was all-encompassing in protect-ing [her]. The [crim]inals he had to deal with, fear of him seized their hearts, and they fled like tits and sparrows with a falcon after them, having aban-doned the gold, silver, and [bronze] of Egypt, which they would have given to these Asiatics to bring about a quick victory for them; [for] the chief men of Egypt were disastrous conspirators and ineffectual plotters[?]. Then every god and every goddess manifested their oracle to the Perfect God (i.e., Seth-nakhte, now become king), proclaiming a bloody victory through him; and the gods pronounced their judgment at break of light . . .

Sethnakhte had rescued Egypt, and a new dynasty had taken power: a new day had dawned.

This was the world in which Sethnakhte's son, Ramesses III was born, lived, and died. He entered life destined for the kingship and remained at the pinnacle of society and power throughout.

The Harem Conspiracy

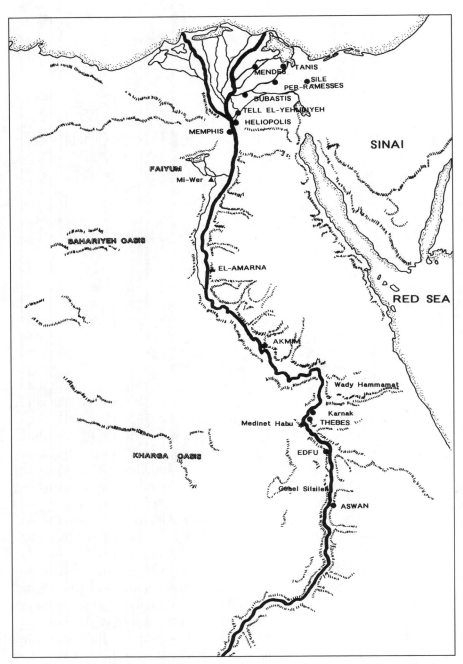

Egypt in the age of Ramesses III

Evidence of a Conspiracy

"Get people together! Incite hostilities in order to provoke rebellion against their lord." He caused a going forth against the royal bark and it was overturned. . . . These were capital offenses deserving of death, the great abominations of the land. . . .

—From the Judicial Papyrus of Turin,
Papyrus Rifaud, and Papyrus Rollin

Our knowledge of the harem conspiracy against Ramesses III comes down to us in a series of documents written on papyri nearly 3,000 years ago. Thought to be once a single book-roll, approximately 50 centimeters high and perhaps as much as five meters in length, it is now fragmented into several pieces.[1] The most complete and lengthy, referred to as the Judicial Papyrus of Turin, contains the actual court transcripts of the trial of those implicated in the conspiracy against the throne. This part of the book-roll is in good condition (except for the beginning, which is in tatters) and beautifully written with letters about 3 to 4 centimeters high and up to 5 centimeters of space between the horizontal lines. The other segments, which are not as well preserved, are investigatory accounts on several of the individuals involved. These fragments are today known as Papyrus Rollin, Papyrus Varzy, Papyrus Lee (1 and 2), Papyrus Rifaud I (A, B, and C), and Papyrus Rifaud II (E).

Unfortunately, the original order of the six surviving sections is unknown. The fragmentation of the original book-roll can no doubt be attributed to a greedy antiquities thief who deliberately cut the roll into pieces so as to realize more money by offering them to individual buyers. The thief appears to have taken some care to cut or tear the papyrus between the columns of text. The book-roll opened from right to left with the script reading in

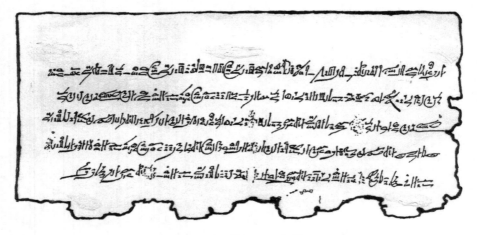

Facsimile of Papyrus Rollin

the same direction. The text is arranged in paragraph-type columns, which consisted of anywhere from 5 to 12 lines.

Apart from the official court record of the prosecution of the conspirators (the Judicial Papyrus of Turin), the investigative reports appear to be written in a specific format: After the introductory line, which states the name of the accused, the text then describes his deed and concludes with the court's verdict and sentencing. Unfortunately for historians, however, one report can straddle two columns: Papyrus Rollin preserves a complete column of five lines, which gives the deed and sentencing of one of the accused, but the beginning of the case report, which named the individual, was obviously in the preceding column, and that segment is lost.

The column of text preserved as Papyrus Varzy lacks an unknown number of words at the beginning of each line and has also suffered damage along the bottom line. But with this column one case ends and another begins, thus giving us information as to the name of the accused. Papyrus Lee consists of two fragments of papyri, each a separate column. The first fragment lacks the top of the column and with it the beginning of the case report containing the name of the accused. Because of their contexts, it appears that Papyrus Varzy breaks off where Papyrus Lee begins, and we may with some confidence fit the book-role together at this point.[2] The second fragment of Papyrus Lee is in much worse condition. It lacks the beginning third of each preserved line containing mainly the end of the report dealing with the verdict and sentencing of the unknown individual.

A major problem in undertaking a comprehensive study of these texts is that the actual documents referred to as Papyrus Rifaud I and Rifaud II have been lost, preserved only in a hand copy made by an early-nineteenth-century French explorer.[3] Unfortunately, J. J. Rifaud was not familiar with the script, and his hastily made copy poses innumerable problems. The original text, as with the other papyri, was written down in the cursive and abbreviated Egyptian script known as hieratic, a method of writing hieroglyphics used by Egyptian scribes in legal, epistolary, and personal documents. Deciphering an ancient scribe's sometimes unique penmanship is often difficult enough, but to do so only from a second-hand copy can be virtually impossible. Consequently, many words and passages, particularly in documents A, B, and C, defy translation.

Rifaud was employed in Egypt by a man named Bernardino Drovetti, whose position as the French consul general in the early 1800s enabled him to amass an incredible collection of antiquities. The Judicial Papyrus was among a number that Drovetti eventually sold to the king of Sardinia, and thence it came finally to reside in the Museo Egizio of Turin.[4] Papyri Rollin and Lee are named after their individual collectors. Papyrus Rollin is housed in the Paris Bibliothéque Nationale, and Papyrus Lee in the British Museum.[5]

It is important to stress that the book-roll was an official government record and as such looks at the event from one point of view to some extent. No information is given that would even remotely give cause for sympathizing with the conspirators. Nevertheless, together these texts relate information of a carefully planned coup d'état. While the details are scanty, they offer a window on a specific time in the distant past when the foundations of the great Nilotic civilization were rocked by a scandalous affair.

Informative and sensational as these documents are, an investigation of the king's reign and what life in Egypt was like during it is needed to understand fully and gain insight into this fascinating historical event. Many of the vital details were not written down or have simply not survived, but complementing straight translation with supporting archaeological evidence can help reconstruct the main elements of the case. The chapters in this book will address the who, why, where, and how of the murder of a pharaoh, striving to fill in the gaps left by Egyptian scribes and the haphazardness of preservation.

The documents of the "harem conspiracy" enjoy many translations by noted experts. The translations that appear in this book, however, are my own. Within the translated texts, bracketed words and ellipses represent gaps in the surviving text; information in parentheses has been added to elucidate the text for the reader. Moreover, with the exception of the name of Ramesses, I will purpose to avoid the later Hellenized version of those Egyptian personal names associated with the reign in favor of the contemporary twelfth-century vocalizations. Also, as a concession to the publishers, the popular spelling of the word *harem* has been used instead of the more correct, Turkish transliteration, *harim*. While the event itself and the identities of those involved have been the subject of much academic debate for almost a century, I offer in this book new, comprehensive interpretations of the case.

Murder at Court

It was a balmy evening in early April 1167 B.C., and the pharaoh Ramesses III was relaxing in one of the harem rooms, his favorite retreat at the royal palace. The evening's enjoyment consisted of sipping wine and playing senet[1] with lovely, young concubines, who were inmates of the royal harem. The old king was content and well satisfied with himself and sublimely unaware that he was about to meet his fate. Without hesitation the women made their long-awaited move to end the king's life and place one of their own choosing on the throne. An armed uprising within the palace ensued. Several of the guards on duty had been rendered inactive. However, the spontaneous popular revolt that had been planned did not materialize. The conspirators had badly miscalculated and were apprehended almost immediately, but the king lay dying.

Ramesses had been on the throne for more than 32 years before he was murdered. The assassination took place while he was residing in the ancient city of Thebes. The king lived most of his life in the capital city of Pi-Ramesses ("House of Ramesses"), located in the eastern Nile delta. A year or two before his death, however, he left the capital and moved more than 400 miles up the Nile to his southern residence on the west bank at Thebes. There, on the occasion of the anniversary of his coronation, while celebrating his long reign with the southern populace, the pharaoh's life came to an untimely end.

The court records tell us that it was the women of the king's own harem, led in particular by a queen named Teya, who initiated the plot to overthrow the king. Teya's son, Pentawere, whom they undoubtedly meant to place upon the throne, was drawn into his mother's plans with his full acquiescence. Later, at his trial "for making rebellion against his lord," the charges against him will read: "his collusion with Teya, his mother, when she was plotting those matters with the women of the harem, and for making rebellion against his lord" (Judicial Pap. 5:7). The idea of a rebellion against the throne was not translated into action until Teya enlisted the help of some court officials outside of the harem proper. A lowly pantry chief, whose name is given as Paibakamana, became Teya's main ally and a prime mover in the conspiracy. With the cooperation of some colleagues—a butler referred to as Mastesuria, an overseer of cattle named Panhayboni, and two administrators of the royal harem, Panouk and Pentau—the groundwork for the coup d'état was laid.

As the royal harem was the private domain of the king, the inmates were sequestered and the quarters declared off-limits to most staff and officials of the palace. With security tight, it was necessary to arrange communication surreptitiously between the harem personnel and their palace accomplices. This was particularly important if they were to garner support for their cause with relatives and the general public outside the palace walls. For this purpose, Panhayboni enlisted the aid of Pairy, the overseer of the king's treasury, to supply him with an entry pass. Once inside, black magic was used to mesmerize the guards so that messages could be relayed without detection.[2] Their messages were then passed "outside to their mothers and brothers who were there, saying: 'Get people together! Incite hostilities in order to provoke rebellion against their lord'" (Judicial Pap. 4:2). Magic was further employed as a means of making the king more vulnerable to attack and thus creating the opportunity to do more dastardly deeds than the transfer of messages: "Now when he effected an entry, the evil things which he was to do . . . were done" (Pap. Rollin 3).

Magic and sorcery played an integral role in Egyptian culture and religion, and the ancients believed in the power of the supernatural emphatically. The women of the harem and their accomplices felt that they could not even hope to succeed without it. Besides the rather mundane task of immobilizing the sentry, they had to remove a king from his throne—a man who by his position was in the full protective custody of the gods. Such an undertaking would require the help of some very powerful sorcerers. To that end, a court magician, Prekamenef, and the king's personal physician, an aristocrat named Iyroy, were induced to take part in the scheme. They in turn inveigled royal librarians, two scribes called Messui and Shotmaadje, who would be useful in securing necessary magical books from the king's library.

Except by innuendo, an attack on the king's person is not spoken of in the extant records. Recently, some scholars have expressed the belief that this incident should not be viewed as a conspiracy aimed personally at

Ramesses III at all, but rather as an attempt to wrest the kingship from the crown prince upon the death of the king.[3] Certainly, it was meant to do the latter, but the time frame of the revolt and various statements made in the trial transcripts and other reports indicate clearly that the conspirators meant the king to die. A supervisor's daybook from a nearby community of royal labor crews reports that work was disrupted for a few days owing to an uprising two and a half weeks before the king's death. This can only be linked to the event referred to in the criminal charges as worded in the court transcripts, i.e., "incite hostilities in order to make rebellion against their lord" (Judicial Pap. 4:2). The implication, therefore, is that the plan was to unseat Ramesses III, not Ramesses IV. It is certain that Ramesses III was still alive to see the criminals apprehended, for it is he who appointed the magistrates who would be put in charge of the legal proceedings. However, he passed away before the trials commenced; he is repeatedly referred to in the written accounts as "the great god" (Pap. Lee 1:3), a term applied only to deceased kings. Furthermore, the king, himself, "says" in a posthumous statement to the court with regard to the prosecution of the criminals that he is now in the company of Osiris, the Egyptian god of the dead. There is no statement that the king died as a result of the conspiracy, but that omission reflects the Egyptians' reluctance to admit that—even though it is repeatedly mentioned that the sun god and protective deity of the kingship, Re, did not sanction the criminals—their gods did, in fact, allow the conspirators some success. One passage not only alludes to an attempt on the king's life but that it was carried through to completion: "he helped them go forth against the royal bark, and it was overturned" (Pap. Rifaud A:3). While it is possible the statement is a literal description of an incident perpetrated by the conspirators, it is more likely that the term "royal bark" is to be interpreted as a metonym for the kingship, much as the presidency of the United States can be referred to as "the White House."

The planned conspiracy was twofold: after the removal of the old king, an armed revolt was to take over the palace in order to displace the heir apparent. The conspirators were obviously confident that the acquiescence of the general populace would follow. The loyalty of members of the military was secured for this purpose: we hear of an army general, Pasai, and a battalion commander, Bonemwese, whose sister, an inmate of the royal harem, was obviously instrumental in his involvement. After what was probably months of surreptitiously sowing the seeds of a rebellion among family members, friends, and military personnel who served under them, they were ready to make their move. "He [Pasai] caused an uprising, which he made fierce" (Pap. Rifaud A:4).

But the uprising did not gain momentum. The attempted coup was quickly and thoroughly squashed, the perpetrators arrested and arraigned before a tribunal handpicked by the dying king.

While in detention, the former general Pasai and some of the others awaiting trial made a move to win favor with two of the judges. Put in the charge of a corrupt chief of police and court bailiff, who were probably former colleagues of the military commander, the inmates were able to arrange a clandestine meeting with two of the appointed magistrates, Mai and Pabasa: "The women went and visited them in the place where they were. There they caroused with them and with Pasai" (Judicial Pap. 6:1). They were found out, and the unethical officials were remanded into custody.

The court transcripts deal with the prosecution of all the persons drawn into the conspiracy, except for Teya and the women of the royal harem. We are never told how many harem women were involved or what their names are. As for the others, the texts disclose a roster of 27 men and 6 women who were arraigned on charges of high treason, plus another 5 men who were indicted for corruption. The surviving investigative reports focus on certain men who appear to have had pivotal roles in the plot to overthrow the king. The men's machinations, said to be done in collaboration with Teya and the women of the harem, were described as being responsible for the magical intervention for the success of the plan and for gaining popular support for and actually carrying out an armed rebellion meant to coincide with the death of the king. The lack of any account of an assassination attempt on the king's life in any of these preserved documents signifies that it was not the men's charge to do away with the king. There is no record of a trial for Teya and the harem women; no dossiers describe their crimes. It is quite possible that this stage of the insurrection, which called for the attempted assassination of the king, or at least a hastening of his death, was undertaken by Teya and her harem friends. Whether the king died as a direct result of an attack upon his person remains unclear, but the trauma of the harem's attempt no doubt contributed to his imminent demise.

The proceedings of the court offer indirect but important clues about the implementation of the plan to overthrow the king and seize the throne. The accused were arraigned in four groups, reflecting the way in which the trial or trials were conducted and the sentencing of the condemned. Before passing away, Ramesses III himself initiated the prosecution of the criminals and appointed twelve judges:[4]

(Judicial Pap. 1:1) [King Wasmuaria-Miamana, life, prosperity, and health, son of Re, Ramesses], Ruler of Heliopolis, [life, prosperity, and health, said] [................] (1:2) [..] the land [..........] (1:3) [......] the whole land (1:4) [................] their cattle. (1:5) [.......] to bring them. (1:6) [.......] everything [.............] in their presence. (1:7) [................] bringing them; while the (1:8) [.........] people, saying: [......] (1:9) [...........] while it is they who are (2:1) the abomination of the land, and I am commanding

the overseer of the treasury, Mantemtowa;

the overseer of the treasury, Pefrawa;

(2:2) the standard-bearer, Kara;

the butler, Pabasa;

the butler, Kedendenna;

the butler, Maharbaal;

(2:3) the butler, Paerswana;

the butler, Djehuty-rekh-nafa;

the king's herald, Parennuta;

the scribe, Mai;

(2:4) the scribe of the archives, Pre-emheb; and

the standard-bearer of the standing army, Hori,

(2:5) to wit: "As for the statements which the people made, I don't know anything about them. Proceed. (2:6) And they will go and they will examine them and they will allow the one whom they would put to death to die by their own hands (2:7) while I am oblivious to it. They shall execute punishment upon the others, likewise while I am oblivious to it. (2:8) For I have charged them (the court) very strictly saying: 'Be careful, and guard yourself from allowing (2:9) people to be punished by a magistrate wrongfully when undeserved.' To them I have said again and again. (3:1) As for whatever has been done; it is they that did it, (3:2) let whatever they have done fall upon their [own] heads; (3:3) while I am immune and protected forever, (3:4) while I am among the justified kings who are before (3:5) Amun-Re, king of the gods, and before Osiris, Ruler of eternity."

Of the 12, 6 magistrates preside over the arraignment of the first group of 21 persons. Individually they were granted a hearing, which was duly recorded:

(Judicial Pap. 4:1) Persons arraigned for the great crimes they had committed and placed in the Court of Examination before the great magistrates of the Court of Examination in order to be examined by

the overseer of the treasury, Mantemtowa;

the overseer of the treasury, Pefrawa;

Pharaoh Ramesses III offers to Osiris, the Egyptian god of the dead,
in a mural from his tomb in the Valley of the Kings.

the standard-bearer, Kara;

the butler, Pabasa;

the scribe of the archives, Mai; and

the standard-bearer, Hori.

They examined them; they found them guilty; they brought their punishment upon them; their crimes caught up with them.

(4:2) The great criminal, Paibakamana, formerly pantry chief.

He was arraigned because of his collusion with Teya and the women of the harem. He made common cause with them and began bearing their messages outside to their mothers and their brothers who were there, saying: "Get people together! Incite hostilities in order to provoke rebellion against their lord." He was placed before the great magistrates of the Court of Examination. They examined his crimes, and they found that he had committed them. His crimes caught up with him; the magistrates who had examined him caused that his punishment be executed upon him.

(4:3) The great criminal, Mastesuria, formerly butler. He was arraigned because of his collusion with Paibakamana, formerly pantry chief, and with the women, in order to assemble enemies to provoke rebellion against their lord. He was placed before the great magistrates of the Court of Examination. They examined his crimes, and they found him guilty. They caused that his punishment be executed upon him.

(4:4) The great criminal, Panouk, formerly superintendent of the royal harem of the house of the harem inmates in the retinue. He was arraigned because he had made common cause with Paibakamana and Mastesuria to provoke rebellion against their lord. He was placed before the great magistrates of the Court of Examination. They examined his crimes, and they found him guilty. They caused that his punishment be executed upon him.

(4:5) The great criminal, Pentau, formerly scribe of the royal harem of the house of the harem inmates in the king's retinue. He was arraigned because he had made common cause with Paibakamana, Mastesuria, and the (above-named) criminal, who was formerly superintendent of the royal harem of the house of the harem inmates in the retinue, and the women of the harem in order to plot with them to provoke rebellion against their lord. He was placed before the great magistrates of the Court of Examination. They examined his crimes, and they found him guilty. They caused that his punishment be executed upon him.

(4:6) The great criminal, Petewentamana, formerly agent of the harem in the retinue. He was arraigned because of his having overheard the matters the men had plotted with the women of the harem, and he had not come forward on their account. He was placed before the great magistrates of the Court of Examination. They examined his crimes, and they found him guilty. They caused that his punishment be executed upon him.

(4:7) The great criminal, Karpusa, formerly agent of the harem in the retinue. He was arraigned because he had overheard the words but concealed them. He was placed before the magistrates of the Court of Examination. They found him guilty, and they caused that his punishment be executed upon him.

(4:8) The great criminal, Khaemope, formerly agent of the harem in the retinue. He was arraigned because he had overheard the words but concealed them. He was placed before the magistrates of the Court of Examination. They found him guilty, and they caused that his punishment be executed upon him.

(4:9) The great criminal, Khaemmalu, formerly agent of the harem in the retinue. He was arraigned because he had overheard the words but concealed them. He was placed before the magistrates of the Court of Examination. They found him guilty, and they caused that his punishment be executed upon him.

(4:10) The great criminal, Sutempidjehuty, formerly agent of the harem in the retinue. He was arraigned because he had overheard the words but concealed them. He was placed before the magistrates of the Court of Examination. They found him guilty, and they caused that his punishment be executed upon him.

(4:11) The great criminal, Sutempiamana, formerly agent of the harem in the retinue. He was arraigned because he had overheard the words but concealed them. He was placed before the magistrates of the Court of Examination. They found him guilty, and they caused that his punishment be executed upon him.

(4:12) The great criminal, Warona, who was formerly butler. He was arraigned because of his hearing the conversation with the pantry chief. He was [standing] near to him, but he concealed them and did not report them. He was placed before the magistrates of the Court of Examination. They found him guilty, and they caused that his punishment be executed upon him.

(4:13) The great criminal, Ashhebsat, formerly assistant of Paibakamana. He was arraigned because of his having heard the conversation with Paibakamana, although he was [standing] far off from him, and he did not report it. He was placed before the magistrates of the Court of Examination. They found him guilty, and they caused that his punishment be executed upon him.

(4:14) The great criminal, Peluka, formerly butler and scribe of the treasury. He was arraigned because of his collusion with Paibakamana; he heard the conversation with him but did not report it. He was placed before the magistrates of the Court of Examination. They found him guilty, and they caused that his punishment be executed upon him.

(4:15) The great criminal, the Libyan, Yeniny, formerly butler. He was arraigned because of his collusion with Paibakamana, when he heard the conversation with him, but did not report it. He was placed before the magistrates of the Court of Examination. They found him guilty, and they caused that his punishment be executed upon him.

(5:1) Wives of the men of the harem gate, who sided with those men who were plotting those things. They were placed before the magistrates of the Court of Examination. They found them guilty, and they caused that their punishment be executed upon them. Total: six women.

(5:2) The great criminal, Pairy, son of Ruma, formerly superintendent of the treasury. He was arraigned because of his collusion with the great criminal, Panhayboni. He made common cause with him in order to incite enemies to provoke rebellion against their lord. He was placed before the magistrates of the Court of Examination. They found him guilty, and they caused that his punishment be executed upon him.

Five men, the pantry chief, Paibakamana; the butler, Mastesuria; the superintendent of the royal harem, Panouk; the scribe of the royal harem, Pentau; and the superintendent of the treasury, Pairy, were indicted for actively inciting rebellion. They were charged either directly or indirectly with collusion with the harem women in treasonous activities. The 16 others, 10 men and 6 women, were prosecuted more or less as sympathizers, including 4 men who were assistants or colleagues from the same palace departments as the 5 previously cited. Also charged, with knowing of the plot to overthrow the king but doing nothing about it, were 6 men who were posted at the harem gate and their wives. All are found guilty and sentenced to be executed.

The indictment of one other person was recorded last in this grouping of men and women:

> (Judicial Pap. 5:3) The great criminal, Bonemwese, formerly battalion commander of Kush. He was arraigned because of the dispatch his sister, who is in the retinue of the harem, had written to him, saying, "Collect people to make war, and come to make rebellion against your lord." He was placed before Kedendenna, Maharbaal, Paerswana, and Djehuty-rekh-nafa. They examined him, they found him guilty, and they caused that his punishment be executed upon him.

Bonemwese was likewise charged with inciting rebellion, but, for reasons that shall be explained later, he was not tried in the same public courtroom as the others. His testimony, instead, was heard privately by four of the judges who held the title of royal butler. Regardless, Bonemwese received the same judgment as his compatriots.

The second arraignment dealt with the prosecution of six men:

> (Judicial Pap. 5:4) Persons arraigned because of their crimes, in colluding with Paibakamana, Pasai, and Pentawere. They were placed before the magistrates of the Court of Examination; they found them guilty; they left them in their own hands in the Court of Examination; they took their own lives; nobody laid a hand on them:
> (5:5) the great criminal, Pasai, formerly overseer of the army;
> the great criminal, Messui, formerly scribe of the House of Life;
> the great criminal, Prekamenef, formerly magician;
> the great criminal, Iyroy, formerly overseer of the priests of Sehkmet;
> the great criminal, Nibdjatfe, formerly butler; and
> the great criminal, Shotmaadje, formerly scribe of the House of Life.
> Total: 6.

From their titles alone, we can ascertain that it was the job of at least four of these men to ensure the success of the action by magical endeavors. The documents tie them directly to the maneuvers of Paibakamana, Pasai, and Pentawere, but there is no mention of any direct link with Teya and the harem women.

At the forefront of the third arraignment stands Teya's son, Pentawere.

> (Judicial Pap. 5:6) Persons arraigned because of their crimes to the Court of Examination, before Kedendenna, Maharbaal, Paerswana, Djehuty-rekh-nafa, and Mayatas-amana. They examined them concerning their crimes; they found them guilty; they left them alone; they took their own lives:
> (5:7) Pentawere, who bore that other name. He was brought in because of his collusion with Teya, his mother, when she was plotting those matters with the women of the harem, and for making rebellion against his lord. He was placed before the judges, in order to be examined; they found him guilty; they left him alone; he took his own life.
> (5:8) The great criminal, Hnetenamana, formerly butler. He was arraigned for the crimes of the women of the harem. He was among them and heard them, and he did not report them. He was placed before the judges, in order to be examined; they found him guilty; they left him on the spot and he took his own life.
> (5:9) The great criminal, Amankhau, formerly deputy of the royal harem in the retinue. He was arraigned because of the crimes of the women of the harem. He was among them and heard them, and he did not report them.

He was placed before the judges, in order to be examined; they found him guilty; they left him on the spot and he took his own life.

(5:10) The great criminal, Pairy, formerly scribe of the royal harem in the retinue. He was arraigned because of the crimes of the women of the harem. He was among them and heard them, and he did not report them. He was placed before the judges, in order to be examined; they found him guilty; they left him alone; he took his own life.

Pentawere and three sympathizers, all of whom in some aspect had direct contact with the harem women, were tried by the same panel of royal butlers (with the addition of one other) as Bonemwese. It would appear that, just before the proceeding, three magistrates were arrested for corruption and another, Mayatas-amana, appointed in their place. Like the accused of the first prosecution, the men of the second and third arraignments were convicted of the crimes charged them, but they were instead sentenced to die by their own hand.

The charges against the accused of the fourth and final arraignment read as follows:

(Judicial Pap. 6:1) Persons punished by cutting off their noses and their ears because they had forsaken the good instructions given to them. The women went and visited them in the place where they were. There they caroused with them and with Pasai. They were caught:

(6:2) This great criminal, Pabasa, formerly butler. This punishment was executed upon him; (but when) he was left alone, he took his own life.

(6:3) The great criminal, Mai, formerly scribe.

(6:4) The great criminal, Taynakhte, formerly bailiff.

(6:5) The great criminal, Naneu, formerly police chief.

(6:6) The person who was going along with them. He was reprimanded severely and was then acquitted; no harm was done to him.

(6:7) The great criminal, Hori, formerly standard-bearer of the standing army.

Following the description of the prosecution of the conspirators, the Judicial Papyrus tells that two court bailiffs and three of the king's appointed magistrates had been caught fraternizing with the prisoners. Of the five men indicted, only one, the standard-bearer, Hori, was acquitted. The others were sentenced to bear their disgrace for the rest of their lives.

Before their trial, many, if not all, of the persons implicated in the conspiracy against the crown underwent intense scrutiny and questioning by state prosecutors and police. The results of their investigation were written down to complete the legal, archival compendium of the whole treasonous affair. Unfortunately, only a few of these reports have survived, and further deterioration of the papyri has denied us the names of the individuals on whom they focus. Still, they provide us with fascinating glimpses of the turn of events.

> (Pap. Rollin) [......Name of accused missing...] (1) He began to prepare magical texts for the purpose of confusing and disturbing, and to make waxen (figures) of some gods and some potions[5] for disabling the limbs of people. (2) They were put into the hand of Paibakamana—Re did not allow him to be pantry chief!—and the other great criminals, saying, "Take them inside," and they took (3) them inside. Now when he effected an entry, the evil things he was to do—but which Re did not allow him to succeed in—were done. He was examined and there was truth in every crime and (4) every evil act his mind planned to do. There was truth in them, and he had committed them together with the other great criminals of his sort. They were capital offenses (5) deserving of death, the great abominations of the land were that which he had done. Now when he realized that these were capital offenses deserving of death that he had committed, he killed himself.[6]

This is the first source that reports the use of black magic in the conspiracy. Magical waxen figures and potions were manufactured for immobilizing people within the palace walls. Those involved with this phase of the plan were presumably expected to dispose of the king's armed guard. The concern shown on the part of the scribes in even recording the perpetrators use of magical procedures is apparent. Insertions were made twice within the dossier to nullify any potent effects the written word might produce: Paibakamana's tenure in office and the evil deeds he carried out were magically obliterated by simple statements that the god Re did not sanction them.

> (Pap. Varzy) [...Name of accused missing...] (1) [........] and he caused the branding irons to be effaced, and then he snatched the palette in his hand and he made a rwd-sign with a iwnw-sign inside it. (2) [.........] It was with this branding iron that says rwd-iwnw that you branded all my cattle. Let it be known that the nature of the branding mark (3) (is such):

> (1) [Sutemhab][7] is the name that Pharaoh, his lord, gave him, but it is the name of a servant of a commoner he had (i.e., he was born with). And

he[8] (Papyrus Lee 1) [was made to take an oath] of the lord, life, prosperity, and health, of loyalty every [time saying: "I did not give] (2) any document from my office[9] to anyone in the country!" But when Panhayboni, who was formerly overseer of herds said to him: "Give me a document for granting me authority and respect," (3) he did (indeed) give him an (official) paper of Wasmuaria-Miamana, the great god, his lord, life, prosperity, and health. And he began (the ritual) of consulting the divine oracle[10] so to delude people. (But) he reached the side (4) of the harem of that other great, expansive place, and he began to use the inscribed waxen figures in order that they be taken inside by the inspector Adi-ram, (5) for staving off one gang of men and spellbinding the others, so that a few messages could be taken in and others brought out. Now when he was examined (6) concerning them, the truth was found in every charge and every evil (act) his mind concocted. There was truth in (the charges) and he did them all, together with the (7) other great villains, who are the abomination of every god and every goddess entirely. The great punishments of death were done to him about which the gods said, "Do them to him."

The partially shredded Papyrus Varzy reports on the embezzlement of the king's cattle. The guilty party was apparently in a position to oversee the branding of the royal herds and, by changing the branding iron itself, was easily able to syphon off a certain number of head without anyone gainsaying him—at least for a while. But what did the theft have to do with the overthrow of the king? It might be that the cattle was a means of bribing others to follow their lead.

The last line of the papyrus fragment ties in neatly with the beginning of Papyrus Lee 1, thus forming a complete dossier. Two important pieces of information are divulged: the methods utilized (and the magic was undoubtedly expected to be effective) in facilitating communication between those within the palace with supporters on the outside, and the access granted to one who, for nefarious reasons, sought to consult the divine oracle.

(Pap. Lee 2) [...Name of accused missing...] (1) [.........] among those [.....] in the container. And he went off [...half a line missing...] his hand limp. Now as for (2) [every crime and every evil he did, he was examined concerning] them, the truth was found in every charge and every evil that his mind concocted. There was truth (3) [in (the charges), and he did them all, together with the other] great villains, who are the abomination of every god and every goddess entirely. They were capital offenses deserving of death, the great abominations of (4) [the land were the things he had done. Now, when he realized that these were] capital [offence]s deserving of death that he had committed, he killed himself. Now when the officials who were in charge of him saw that he had killed himself, (5) [no punishment was exacted upon him, the abomination of] Re entirely, for which the divine decrees say, "Do it to him."

As much as half of this account is missing, leaving us with only tantalizing bits, such as a container of some sort being utilized to effect some sinister deed.

(Pap. Rifaud A) [.....Name of accused missing...] (1) [...] and he [came to prominence through] the power of the Lord of the Two Lands, Wasmuaria-Miamana, life, prosperity, and health, the great god, and he did all sorts of good things for him everyday. He made him overseer of the army [...] a great official of the land. The king, Wasmuaria-Miamana, life, prosperity, and health, (2) the great god, his lord, gave him very many [favors]. He gave him temples[11] and he bestowed upon him the commission, but he did not do his duty. In spite of the many good things the king, Wasmuaria-Miamana, the great god, had done for him, (3) he attached himself to those other great villains, and as a great official of the land he caused a going forth against the royal bark and it was overturned. He forgot the many good things the king, Wasmuaria-Miamana, life, prosperity, and health, had done for him. (4) He caused an uprising, which he made fierce and [.....] like Sekhmet. [He committed] those crimes, the abomination of the great gods of the land, in forming a conspiracy against his lord, life, prosperity, and health, who made him (5) and the other criminal of his sort. He began to overturn the protections together with the other great criminals of his sort, (namely) the one whom Re did not authorize to become pantry chief, and the one whom (6) Re did not authorize to become the overseer of the [.....] of the treasury of Sekhmet, while they contended (legally) with [Paba]sa, the other great criminal of his sort. He began to overturn the protections. (7) He ignored the good things that were done for him. He performed the work of his father [......] Mahu, [.......], the great god [........] the king, Wasmuaria-Miamana, he being a scribe (8) [who made a conspiracy] against his lord, life, prosperity, and health, who made him and who created his office. He forgot the many kindnesses Wasmuaria-Miamana, life, prosperity, and health, the great god, (9) his lord, life, prosperity, and health, had done for him [and the other great criminals of his sort, (namely)] the one whom Re did not authorize to become pantry chief, and the one for whom Re did not allow the land to rebel. . . .

The military-led, armed rebellion that ensued as part of the plan to unseat the king is here revealed by the royal archivists for the first and only time. The overturning of the royal bark may be a reference to an attack on the king's person, presented in terms obscure enough to be acceptable for the official record.

(Pap. Rifaud B) [...Name of the accused missing...] (1) "[....] the one who with the child of a townsman [....] for the one whom Re did not authorize to become [....] (2) [.....] He gave to him his daughter for wife, he being a criminal of [.....] He acted, he made for himself a good name (3) [...] And he united with them [against his] lord, life, prosperity, and health. He gave to him a few of their sort. (4) [...], he acting in the capacity of overseer of the priests of Sekhmet, mistress of [....] After they contended with [.....] (5) [...] and he commanded him as the overseer of priests of Sekhmet [...], while leading (6) [....] the other great villains of his sort. The crimes, the great abomination [of all the gods of the land....], (7) [....] the other villains and this other great criminal of their sort [.....]" [remainder lost]

A relationship through marriage between two of the conspirators is the only substantial piece of information hitherto unrecorded that can be salvaged from the undecipherable script of this section.

(Pap. Rifaud C) (1) [Bon]emwese, he being the overseer of the Medjay[12] [and he achieved] a good lifetime. He exercised his command of the warriors therein it and he attained old age. (2) [.... He] transgressed [against the] great [gods] of the land [......] see [......] overseer of the priests [........] of Amun [.....] the overseer [....] (3) [......] of Pre to the place although its name is not known. He was made by the king, Wasmuaria-Miamana, life, prosperity, and health, the great god, the father of the king (4) [......] the [chambers?] of the house of life [........] and he entered and he found the writings of his father. The battalion commander, he dwelling in [.....] (5) [.....] the agent and the chief of the Medjay who gave to him the *hk3w*[13] documents and he saw his lord, life, prosperity, and health, and he [feared] and he gave him a few of that sort [......] (6) [.......the other great criminal of his sort, namely the one] whom Re did not authorize to become overseer of the priests of (7) Sekhmet [......][14]

The incomprehensible secondhand copying of this document leaves only a tantalizing glimpse of a perhaps unexpected encounter between the accused and the king. At the end of the second line, the scribe refers to Ramesses III as the "father of the king," further proof that a successful regicide did occur and confirming that, by the time of the trials, a new king, Ramesses IV, had ascended the throne.

(Pap. Rifaud E)[15] (1) "The great criminal, destitute and deprived of his name, the butler Maadje whom Re did not authorize to become scribe of the house of life!—small and insignificant. (2) That which Ramesses III, life, prosperity, and health, the great god, his lord, did for him when he was a scribe of the house of life, small and insignificant: (3) he procured him his sustenance, and he procured for him all that was good in the land. He made him a butler and began to protect him [...] (4) but he began to conspire against him in his palace, life, prosperity, and health, with each of those who conspired, after having acquired prestige.

(5) That which Ramesses III, life, prosperity, and health, the great god, his lord, did for him: He filled him with certain [...], (6) daily—Re did not allow him to become butler!—The king sought him out when no one knew his name. He made his fortune as (plentiful as) (7) sand and every good thing of the country by means of his efficiency, but he ignored that which Ramesses III, life, prosperity, and health, the great god, his lord, did for him; and he carried out the bad deeds, the abominations of (8) the great gods of the land [...] he went forth (?) and he was seized (9) and he was placed before the magistrates in the court of examination and he was examined. There was truth in them (the charges); he had done them without exception."

A second complete dossier is afforded us with Rifaud E. Interestingly, the document does not provide any account of the role the individual played in the uprising. It merely denigrates his character. The entire diatribe in effect tells us the villain "bit the hand that fed him."

What is clearly missing from the trial transcripts and the investigative reports is testimony made by the accused—or by anyone else, for that matter—in their own defense. Such testimonies do exist from ancient Egypt, giving evidence of a person's prerogative to defend themselves against charges brought against them, but perhaps because of the magnitude of the crime the court would not lend credence to the traitors' actions by recording their words for posterity. Only in Papyrus Lee is one of the accused quoted in a statement, and that quotation, an oath of innocence, is admitted as evidence of perjury, recorded to further defame his character.

The unsatisfying incompleteness of the judicial records invites us to delve further to uncover the actions of the key perpetrators on that fateful day. It may be possible to identify the unnamed miscreants of the investigative reports with a little detective work, but first it is necessary to examine the king's background and that of his family. A beloved ruler is not assassinated by those close to him without good reason. What was it that prompted these people to take such desperate measures?

Docket of the Accused

Name	Title	Charges	Verdict	Sentence
Pentawere	king's son	collusion with Teya and harem women inciting a rebellion	guilty	suicide
Paibakamana	pantry chief	collusion with Teya and harem women inciting a rebellion	guilty	execution
Mastesuria	butler	collusion with pantry chief and harem women inciting a rebellion	guilty	execution
Panouk	overseer of the royal harem	collusion with Paibakamana & Mastesuria inciting a rebellion	guilty	execution
Pentau	scribe of the royal harem	collusion with Paibakamana, Mastesuria, Panouk, and the harem women inciting a rebellion	guilty	execution
Panhayboni	overseer of cattle	inciting a rebellion	unknown	unknown
Pairy, son of Ruma	overseer of the treasury	collusion with Panhayboni accessory to treason	guilty	execution
Bonemwese	battalion commander of Kush	collusion with the harem women inciting a rebellion	guilty	execution
Pasai	army commander	collusion with Pentawere & Paibakamana inciting a rebellion	guilty	suicide
Prekamenef	magician	collusion with Pentawere, Paibakamana, and Pasai treasonous use of black magic	guilty	suicide

Docket of the Accused, continued

Name	Title	Charges	Verdict	Sentence
Iyroy	overseer of the priests of Sekhmet,	collusion with Penta-were, Paibakamana and Pasai treasonous use of black magic	guilty	suicide
Messui	scribe of the Sacred Library	collusion with Penta-were, Paibakamana, and Pasai	guilty	suicide
Shotmaadje	scribe of the Sacred Library	collusion with Penta-were, Paibakamana, and Pasai	guilty	suicide
Nibdjatfe	butler	collusion with Penta-were, Paibakamana, and Pasai	guilty	suicide
Hnetenamana	butler in the royal harem	failure to come forward	guilty	suicide
Amankhau	second-in-charge of the royal harem	failure to come forward	guilty	suicide
Pairy	scribe of the royal harem	failure to come forward	guilty	suicide
Peluka	butler and scribe of the treasury	sympathizer	guilty	execution
Yeniny	butler	sympathizer	guilty	execution
Ashhebsat	assistant to the pantry chief	sympathizer	guilty	execution
Warona	butler	sympathizer	guilty	execution
Petewentamana	(security) agent of the harem	failure to come forward	guilty	execution
Karpusa	(security) agent of the harem	failure to come forward	guilty	execution

Docket of the Accused, continued

Name	Title	Charges	Verdict	Sentence
Khaemmalu	(security) agent of the harem	failure to come forward	guilty	execution
Khaemope	(security) agent of the harem	failure to come forward	guilty	execution
Sutempidjehuty	(security) agent of the harem	failure to come forward	guilty	execution
Sutempiamana	(security) agent of the harem	failure to come forward	guilty	execution
wives of the (security) agents of the harem		sympathizers	guilty	execution
Pabasa	royal butler and appointed judge	mingling with the prisoners	guilty	mutilation
Mai	librarian and appointed judge	mingling with the prisoners	guilty	mutilation
Taynakhte	bailiff	mingling with the prisoners	guilty	mutilation
Naneu	police chief	mingling with the prisoners	guilty	mutilation
Hori	standard-bearer and appointed judge	mingling with the prisoners	acquitted	reprimand
Teya	queen	regicide	unknown	unknown
women of the royal-harem-in-the-following		regicide	unknown	unknown

CHAPTER TWO

A House Divided

Ramesses III was probably born and raised in the environs of the eastern Nile delta. Little is known about his family background except that he was the son of the pharaoh Sethnakhte, born of the queen consort, Teya-Maienese. When his father claimed the throne after a brief struggle, Sethnakhte became the first pharaoh and patriarch of the Egyptian Twentieth Dynasty. In a surviving document from his reign, Ramesses recounts his own accession to the throne of Egypt upon the death of his father:

> He [Sethnakhte] appointed me to be hereditary prince in the place of Geb (i.e., on earth), I was the great chief mouth[1] of the lands of Egypt and commander of the whole land united in one. He (the king) went to rest in his horizon, like the gods; there was done for him that which was done for Osiris; he was rowed in his king's barge upon the river and rested in his eternal house west of Thebes.[2] Then my father, Amun-Re, lord of gods, Re-Atum, and Ptah,[3] crowned me as Lord of the Two Lands on the throne of him who begot me; I received the office of my father with joy; the land rested and rejoiced in possession of peace, being joyful at seeing me as ruler of the Two Lands. . . . I was crowned with the atef-crown bearing the uraeus; I assumed the double-plumed diadem. . . . I sat upon the throne of Harakhte (the kingship). I was clad in the regalia, like Atum.[4]

Upon his coronation, Ramesses adopted a throne name and royal title befitting the pharaoh of Egypt. He was henceforth called "Mighty bull, great in royalty; Strong and Valiant like his father, Montu;[5] Rich in years like Ptah; Sovereign who Protects Egypt and Chastises the foreigners; The King of Upper and Lower Egypt, Wasmuaria-Miamana; the Son of Re, Ramesses, Ruler of Heliopolis."

The date of Ramesses' accession, the first month of Shomu, day 26 by their calendar, fell on March 7, 1199 B.C. Surviving texts and monuments from his reign reflect a dynamic and illustrious career. During the first half of Ramesses' reign, Egypt was beset by invaders coming from the west and northeast, originating as far away as the Greek Islands. In his fifth year the first assault by the Libyans took place on Egypt's western frontier.

While always a thorn in the side of dwellers in the Nile Valley, the old Libyan clans that had inhabited from time immemorial the oases nearest the river had never been a significant problem for the Egyptians. In the early decades of the fourteenth century, however, a new tribe, the Meshwesh, appeared in the region, and about a century later a second and even more formidable people, the Labu, loomed up on the western horizon. The Meshwesh were probably indigenous to North Africa, but the fair complexion of the blue-eyed Labu betrays a northern origin. The Egyptian army was able to repulse them but were forced to fight them again in Year 11. This final confrontation was a total victory, and the Libyan forces were routed by Pharaoh's army. As pharaoh, Ramesses took all the credit. He boasted of the campaign: "See, I destroyed them and slew them at one stroke. I overthrew them, felled them in their own blood and turned them into heaps of corpses." While we are not told of Egyptian casualty figures, the enemy's casualties on the earlier campaigns were enumerated by cutting off the hands and phalli of the slain. The final tally: "hands–12,659; foreskins–12,859; and captives–about 1,000."

In the closing years of the thirteenth century, the Egyptians had to contend with a second menace, which, like the threat from North Africa, took the form of a movement of peoples. The Libyan forces had been accompanied by a curious group of sea pirates, who came in ships from the north to attack the Delta. The outlandish costume of these maritime brigands attracted the attention of Egyptian artists, and on the walls of the mortuary temple of Ramesses III at Thebes they left a fine pictorial record of the newcomers. Some wore curious soft hats, reminiscent of a chef's cap; others had helmets with an enormous feather crest, or a ball and crescent decoration. Most carried long swords of iron and wore body armor. The pirates were not of a single race, but comprised several federated tribes. The tribal names—Lukki, Eqwesh, Turash, Shekelesh, Shardana, Denyen, Chekel, Peleset—are unlike ethnic designations encountered anywhere else in the Near East, and it was already clear to scholars a century ago that we should look to western Asia Minor and Europe for their place of origin. The Egyptians, who had rarely if ever encountered them previously, called them collectively the "Peoples of the Sea."[6] It was they who became the greatest challenge of Ramesses' reign and the true test of Egypt's stamina as a world power.

In Year 8 the confederacy of seafaring peoples made an attempt to conquer and displace the population not only of Egypt but of the entire Near East, as far as modern-day Turkey. Around 1230 B.C. factors unclear today were uprooting sedentary communities along the Adriatic coast of northern Greece, in the Cyclades, and along the coast of Asia Minor. At the same time western Asia Minor was in turmoil. The Hittites had suffered a grievous crop failure, and Egypt and Ugarit had dispatched shipments of grain to the stricken country. Accompanying the economic disaster came an invasion by a people later to be called the Phrygians, who were making their way from the Balkans across the Bosporos and into the western provinces of the Hittite Empire. In the east, in the highlands of Armenia, the Mushki (biblical "Meshech") were carving out a principality for themselves in defiance of Hittite authority. Population pressure, the uncertainty of livelihood, and the inability of political institutions to provide security made life intolerable throughout the Near East: people left home, looking for new lands. Across the ancient world flowed the largest and most destructive migration it had ever known. In Egypt, the object of the movement, the immediate effect was, strangely, negligible, at least in comparison to the fate of Asia Minor, Syria, and Palestine.

From the Adriatic and the Peloponnese, from the islands of the Aegean and the coast of Asia Minor, the displaced peoples gravitated in a southeasterly direction to the vicinity of Rhodes. Late Greek legends suggest that it was there that a federation was formed, probably under the leadership of the Peleset. The ships of the federation led the way along the coast, the wives and children of the warriors following on land in their two-wheeled oxcarts with all their worldly possessions. They came to stay. Their onslaught began with the Hittite Empire in Asia Minor and moved south through Syria and Palestine. Every city and town in their path was devastated. In a letter found at Ugarit, the king of Cyprus warns the king of Ugarit that the ships of the enemy have been sighted and advises military preparations. Soon the Syrian coast was under attack: "My father, behold!" the king of Ugarit writes back, "the enemy ships came here; my cities were burned, and they did evil things in my country." Soon Cyprus was overwhelmed, and the king of the Hittites had to contend with enemy ships based on that island: "Against me the ships from Cyprus drew up in line three times for battle in the midst of the sea. I destroyed them, I seized the ships and in the midst of the sea set them on fire." Nevertheless, it must have been a short-lived victory. The Hittite Empire soon disappeared beneath the waves of Phrygian and

Mushkian invaders. The great city-states of the Levantine coast—Alalakh and Ugarit—were razed to the ground and never again occupied.

Egypt came face to face with the advancing horde on the southern coast of Palestine. War reliefs on temple walls built under Ramesses III show that a tremendous battle on both land and sea ensued. The Egyptians lured the fleet of the enemy into the confines of a harbor or inlet, where they were set upon by the Egyptian ships. At the same time, the land forces of Pharaoh brought a halt to the enemy foot soldiers, forcing the wagon train to flee. In a speech to his court, Ramesses graphically describes the engagement for posterity:

> No land could stand before their power: Khatti, Kode, Carchemish, Arvad, and Cyprus were devastated. . . . A camp was set up in Amurru, and they desolated its people and its land as though they had never come into being. They came forward to Egypt. . . . I established my frontier in Palestine. . . . I prepared the harbor with warships, galleys, and barges. They were completely manned from stern to stern with valiant warriors. . . . (On land) the chariotry consisted of able warriors and all competent officers. . . . As for those (enemies) who reached my border, their seed is no more. Their hearts and souls are finished for all eternity. As for those who came forward upon the sea . . . a trap was prepared for them. Those who entered were dragged up, overturned, and laid low upon the beach, slaughtered in heaps of corpses. . . . I did not permit the foreigner to see the borders of Egypt.[7]

While the record is one-sided, there can be no doubt that the victory was Egypt's. The Peoples of the Sea were stopped, the confederacy broken up. Some were taken into the Egyptian military establishment or forcibly settled on rural estates. Others moved away, disillusioned in their abortive attempt, and a cursory glance at Mediterranean topography reveals their final distribution. The Shekelesh, in all probability, found a home in Sicily, to which they bequeathed their name; and in like manner some of the Shardana became the eponymous inhabitants of Sardinia. The Chekel settled partly in Cyprus and partly in the plain of Sharon in northern Palestine. The only people not to suffer serious spatial separation from their former objective were the Peleset, who probably came into a treaty relationship with the Egyptians and were allowed to settle on the broad coastal plain north of Gaza. Ultimately, they gave their name to the country, Palestine, and the Hebrews were later to make them a byword as the Philistines.

With the final defeat of the Peoples of the Sea, Ramesses' ability and credibility as a competent ruler were further established. The king now unabashedly claimed: "I have caused the women of Egypt to walk freely wherever she would, unmolested by others on the road. I allowed the soldiers and charioteers to sit idle during my time, and the mercenaries lay at night in their villages without any dread." Peace had been restored and the boundaries of Egypt made secure.

But the war years had taken their toll on the economy, and even Ramesses could do little about that. No bravado statement by a king could mask the true state of the nation. The invasion of the Sea Peoples had severely crippled Egypt. The pharaoh's land found itself cut off from the lands formerly part of the Hittite Empire, to which its merchants had had access for more than 70 years. The silver and copper of Anatolia were no longer available, and iron, which other states of the Near East were beginning to use on a wider scale, was not to be found in Egypt. Moreover, exhaustion appears to have afflicted the native mining operations. Within a generation of the death of Ramesses III the Sinai mines shut down, and records of mining and quarrying in Nubia cease at about the same time.

The Libyan wars had ravaged the Delta, Egypt's breadbasket, and the result was a rampant inflation from which Egypt could not easily recover. Fifteen years after the last war, Egypt was in a deplorable condition. A scarcity of grain left many of the granaries empty. Since it was from state granaries that the masses of government workers were paid their wages, frequently their wages were in arrears or not forthcoming at all. Early in Year 29 the situation came to a head and a general strike was called in the Theban area: "The workmen passed over the five checkpoints of the necropolis and said: 'We are hungry! Sixteen days have gone by in the month!' and they sat on the outskirts of the estate." Three officials sent off from the town to investigate the stoppage of work could not cajole the men back to their jobs. Two days later, when the strikers marched on government offices, the chief of police came to see what was going on. When he realized he was powerless to stop them, he went to fetch the mayor. At length, a legation of police, priests, and the mayor confronted the strikers and was told: "it's because of hunger that we have been driven to this. There's no clothing, no oil, no fish, no vegetables. Send to Pharaoh, our good lord, concerning this." The members of the legation heard them out and were able to gather together enough provisions from the government storehouses to pay them for the month. Although the immediate crisis was resolved, strikes continued sporadically for the remainder of the year. The pattern was always the same: the workmen would walk away from their work area, sit down in front of the local government administration buildings, and refuse to work until they were paid. The prime minister himself was obliged at one point to go up and down the Nile scrounging the wherewithal to pay them. What followed the events of Year 29 is unknown, but there were probably other strikes. The economy actually worsened during the subsequent reigns of Ramesses' sons. Since the glorious days of Ramesses II, Egypt relied heavily on revenues from her far-reaching empire. After almost 30 years of Ramesses' reign, Egypt's control over the rest of the Near East waned considerably, and incoming taxes from the territories dwindled. Ramesses III had failed to restore Egypt's empire, and without it there was no hope of renewed prosperity.

Apart from his political achievements, little is known of Ramesses' personal character. In a posthumous document completed by the king's son and successor, Ramesses IV, in which his father's financial gifts to the temples are inventoried, he endows his father with many noble virtues, most notably that of philanthropy toward his whole realm. It may be, however, that the son "doth protest too much." Indeed, later classical tradition remembers this king as a ruler who lived well and amassed riches but, because of his niggardly and miserly character, did little to spread the wealth. The size and magnificence of his palaces and mortuary temple attest to this. The king went so far as to boast of the riches in his palace in Thebes, speaking of his tableware being of fine gold, silver, and copper too numerous to count and of a multitude of foodstuffs, such as bread, beer, wine, and fatted geese and oxen, daily offered to the god. All this while the poor of Thebes hungered?

Further evidence on Ramesses' character is adduced in the transcripts of the trial. In them the king absolves himself of exacting vengeance upon the perpetrators; he explicitly states that he does not wish to know who they are and that he wants no part in their conviction and sentencing. Also, he expresses righteous concern over the possible prosecution of innocent people. If the statements were not merely legal formulas, they may have been an attempt by Ramesses and his heir to leave the realm with a last impression of the king as a fair and magnanimous man. If so, why was this necessary? Was the king, in actuality, known to be a vindictive person? One cannot say with any certainty; there is always the danger of reading too much between the lines. On the other hand, one cannot help but form an opinion of the man when reviewing the facts of his reign. From his numerous bombastic speeches inscribed on the walls of his mortuary temple, his self-satisfaction is undeniable. The king appears to have had a predilection for assembling his family and staff in the courtyard of his temple to regale them with the wonder that was Pharaoh. Apart from his usual captive audience who are in the immediate environs of his place of residence—"the king's children, king's butlers, magistrates, courtiers, and every officer of the army and chariotry"—a larger assembly was at times required: "the entire land gathered together in one place, the [royal] entourage, all the citizens of the land of Egypt, generation-levies, and all young people of this land." The king's speeches often began with a phrase such as: "Listen up! I'm speaking to you." Ramesses makes the point often that nothing goes awry with their pharaoh in charge: "My plans succeed," he says; "my plans come about without fail"; "what I want comes to pass; my counsel and my plans are sure." The court, quick to acquiesce in this judgment, responds: "Thy resolve is strong, thy plans effective," "thy counsel is good," "thy plans and thy counsel is what comes to pass." One arguable assessment of Ramesses III: a ruler who is in essence a pompous windbag.

Ramesses III and His Queens

Ramesses married early in his adulthood. In keeping with tradition, the queen consort bore the title *ḥmt-nsw wrt,* "The Great King's Wife." As the chief royal wife, she held the highest rank to which a woman of the realm could aspire, and as such she could command a great deal of power and wealth. In the past, there were those who resided in their own palace, separate from that of their husband and his harem, and possessed extensive estates, which were staffed by a multitude of servants and retainers. In fact, some of the most influential men in the country acted as stewards of the queen's estates, tutors of her children, and personal secretaries. Strategically, she had no less than the throne of Egypt at her disposal. Although one could point to exceptions, the chief royal wife was the de facto propagator of the kingship. The king might have any number of children by wives of lesser status and concubines, but it was the queen's children who would have prior claim to the throne.

During Ramesses III's reign, at least two women emerged as queen consort. One was a noblewoman by the name of Ese Ta-Habazillatu ("Isis, she [born] of Habazillatu"). Depicted on a statue of Ramesses III, she bears the title "The Great King's Wife."[8] In her tomb and elsewhere, she is also entitled "King's mother" of Pharaoh Ramesses VI, confirming that she not only outlived her husband but survived through three more reigns.[9]

Her matronymic tells us she was the daughter of a foreigner called Habazillatu, whose name is West-Semitic for "meadow flower." Habazillatu was probably a commoner and one of many foreigners brought into Egypt under the Ramessides. A good number of these immigrants naturally settled in the eastern Delta region. It may be significant that, during

"The Mistress of the Two Lands, Ese," depicted in full queenly regalia on the walls of her tomb in the Queen's Valley. (Courtesy of Dr. Christian LeBlanc)

his reign, Ramesses III paid particular homage to the ram-headed god, Banebdjed, a deity whose cult seat was the city of Mendes, located on a eastern branch of the Nile in the Delta some 25 miles northeast of the Egyptian capital, Pi-Ramesses. Furthermore, one entire wall in Isis's tomb is decorated with the queen making offering to this god, as does her son Ramesses VI in an inscription from his reign. The special reverence given to the chief deity of Mendes is reason to suspect that Habazillatu may have resided and, perhaps, raised her daughter, Ese, there. One wonders whether she lived long enough to see her daughter become queen.

As for the king's other queen, nothing definite, including her name, is known. In fact, her very existence is accepted by scholars mainly on the basis of negative evidence: some of the king's sons did not claim Queen Ese as their mother in spite of the fact that they held high honorary posts that suggest they were in the line of succession; therefore one might argue there must be another great royal wife. It is this author's contention that the identity of this queen, whose name has been possibly deliberately suppressed, is none other than Teya of the conspiracy documents.

For more than half a century Egyptologists have been debating family relationships within the Egyptian Twentieth Dynasty. "Who was related to whom" has been the subject of many a scholarly article, but the arguments deal primarily with who may be Ramesses III's sons and grandsons and who may be the sons of Isis Ta-Habazillatu. The identity of Teya has been extraneous to this debate since Egyptologist James Henry Breasted first speculated in the early 1900s that Teya was most likely a "secondary" or "lesser" wife of the king. With little evidence to go on, Egyptologists have accepted his pronouncement almost without question. Perhaps it is time to look at her from a different perspective.

Teya and the harem women implicated in the conspiracy are spoken of in the most general terms. Nowhere do their titles indicate a particular rank. Indeed, except for Teya, they remain nameless. This, of course, is a deliberate denigration on the part of the court scribes in order to assign them as little importance as possible. But, in the case of Teya, there is perhaps something more at stake. Not only is Teya's rank suppressed, but also that of her son Pentawere. Notably, he is the only *male* in the transcripts who is so treated. That Teya is named and singled out in context from the other women, "Teya *and* the women of the harem" (Judicial Pap. 4:2) gives the definite impression of a woman of superior rank in relation to the others. Moreover, if Teya were merely one of countless women in the king's harem, why would so many officials at court, some extremely high ranking, sympathize with her and, more to the point, be willing to promote her son Pentawere over the king's appointed heir?

Why would any of them expect him to be acceptable to the people of Egypt? Why would the powerful garrison of Kush have thrown in its lot with the conspirators? Quite simply, neither army nor officials would have done so had not Pentawere a mother of exalted rank and thereby a legitimate claim to the throne. Court authorities were not likely to put down in writing for posterity Teya's and Pentawere's elevated rank, as any suggestion of justifiable motive would weaken the case of their accusers.

There is every reason to believe, therefore, that Teya enjoyed an erstwhile rank higher than that of ordinary spouse; and in the contest of queenship this could only be that of *ḥmt-nsw wrt,* "great king's wife." It is entirely understandable that all textual references to Teya's exalted status dating from before her arraignment should have been later expunged by the authorities. There is, however, a strong circumstantial case to be made.

On the west bank of the Nile at Luxor is the ancient necropolis today known as the Valley of the Queens. The area, known by the ancients as *t3 st nfrw (Ta set neferu,* "the place of beauties"), was the burial ground of the royal wives and royal children of the Nineteenth and Twentieth dynasties.[10] The dispersal of the tombs within the valley reveals not only a chronological grouping but a familial one as well. Interestingly, the family members of Ramesses III are grouped in two separate locales within the valley: at the westernmost end of the main wadi are the tombs of Queen Ese (QV51) and two of Ramesses III's sons, Ramesses (QV53) and Amanakhopshaf (QV55); located in a peripheral wadi that branches off to the southwest from the main thoroughfare are tombs of three more sons of Ramesses III, Prehiwomnef (QV42), Sutakhopshaf (QV43), and Khaemwese (QV44).

The distancing of these two tomb groupings in itself suggests a separation of branches of the family. At some point in Ramesses' reign a tomb was excavated for Queen Ese. It is reasonable to suppose that in close proximity are the tombs of her own children. Although Ese is not mentioned by name in the tombs of Ramesses and Amanakhopshaf, both state they are "born of the Great King's Wife." In line along this same southern flank are two more tombs, which, judging from their position, were likely meant for the offspring of Ese and the king. One designated as QV54 was never completed; the other was inscribed for the "King's Daughter," Tyti (QV52). Tyti's other titles reveal that she later married a king, became his chief consort, and produced a son who eventually gained the throne.[11]

Well out of sight from the tombs of Ese and her children are the tombs of the princes Prehiwomnef, Sutakhopshaf, and Khaemwese. Unlike the tombs of their half brothers, there is no textual reference in these tombs to the mother of the tomb's occupant, although a scene in Prehiwomnef's

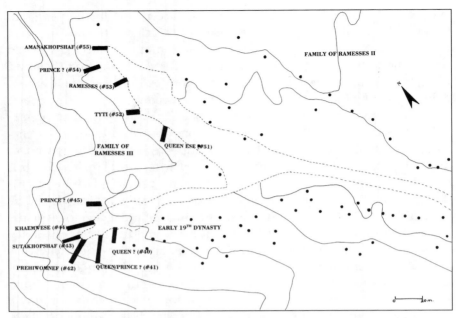

Plan of the Valley of the Queens showing the disposition of tombs
of the two branches of the king's family.

tomb depict's a queen in full regalia making offering to Osiris undoubtedly on behalf of her deceased son. The three brothers' tombs, designated
QV42, QV43, and QV44, are at the end of the side valley. Flanking them
on both sides are tombs QV41 and QV45, neither of which is decorated
but which are, architecturally, contemporary to the others. It is tempting
to see tomb 41, situated at the forefront of this group, as the unfinished
resting place of their mother, Ramesses III's "other" queen consort, Teya,
or perhaps of their disgraced brother, Pentawere.[12] Tomb 45 might
equally be considered for Pentawere or another full brother.

The names of royal women in the reign of Ramesses III are curiously
scarce. Neither in the king's tomb or in any inscription of his reign does
he name his own mother—an uncommon oversight.[13] Apart from the
single statue inscribed with Queen Ese's name mentioned above, there is
no other mention of her. Although her tomb was probably excavated in
her husband's reign, her name was not added until her son,
Amanakhopshaf, ascended the throne as Ramesses VI. In the great mortuary temple of the king, still standing on the west bank of the Nile at
Luxor, several depictions of a "Great King's Wife" appear on the walls,
but none bears a name. Even his daughters, pictured twice in procession

and offering to their father, remain anonymous. While there is no basis for an accusation of misogyny—even his male children share this oblivion in his temple—one cannot help the impression that in this king's reign women were relegated to the background more than usual. Therefore, the absence of Teya's name from the monuments cannot be used to bolster the case that she was a woman of unexceptional rank.

To both of Ramesses' queens were born at least ten sons, if Pentawere is included. As mentioned above, five are attested in their lavish tombs in the Valley of the Queens. An inscription in one notes that the tombs were a gift from the king to "the *principle* royal children," a reference that distinguishes those born of his chief wives as opposed to the children of the women of his harem.[14] This ranking of his own children is again documented and illustrated in terms of the protocol at court on the walls of the king's mortuary temple. In reliefs depicting the religious festival for Min, the Egyptian god of royal procreation and legitimacy, Ramesses III is shown being carried on his palanquin from the palace by his sons, who are again called "the principle royal children."

Following behind the king's carrying chair are various attendants who are in turn followed by "royal children in the following of his majesty." Bringing up the rear in the procession are military officers who carry the king's accoutrements. Their placement in the ceremonial parade bespeaks their position as "second-rung" children of the king (of which he probably had many). After all, Pharaoh's epithet "Mighty Bull" was taken seriously, and the king was expected to be a formidable procreator, fertility being a sign of royal greatness. In this respect, as in others, Ramesses III tried desperately to emulate his great predecessor, the magnificent Ramesses II. Besides having a godly life span of nearly 90 years, 67 of which were spent on the throne, Ramesses II boasted more than a hundred offspring. Ramesses III went so far as to give his own sons the same names and posts as the crown princes of Ramesses II.

Some of the king's children are named as they appear in procession in a now famous series of reliefs on the walls of the king's mortuary temple located on the west bank of the Nile at Thebes. The reliefs cover two walls, spanning both sides of an entrance portal to the first hypostyle hall. On the right side, 19 princes parade in attendance. A mirror image of this scene appears on the left side, except that after the thirteenth in line, figures of 14 princesses are substituted to fill the remaining sections of wall. A bordered column before the first 10 figures on both sides of the portal indicates that names and titles were to be inscribed (the others being left anonymous), signifying their exalted rank as the "principle" sons of the king and, consequently, their prior claim in the line of succession.

Although the scene itself was completed under Ramesses III, the textual identifications were filled in at a later time. That is evident by the inscriptions for the first three figures, whose assigned names are enclosed in a royal cartouche. As is true in other reliefs in the temple in which his sons, wife, and daughters appear, Ramesses III did not allow the mention of their names. The prohibition was apparently corrected in the reign of Ramesses VI, some 11 years after the death of his father.[15] Even after that time, given the importance of seniority in terms of royal succession, one would expect that the princes appear on the walls according to their order of birth.[16] If so, the scene of reliefs presents a fascinating insight into the troubles that ended Ramesses III's life.

The principle sons of the king appear in the following order as filled in later: Ramesses (IV), Amanakhopshaf (Ramesses VI, in the second and third position), Sutakhopshaf (Ramesses VIII), Prehiwomnef, Manthikhopshaf, Mayatum, Khaemwese, Amanakhopshaf, and Maiamana.

Queen Ese bore the king his first son. He was named Ramesses in imitation of the first-born son of Ramesses II by his queen Istnofret, but unlike his namesake he survived the reign of his father to ascend to the kingship. His mummy reveals that he was a man in his fifties at the time of his death, after a brief six years on the throne. Being the eldest and a teenager by the time his father gained the throne, Ramesses must have been groomed for the kingship early in his father's reign. In a religious festival recorded on the walls of the Temple of Amun at Karnak dated to Year 22, the prince is pictured in attendance with his father. By this time, he had already been accorded the position of commander in chief of the army. Apart from the honorific title of crown prince, this most prestigious military appointment was traditionally given to the son who was expected to succeed his father. In this the top-ranking office, numerous generals—and, thus, the entire standing army—were subordinate to him.[17] It is important to note that Ramesses is the only one of the king's sons to hold this post. His premier position over the king's other sons is further illustrated in the festival of Min where, identified as the crown prince and commander in chief of the army, he stands at the forefront of his father's palanquin leading his brothers. As the first son in line in the procession of princes, Ramesses is entitled "Fan Bearer on the King's Right, Crown Prince, King's Scribe, and Commander in chief of the Army," followed by his name in a cartouche.

At the same festival recorded at Karnak, a younger brother, identified as the commander in chief of the chariotry, Amanakhopshaf, stands behind the prince Ramesses, In the procession of princes, the second *and* third figures following Ramesses are designated for a brother who later gains

Two nearly identical scenes depicting a procession of princes graces the walls at the Rames-seum, the mortuary temple of the great Ramesses II. The top photo depicts three crown princes (the first two of whom were probably deceased by the time the relief was carved) dressed in full regalia befitting their station. The bottom photo shows the thirteenth prince in line identified with the cartouche of Merenptah. It is obvious that the artists of Ramesses III's court almost slavishly copied it for their sovereign's own mortuary complex. In the earlier scene, the sons of Ramesses II appear by name in their order of succession. This long-lived king survived his first twelve sons, three of whom had been designated in their lifetimes as the "heir apparent." When the next prince in line, a son named Merenptah, finally succeeded to his father's throne, the royal stonecutters duly inscribed their new king's cartouche before the thirteenth figure in the procession, giving evidence that the relief was made to mirror the actual protocol of the princes in courtly ceremonies.

the throne as Ramesses VI.[18] Preceding his royal cartouches, one of which includes his birth name of Amanakhopshaf, are the princely titles "Fan Bearer on the King's Right," "Crown Prince," "King's Scribe," and "Commander in chief of the Chariotry of the Victorious King." The same titles appear in tomb 55 in the Queen's Valley made for one, Amanakhopshaf. We would naturally assume they are one and the same, if not for one thing. The burial chamber of tomb 55 holds a red granite sarcophagus, remains of a wooden coffin, stylistic of this period, and the bones of a young man. One must conclude that the tomb's owner, Amanakhopshaf, who is attested as the son of Queen Ese and pictured as a young boy on the tomb's walls, died during his father's reign and was laid to rest here.

The prince who became King Ramesses-Amanakhopshaf VI, in keeping with tradition, was buried in the Valley of the Kings. So who was he? We know that Pharaoh Ramesses-Amanakhopshaf VI was born of Queen Ese from her tomb, which was decorated owing to the generosity of her enthroned son. In addition, the ninth figure in the procession of princes is named for the "Fan Bearer on the King's Right, King's son of his body, Ramesses-Amanakhopshaf." The plausible explanation is that the queen's second-born son, the crown prince and the first named commander in chief of the chariotry, died in his youth. At some point during the reign, the queen gave birth to a third son, who was named Amanakhopshaf in honor of her beloved lost child. In inscribing the names of his brothers on the temple walls, Ramesses-Amanakhopshaf VI usurps the position originally meant to depict his like-named brother and also assumes his titles—after all he did gain the kingship over the others in line—but preserves the correct ordering by inserting himself as the ninth-born son. One wonders whether Queen Ese was influential in having her younger-born Amanakhopshaf "moved up" in the order of succession and put in the place of her deceased child during the king's reign, something that would have surely enraged his half-brothers and their mother.

That Ramesses-Amanakhopshaf VI would assign himself two positions in the procession is puzzling. What justification could there have been for what appears to be the deliberate omission of the name and titles of the prince next-in-line? If the second-born son of the king was none other than Teya's firstborn, Pentawere, the answer is obvious.

This hypothesis is further supported by a relief on the wall of a small backroom chapel in the same temple. Here King Ramesses III is shown receiving offering from eight sons.[19] The princes are lined up in two rows of four, and, while their names are left blank, the titles of the two leading princes are inscribed before them. The prince leading the row pictured at bottom holds the post of commander in chief of the army, whom we can

The son of Queen Ese, Prince Amanakhopshaf,
who passed away while in his youth during his father's reign.

plausibly identify as Prince Ramesses, the king's heir apparent. The prince
leading the top row is not only designated as a crown prince, however,
but is entitled commander in chief of the "menfat" *(mnf3t),* a segment of
the army consisting of an elite group of foot soldiers. This is a title not
claimed by any of the other sons in the procession scene or elsewhere.

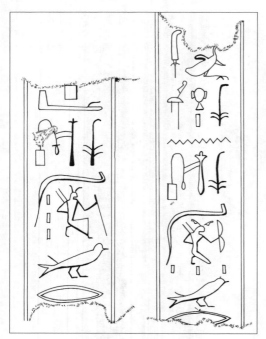

A comparison of the two titles of the rival heirs apparent as inscribed on the wall of the chapel: "Crown prince, King's Scribe, Commander in chief of the Menfat" (left); "Fan Bearer on the King's Right, King's Scribe, Commander in chief of the army" (right).

The figure thus qualified is unique. He does not occupy a titular position as inscribed among the sons in the processional scene, but in the chapel relief is pictured as a prince of elevated rank. Who could he be? He is clearly not Ramesses, Amanakhopshaf, Sutakhopshaf, Prehiwomnef, Manthikhopshaf, Mayatum, Khaemwese, or Maiamana. Under these considerations it is most tempting to identify the mysterious individual with the unfortunate son, cast into oblivion by a rash act, who masquerades in his shame and indignity as "Pentawere, who bore that other name."[20]

The royal sculptors conveyed an even greater importance to the two leading princes in the chapel scene and the first three figures of the processional scene by depicting them in more formal regalia than those that follow. These five are attired in a long, flowing robe with cape and full wig while the others are shown bare-chested, wearing a short kilt with shaved head and sidelock. Ramesses, Amanakhopshaf, and the unnamed prince of the chapel relief are the only princes depicted on the temple walls that bear the title of "crown prince," suggesting a correlation between their rank and their costume.

The second son born to Teya was Sutakhopshaf. This man not only survived the reign of Ramesses-Amanakhopshaf VI but was still alive some seven years later to ascend the throne as Ramesses VIII. In the processional scene he is the fourth figure in line and here entitled "Fan

Line drawing of a relief in the king's mortuary temple showing an unidentified crown prince, most likely Pentawere, entitled "commander in chief of the elite foot troops" presenting offerings to his father, Ramesses III.

Bearer on the King's Right, King's Scribe, Commander in chief of the Chariotry of the Victorious King."[21] Sutakhopshaf is identified as Ramesses VIII by his royal cartouche, which the royal sculptors had to squeeze in the space between the earlier inscribed column and the skirt of his garment. The figure's dress was also altered from the short kilt to the long robe and the outline of a full wig with uraeus carved on his head, further underscoring the significance of the princes attire.

An old man by the time he was crowned, Sutakhophshaf survived only one year as king. It is unlikely that he ever expected to become king, and it was probably thought that when he passed away he would be interred in the tomb made for him in Valley of the Queens. But this tomb, 43, was never utilized for burial. The titles carved on the tomb's walls reveal the prince's appointment during the reign of his father, as "First Charioteer of his Majesty, Charioteer of the King's Barracks of the Residence of Ramesses III." This post does not correspond exactly to the elevated one assigned him on the temple wall; in fact the latter is identical to the title claimed by the second in line, Amanakhopshaf. It may be that Sutakhopshaf was promoted to the higher position by his regent brother. The prince is further noted as "Senior King's Son," an honorific epithet perhaps accorded as a sop to a male offspring who, although close in age to his older brothers, was not to be dubbed crown prince.[22]

Before Queen Ese produced her third male offspring, Amanakhopshaf the younger, Queen Teya had given the king his next six sons. Following Pentawere and Sutakhopshaf, Prehiwomnef was born. The burial chamber of his tomb, 42 in the Valley of the Queens, holds a sarcophagus that had been originally made for a queen, perhaps proof that Prehiwomnef died unexpectedly and accoutrements for his burial had to be hastily assembled. While alive, the prince was distinguished as a "First King's Son" and held the position of "Great Chief Charioteer of His Majesty," but not for long.[23] His younger brother, Manthikhopshaf, later assumed his post, proving that the king, Ramesses III, buried his son during his lifetime. These two brothers were named after the third- and fifth-born sons of Ramesses II, who had also been appointed as the king's chief charioteer in succession.

Nothing more is known about Manthikhopshaf, as no other monument, tomb, or text bears his name. It has been speculated that this prince lived to see at least two of his brothers reign as king and fathered the child who would later become Ramesses IX.[24] Better known is the brother who was Manthikhopshaf's immediate junior, Ramesses-Mayatum. Late in his father's reign, he was installed at Heliopolis as high priest of the cult of the sun god, Re, a position he retained throughout the reign of Ramesses V.[25] It is likely that when Mayatum passed away he was buried in Heliopolis, as were others who had held this office.

The "First King's Son and Sem-Priest of Ptah," Khaemwese, was the last son Teya would bear. The creator god Ptah reigned supreme in the city of Memphis, and being in the service of the cult of this god the prince would have been stationed in Memphis, some 500 miles north of Thebes. How long he was in residence there is uncertain, but if Khaemwese was still alive by the end of his father's reign he would not have been present when his mother and brother made their move. The prince was interred in the tomb given to him by his father in the Valley of the Queens. The beautifully preserved paintings depict a young boy dutifully in step behind the king.

The youngest son of Queen Ese was Miamana. As the last of the principal sons of Ramesses III, he was positioned in the protocol at court as "fan bearer on the king's right," as were his other brothers. Since we know of no post that was conferred on him during the reign, he might have been very young when his father was assassinated.

An adolescent Prince Khaemwese portrayed as fan bearer
on the right of the his father, the king.

To be the matriarch of a generation of future kings is an incomparable accomplishment for any woman. Ese and Teya were rivals for this legacy. Giving birth to several sons, in spite of the high child mortality rate and a long-lived husband, was good insurance that one of their offspring would spawn a dynasty of rulers. While most wives of the Egyptian pharaoh would have thought themselves and their offspring fortunate to be in such a position of power, there would be those whose ambitious and volatile nature could never be satisfied with second best. Teya was, perhaps, such a woman. It is easy to think the worst of her: greedy and hungry for power, wanting a prominent place for herself in history, driven by purely selfish motives. But she is, perhaps, worthy to be given the benefit of a doubt. It is not so unlikely to think that her reasons for wishing the king dead were understandable or even noble. The sight of her son, a son of Pharaoh's, so able and, in her mind, so deserving of the kingship, overshadowed and displaced by the offspring of another woman, may have been too much for her to bear. What a trick of fate to be so close to the throne and yet so far. We cannot rule out the possibility that the king or, perhaps, the crown prince, Ramesses, had a cruel nature.

Whatever Teya's reasoning, dissatisfied she certainly was. For her part, Teya was able to gain the confidence and support of a close circle of harem women. One woman, in particular, proved herself useful by having a brother who controlled a battalion of archers stationed in Nubia. It fell to her brother, Bonemwese, to rouse the public and, in particular, join with the general Pasai in mobilizing troops for an armed rebellion against the throne. Her letter to her brother would later be submitted as evidence for his conviction. It is not obvious what these women of the harem had to gain by the king's overthrow. Personal greed could *not* have been the reason they committed high treason. The king and royal family stood at the apex of the social pyramid. In their close association with them the women of the royal harem already had more in terms of material wealth and creature comforts than most of the people of Egypt could hope for. Apart from Teya their station in life would not significantly advance even with the succession of a new king. This is particularly true of the women implicated in the conspiracy who are called the "harem women who are in the following." As such they were a select group of the king's harem, probably chosen by the king himself to be in his personal entourage that traveled with him and made appearances at religious festivals and other public ceremonies.

If their lot in life would not substantially improve from their present privileged and comfortable existence, then their wish to see the king dead and the heir apparent overthrown may have stemmed from a purely personal dislike. One wonders whether these wellborn Egyptian women harbored resentment for servitude to a queen who, unlike themselves, did not come from noble, native stock but was merely the daughter of a reviled Canaanite. But one gets the impression that they were driven by something more than personal feelings of dislike or petty revenge. In view the fact that the harem women and their male cohorts

The women of the royal harem are shown in perpetuity serving the king
on the high-gate of the Ramesses III's mortuary temple.

believed that, once their plan was put in motion, the rest of the court
and the public would rally behind them, they surely felt their cause to
be a just one. The depressed economic state of the country may have
taken its toll on their extended families more severely than we can today
realize and perhaps for that reason the women of the harem were willing
to risk their lives to effect a change in the kingship.

Two queens vying for the supremacy of their sons appears to have lit
the fuse to the explosive incident that would claim the life of pharaoh.
But such a hostile predicament could only ferment under circumstances
already present in the disposition of the palace community. An examination of the long tradition of the Egyptian royal harem is essential to un-
derstanding how and why such treachery was fostered.

Ramesses' Family and the Line of Succession

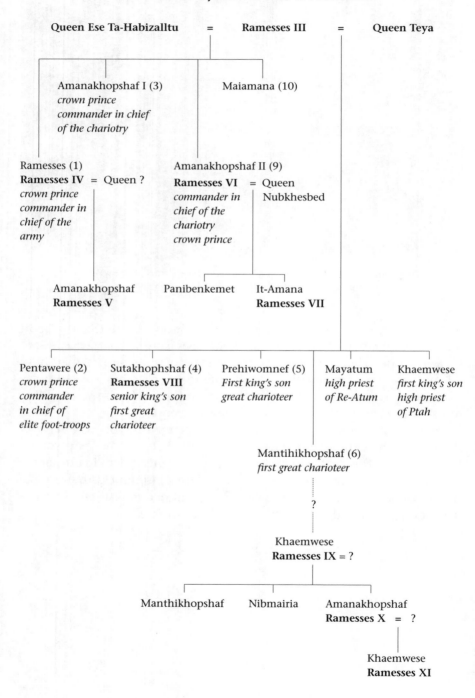

CHAPTER THREE

The Royal Harem

When Ramesses III gained the throne in the early part of the twelfth century B.C., he inherited as part of his sovereign domain a social network that unquestionably can be identified, even by our own modern definition and prejudices, as a royal harem. The Egyptian royal harem was in essence an extension of the king's household and as a cultural entity can be traced back to the beginning of the Old Kingdom. But the organization, operation, and evolution of this select community throughout Egyptian history has left very few traces in the archaeological record. Most of our evidence, meager though it is, comes from texts. In the physical sense, the royal harem was a consortium of women, handpicked by the king and housed in separate quarters of the king's palace and in other royal residences throughout the country. It was every king's privilege to set up a harem, and the size of a king's household no doubt corresponded to his financial capacity to sustain its numbers. The future Ramesses II acquired a harem of his very own when he became the heir apparent to the throne as a gift bestowed upon him by his father, Seti I.

For many, the word *harem* conjures up images of veiled dancing girls and bejewelled sultans reclining on velvet cushions in chambers decorated with diaphanous curtains. Such dramatic license must of course be discounted as superficial and skewed. The reader should also be aware that *harem* is used here as a convenient tag to introduce a recognizable cultural phenomenon that has existed in various societies around the world throughout history. While some elements of this social ordering reflected in southeast Asia, Turkey, or Baghdad (familiar to us through stories like the "Arabian Nights" or "Anna and the King of Siam") invite valid anthropological comparison with ancient Egypt, the cultural variants are important in providing an accurate picture.

The word *harem* comes from an Arabic root meaning "forbidden," which conveys the same expression of inviolability as the ancient Egyptian terms. Notably, in ancient Egypt, as in the rest of the Middle East and elsewhere in the world, what was meant by *harem,* despite all that it implies to us today, was merely a designation for the site of the women's residence. The words *ipt* (pronounced epet)

and *ḫnrt* (pronounced hen-er-ret)

denote the actual domicile that housed the women. By late New Kingdom times, the first had become old-fashioned, and the second word, *ḫnrt*, was much more common. The occupants of the *ḫnrt*, i.e., the women themselves, were called *ḫnrwt* (henerut). A good literal translation of the word *ḫnrt* was "place of seclusion," and *ḫnr* or *ḫnrwt* meant "the secluded ones" or "those of the place of seclusion." The same words were used to denote prison and prisoner.

In neighboring lands, the words for harem similarly express this ultimate form of female isolation: the word *tubqum*, literally meaning "inner corner," designates the harem section of the palace in the kingdom of Mari; in ancient Hebrew, the word *penima,* meaning "inside," denotes the women's quarters; and the Assyrian word for the harem apartments, *bitāt,* literally translates as "interior."[1] The physical separation of these women from the public and the rest of the court is supported by architectural evidence. Archaeologists have, with some success, been able to identify sites as harem residences, or parts of the royal palace as the private quarters of the harem. Excavation of the royal palace at Mari revealed that the harem quarters were indeed in the corner of the building, far removed from the main gate. There are also Egyptian tomb reliefs that show plans of a palace with the harem apartments located at the back of the complex, away from the main entries. The foremost members of the royal harem were housed in the pharaoh's palace estate in the capital city, but harem residences existed in other cities throughout Egypt and were often established in areas favored by a particular king. For instance, the pharaohs of the twentieth to seventeenth centuries B.C. were fond of a locale in the lush, lake area of the Faiyum, where hunting and fishing were particularly good.² Here was founded a harem palace called Mi-wer, an estate that continued to flourish through Ramesses III's reign and into that of Ramesses V.³

Harems located outside the capital provided accommodation for the king and his entourage on state visits or vacation retreats to the area. Although the royal harem was specifically built as a pleasure palace solely for the enjoyment of the king, it operated in every other respect as a productive government institution. During the king's long absences, the harem palace functioned to sustain itself and sometimes produced a valuable commodity. Farmland and cattle were given over to the estate, as well as field hands to tend them. An array of servants was also required to maintain the palace and to see to the needs of the inmates. This occasioned the employment of a hierarchy of administrators, who were titled "overseers of the harem," to keep accounts, tally payments to workers, take inventories, and keep things running smoothly. These officials and workers settled their families in the area around the harem palace, and a thriving community emerged of which the harem proper was the integral center.

The ladies of the harem did not sit idle. They functioned as productive members of the estate. Archaeological evidence uncovered at Mi-wer attests to their participation in the weaving industry as spinners or supervisors of trainees. The manufacture of textiles was obviously a source of pride to the women and, possibly, a means of advancement in the social hierarchy within the harem. A small, wooden statue found in the excavations of the harem quarters bears the inscription of a certain woman of the harem: "Teya, chief of weavers."⁴ But in spite of whatever daily chores were expected of them, there is no doubt that the lifestyle of the inmates was sophisticated, the standard of living luxurious. The women were garbed in the finest linen and their hair and body scented with perfumes and fragrant oils. In the time of Ramesses III, the harem ladies were dressed in a full-length, flowing, pleated robe that was draped over their shoulder and knotted beneath one breast. Beneath this diaphanous garment was an underdress of slightly heavier cloth. Their feet were shod in open sandals that could be made of either leather or papyrus reed. The body oil they disposed of in abundance was a very expensive commodity, some imported from foreign lands, and were given out sparingly as pay to the rest of the population. One court official of the Eleventh Dynasty boasts that he actually was in charge of doling out precious ointments to the king's ladies. This was true of the perfumes as well, which included exotic and local fragrances such as myrrh, frankincense, jasmine, and lotus.

They were adorned with jewelry given as favors and rewards by the king, including broad collars, armlets, bracelets, pendants, brooches, and earrings made of gold, silver, lapis lazuli, carnelian, colored glass, and faience. Besides obviously being a source of wealth for these women, they were ornamental status symbols among the rank and file of the harem. Artifacts recovered from palace estates show an abundance of items of vanity. Bronze mirrors, combs, hairpins, cosmetic implements and jars, razors, tweezers, and even hair curlers attest to the women's preoccupation with their toilet. Their elaborately coiffed long hair was styled in braids and tight curls by attending maids. They applied rouge to their cheeks and lips in the form of powder extracted from the henna plant and black kohl to their eyebrows. Encircling the eyelids with kohl made of dark green malachite added radiance and defined the look of the famous and beautiful Egyptian almond-shaped eyes.

The harem residence was part of a king's palace and set up strictly for his benefit. Inlaid furniture of ebony and cedar and opulent decorative ornaments found in harem apartments indicate lavish and richly appointed surroundings in a garden setting. It was the king's comfort that took priority on his occasional, if not regular, visits to a particular retreat, and the primary duty of the inmates was entertaining the pharaoh. Wall reliefs show harem women dancing and singing to the music of harps and lutes and playing board games. Specially trained people were often employed to instruct them in arts and music. The blind harpist, a figure common at court and banquets of the aristocracy, may well have been one who not only entertained the court ladies but taught them his songs. The lyrics of one of the most famous harper songs describe a philosophy of life perhaps followed by the women in the royal harem:

> Spend the day merrily!
> Follow your heart as long as you live!
> Put myrrh upon your head and clothe yourself in fine linen!
> Put garlands on the body of your beloved!
> Set music before your face until the day of mourning!
> Make holiday and do not weary of it,
> For none can take his goods with him;
> And none that has departed can come again.[5]

A Greek historian relates that the women in the Persian royal harem slept during the day, so that they could be fresh to entertain the king at night with singing and music. A document from the Persian court describing the king's anticipated visit to his harem describes the event as it must have occurred in harems of all lands: "The women are reclining on the lovely couch with cushions; they adorn themselves with clips, with square earrings and a necklace decorated with gold: 'When will the master come to us? When will we have the pleasure of experiencing love with our bodies!'"[6] Plans of harem quarters show storerooms housing musical instruments and apartments where women are preening themselves.

It is not altogether clear how women were chosen or inducted into the royal harem, and there are no documents specifically defining the hierarchy of women within the harem. Most of the information regurgitated in secondary sources concerning the workings of the Egyptian royal harem is based on inference, but indirect textual sources and the titles borne by the ladies at court imply a defined ordering. On tomb and temple walls, daughters of wealthy aristocrats proudly bear the title of ḫkrwt-nsw (heckar-ret-nes-u), "royal ornament,"[7] or ḥsyt-nsw (hesi-et nes-u), "king's favorite." From the New Kingdom on a particular coiffure appears to be peculiar to them: from the top of the head a thick lock of hair, shoulder length or longer, is thrown slightly forward over one side of the head. The strands are either braided or tightly curled and held in place by a hair clip. Depictions of some of these maidens show them to be wearing a tall, ornate fillet or headdress. This same headdress has been noted on wall reliefs from palace apartments showing harem girls attending the king.

While the titles of "royal favorite" and "royal ornament," especially when held by young maidens wearing the unique fillet, are suggestive of harem residency, there are instances of these titles being held by women who are the wives of high-ranking courtiers. It may be that many girls who once resided in the royal harem and many who were perhaps born there may have been given as wives, a gift from the king to favored court officials, and therefore may already have held the title before their "marriage." In the Turkish harem system, the indulgent sultan at times married off some of his aging women instead of retiring them to Eski Serai, a seraglio set up for dowager wives and matronly inmates. That this practice was occasionally carried out by Egyptian kings is remarked upon in a line from an instructional papyrus of Ptolemaic date.[8] In it, an unnamed "wise man" adumbrates the many benefactions accredited to the goodness of god among which is the woman of the royal harem who is given another husband. More to the point, however, is that this event is cited as a gift from god! Obviously, growing old and languishing in the royal harem was not considered an enviable fate. It is also probable that many officials' wives simply had the title "royal ornament" honorifically bestowed on them by royal favor. In this context, the title is best interpreted simply as "court lady" or "lady-in-waiting."

Maidens of humble birth sometimes found their way into the royal harem, chosen probably for their beauty. We know that one girl who was the daughter of a servant was among them. The royal archives document the pharaoh Amenhotep III literally ordering young women by mail at a price of 40 pieces of silver each, along with the demand that they be beautiful but not possess shrill voices. One ancient Egyptian folktale tells of a beautiful woman who is brought to the attention of the king and becomes his mistress. Pharaoh is so taken with her that he listens to her every word and gives her anything she desires. She pours his wine, accompanies him on various outings, and is even at his side at official royal appearances. Pharaoh bestows upon her the rank of *špst wrt* (shepset weret), which is equivalent by modern standards to that of "dame." But this is a designation well documented for aristocratic women of all stations in the realm and one so general in description that one cannot always identify a member of the royal harem by this title alone.

It is only those women entitled *ḥmt-nsw* (hemet-nes-u), or "royal wife," whose presence in the royal household is self-evident. Since Egyptian sources do not specify what governed a woman's elevation to the status of king's wife, it may be useful to draw on documentation of the Ottoman Empire with respect to the sultan's seraglio. The hierarchy of the Turkish institution was well defined and rational: the sultan might have wives and any number of concubines, but he had only one mother and she alone was the head of the harem. As *Sultan Validé,* she ruled over the other women as long as she was alive. When she passed away, that honor fell to the chief wife, or "First *Kadin.*" That this was the case in the Egyptian royal harem is implied by the graphic evidence. In scenes on temple and tomb walls, the mother of the king is often pictured standing behind her enthroned son. Chronologically, most of these are dated to the early years of the king's reign. When later she is replaced by Pharaoh's principal wife, entitled *ḥmt-nsw wrt* (hemet-nesu-weret), "Great King's Wife," we might assume that the dowager queen has passed away.

The *kadins,* the equivalent of a legal wife, of which the sultan could have only four at one time, followed in rank behind the "First" according to seniority.[9] From his numerous concubines, or *ustas,* the sultan singled out some to share his bed. They then had the opportunity to be raised to the status of *ikbals,* "king's favorites." In the event of the birth of a male child and the growing affection of the sultan, a fortunate concubine could ascend to the rank of wife. A similar ranking of harem women is confirmed for the Assyrian harem as well and is mirrored in the Egyptian culture by the titles *ḫkrt-nsw* (king's ornament) and *ḥsyt-nsw* (king's favorite).[10] As for the royal wife, *ḥmt-nsw,* there is no evidence

Daughters of foreign chieftains ensconced in the royal harem of Amenhotep III
are pictured for posterity on the walls of the tomb of the queen's steward, Kheruef.
(Courtesy of The Oriental Institute of The University of Chicago.)

that a pharaoh was limited to four in number, but one can readily believe that giving birth to a son of Pharaoh would be useful in attaining
the privileged position of wife.

There is substantial evidence that the royal harem was the destination
of foreign princesses and their entourages given to Pharaoh in the name
of diplomacy and as political favors by their head-of-state fathers. One
such princess, from the land of Mitanni (modern northern Iraq), given
to Amenhotep III, came to Egypt with 317 maidens in attendance. They
were received by the pharaoh and then all promptly placed in an isolated harem estate, where very little is heard of them again. The same
king also received a second Mitannian princess into his harem, as well as
two Syrian princesses, two Babylonian princesses, and one princess from
Arzawa (modern southern Turkey). The daughters of these foreign chiefs
can still be seen today, depicted in relief in attendance at the king's coronation jubilee in the tomb of the king's courtier, Kheruef, located on the
west bank at Luxor.

Inscriptional records concerning these foreign princesses relate that
the title "royal favorite" was applied to them once they entered
Pharaoh's harem. There were a few who managed by sheer force of per-
sonality to rise from the obscurity of the royal harem into historical
prominence. One such woman was a princess, who might also have
come from Mitanni, named Kiya, given in marriage to the pharaoh
Akhenaten. Kiya was not only called the commonplace "royal favorite"
but also held the rank of ḥmt-nsw (king's wife) and "greatly beloved
one." She was not, however, the "Great King's Wife": that honor belonged to the beautiful queen, Nefertiti. She therefore had no claim to
wear a royal crown or to enclose her name within a cartouche. But,
while such marks of a queenly status are absent, Kiya appears to have
had exceptional privileges. For one thing, there was a series of small
chapels erected in her honor at the new capital city. Her select position
at court did not last very long, however, since there is evidence that Kiya
was not liked by the princess, Meritaten, Nefertiti's daughter. When Meritaten succeeded her mother as queen, she removed Kiya's name from
existing monuments and mutilated her image wherever it was found,
taking pains especially to excise the eyes. Another foreign princess, this
one of Hittite extraction, whose marriage to Ramesses II was meant to
solidify a shaky alliance between two great powers, Egypt and Khatti
(modern-day Turkey), was elevated to "chief royal wife" sharing the
queenly crown with Ramesses' Egyptian-born wife, Nefertari. Her arrival
in Egypt is recorded on a stela at Abu Simbel with the comment: "Thus
his majesty saw that her face was beautiful, the likeness of a goddess.

The daughter of the prince of Khatti was beautiful in the heart of his majesty. He loved her more than anything else, as something beautiful, given to him by his father the god, Ptah." The official marriage announcement stated that she resided in the royal palace in the capital city and was daily in the company of the king. Monuments at the Egyptian capital bore her name with full queenly titles, and her name was recounted centuries later in legend. After residing some forty years in the capital city, the now dowager queen departed to live out the rest of her life in the harem residence at Mi-wer, which had perhaps become the Egyptian equivalent of the Turkish sultans' Eski Serai.

Other foreign women, a number of them carried away to Egypt as booty from successful military campaigns, were inducted into the king's harem. Amenhotep II captured 323 daughters of Palestinian princes as well as 270 of their female court singers. The Mari king, Zimri-lim, also captured hundreds of women on an invasion of a nearby state and shipped them to his capital, where most would serve as weavers. A message to the king's chief wife accompanied them specifying that about 30 of the most beautiful, "from the tips of their toes to the hair of their head without blemish," be selected for his harem. He further instructed that the status on their entry papers be changed and that enough rations be given them "so that their appearance does not suffer." Later, Zimri-lim thought better of having his wife choose the females and countermanded the order.

Regardless of a woman's status within the royal harem, whether "royal ornament" or "king's wife," she was, as all were, Pharaoh's chattel. In return, she was well provided for and protected. Her seclusion from society, clearly indicated by the Egyptian words for harem, resulted from her being included within the king's sphere of protection. Communication with her family, by way of visits and letters, was occasionally allowed but severely restricted. The documents of the harem conspiracy against Ramesses III illustrate that the restriction was enforced, though eventually this element of security was breached.

The women's segregation even from other members of the court is illustrated in a famous letter from the Babylonian king, Kadashman-Enlil, who complained that he had received no word from his sister since she was given to the pharaoh in marriage. The concerned brother wrote: "My sister, whom my father gave to you, is with you there, but no one has seen as yet, whether she is alive, or whether she is dead." With his harem assembled before him, Pharaoh singles out one of the women and says to the Babylonian messengers who had delivered the letter: "Behold, your mistress who stands before you!" But the Babylonian princess is not permitted to converse with them, and the messengers depart, doubtful of her identity. When Kadashman-Enlil hears about the audience with Pharaoh, he suspects the worst and again sends off a message: "Perhaps she is the daughter of a beggar, she whom my messengers have seen. Who is to tell them: 'Yes, it is indeed she'? For she did not open her mouth nor say anything to them." To this Pharaoh protests, "If your [sister] were dead, who then would conceal anything, [or why] should we cause another to take her place?" There is no further communication concerning this princess, and we are left to wonder whether she was ever heard from by her family again. It is surprising that the Babylonian king could be so outraged by the fact that his messengers were not allowed conversation with his sister, a royal harem inmate, when his own harem operated with similar, if not more stringent, restrictions. In fact, a royal decree of that empire asserted that no one was permitted to approach any harem lady nearer than seven paces. There was even a law that forbade male servants to be in view of the women when watering the harem gardens. From tomb reliefs, which show doorkeepers on duty at harem apartments, and from the harem administrative titles that abound in the textual record, it is clear that the women of the Egyptian harem were just as rigorously guarded. Women in royal harems all over the Near East—Babylonia, Assyria, Israel, and Mari as well as in the later institutions of the Ottoman and Arab empires—were under the guardianship of eunuchs. The reason for employing eunuchs is obvious, and even they were grilled and closely monitored to see that nothing improper occurred, but there is no evidence that the Egyptian king adopted such measures. In fact, the Turin Judicial Papyrus offers evidence to the contrary in its description of the prosecution of the wives of the harem doorkeepers.

In records of the Assyrian and Turkish empires, it is noted that the administration of the harem, the guards and the women, were under the strict supervision of one official, called the "Chief Black Eunuch" in Ottoman Turkey and the "Great One of the Palace" in Assyria. He actually filled the post of steward to the queen and as such acted as liaison between the queen and the harem women and the king. In both empires, he was one of the most powerful men at court. For comparison we may look to the most famous "Steward of the Great King's Wife" in Egypt, a man called Kheruef, who served Queen Teya, the consort of Amenhotep III. Kheruef's tomb is one of the most artistically beautiful tombs in the Theban necropolis, and its size and appointment indicate a person of high status in the royal palace. Along with foreign princesses, royal princesses and other harem ladies are prominently displayed in procession on its walls.

In whatever culture or time period harems are found, they are repressive at best and have been aptly referred to as "a particularly benign form of slavery."[11] Nevertheless, in spite of their incarceration, the women of the Egyptian royal harem were not necessarily ill used. Ancient Egypt was in essence a hierarchical despotism, and as such the movements of most of the population were more or less monitored. Craftsmen at work in the royal necropolis and field hands employed on royal and temple estates lived with their families within guarded confines. In exchange for their services, they received wages in the form of food, clothing, and other commodities. Today, freedom of movement is viewed as an inalienable right, but to the ancients it was a luxury they could not afford to hold dear, nor did they particularly desire it. Life was extremely difficult in antiquity. The state offered the best means of survival in a world where famine and disease were widespread. Not to report to the state your whereabouts, not to make yourself available for work, would mean you would surely starve. The women of the royal harem could not come and go as they pleased, but they lived a life of relative ease and received the best that life had to offer. In comparison to the everyday life of the common woman, there is reason to suspect their willingness, even eagerness, to become part of the king's household.

The ladies of the royal harem could also expect to be provided with, if not an opulent burial, at least one that would ensure that their elite standing would continue in the next life. The care and preparation of the corpse, the performance of the essential religious rites, the size of the tomb, and the richness of the funerary effects were all of great consequence for a person's entry into the afterworld. Chance finds of funerary items offer important clues as to how and where the ladies of the royal harem were buried. In 1904, a French archaeologist, Georges Legrain, purchased about forty inscribed canopic jar fragments from a dealer in Luxor, who no doubt acquired them by clandestine digging on the West Bank.[12] Two of the jars had been made for royal princesses, but the others belonged to the women of Amenhotep III's harem. Besides name and title, that of "King's Ornament," several of the pieces imparted their owner's character-revealing nickname: "the much sought after one"; "she hot-tempered like a leopard"; "the catlike one."

Although no precise location can be ascribed to the fragments, several places of origin have been suggested: Legrain believed that the women were buried in the Valley of the Queens, a few kilometers northwest of Amenhotep's palace. However, considering that the countless harem women were of dubious importance in the court hierarchy, it seems unlikely that they each would be accorded the privilege of a grandiose, decorated tomb in an area reserved for queens and hereditary princes. Howard Carter thought that they came from undecorated pit tombs located on the plain to the northwest of the ruins of Amenhotep's palace and before the entrance to the Valley of the Queens, an area within walking distance to the Theban palace of Ramesses III. The pit tombs had been thoroughly looted, but Carter reported that information from locals living in the area led him to believe that they were the graves of harem ladies. Given their size and proximity to the palace, this is probably a more reasonable assumption.

The harem women were by no means exchanging their subjugation for material wealth and comfort. Despite their official service to the king, there is every indication that in practice things were quite equitable. A literary account concerning the women of the pharaoh Sneferu's harem highlights the fact that they were anything but obsequious. The anecdote recounts a day when King Sneferu was suffering from boredom and, in a state of depression, called for his chief majordomo to advise him on a means of entertainment. The king's man came up with a splendid idea: "May your majesty proceed to the pleasure lake of the palace. Fill a boat with all the beautiful girls of your household. Your majesty's heart will be refreshed by seeing them row up and down." The king replied: "Indeed, I shall go boating. . . . Let there be brought to me 20 women with the shapeliest bodies, who have not yet given birth. Also let there be brought 20 fishnets and give these nets to the women to wear in place of their clothes!" All was done as his majesty commanded, and "his majesty's heart was made glad at seeing them row." Now obviously sexual exploitation was something the king could get away with, but the story continues: "While the girls were rowing for his majesty, the girl who was at the lead oar, fingered her braids and a turquoise pendant she was wearing fell into the water." She stopped rowing and taking her lead so did all the others. "His majesty said to her, 'Why have you stopped rowing?' She replied, 'Because my pendant of turquoise fell into the water.' Then his majesty commanded her, 'Row! I shall replace it for you.' But she replied, 'No! I want that one!'" And in spite of the mighty pharaoh's commands, the girls refused to row. The king was nonplussed. He was also stuck in the middle of the lake. He had to call to the shore for his majordomo for assistance. The rowing party did not continue until the girl's pendant was recovered from the lake bed, 21 feet below the surface.[13]

Apart from the restrictions placed on the women in the king's harem, ancient Egyptian society offered women in general more freedom and put them legally on a more equal footing with men than women in most countries of the Middle East and North Africa today. For instance, women could own property and dispose of it according to their own wishes, adopt children, effect financial contracts, and execute wills, all without the concurrence of a husband. Among the common people, women were an indispensable segment of the labor force. They worked side by side with men in the fields and workhouses, picking fruit, gathering crops, weaving cloth, and making bread. Women of the lower classes also served as domestics and servants to royalty and the aristocracy. They can be seen in relief and painting, serving food and drink, making beds, attending to the mistress's toilet, and carrying accoutrements. But much of what we know of the social status of women centers on the aristocracy. It was only members of the upper class, which included, of course, the extended royal family, who could afford to build large, substantial domiciles, operate estates, own a wealth of material and luxury items, have statues carved in their likeness, and their faces and names reproduced on tomb and temple walls. Women's secondary posture on statuary and their diminished exposure in their husband's tomb indicate that a woman's position in life was often irrevocably tied to the status of the man she married.

This is particularly noticeable in the religious sector, where women of noble birth who actively participated in temple rituals and served in the cult of a particular deity often held what would be the female counterpart of their husband's position. As documented on the walls of the tomb's of their husbands in the Theban necropolis, one often finds that the wife of the high priest of Amun holds the appointment "Chief of the harem of Amun." Similarly, the wife of the high priest of the god, Khonsu, or of Montu or Thoth, is named as chief of the harem of that deity. The wives of the lesser priests are attested as "sistrum player" or "songstress" within the cult their husbands served, their duties at times self-evident. For the most part, the purpose of women's involvement in cultic rituals and events, both at the local and state level, was to supply musical accompaniment. In this context, some scholars have convincingly argued that the term ḥnr, commonly translated as "harem," should here be deemed a term synonymous with "musical troupe." The chief of the ḥnr not only took part in the musical performances but acted as supervisor to the other women and, in some instances, as superintendent of the temple stores.

In one sector of Egyptian religious life, the cult of Hathor, women appear to have held sway. The cow goddess, Hathor, was the patroness of women and childbirth, and in that realm a male's presence was not appropriate. Women functioned as priestesses in the cult's rituals, which were mainly musical processions of offering and adoration. In the

Middle Kingdom, the position "prophetess of Hathor" was held by daughters of regional overlords, which bespeaks attribution to their father's political stature.

As mentioned above, the wives of officials in the government were often provided with the title "royal ornament." There does not seem to be any real function attached to the title except what the title thus translated might imply: these court ladies were allowed a place with their husbands at royal audiences, more or less for the sake of being "decorative." In some cases, a particularly high-ranking courtier could secure a position for his wife or his daughter within the royal household. The position was almost exclusively that of "royal wet nurse," an extremely influential and rewarding situation for the woman, both for herself and, perhaps more importantly, for her children. Nursing the future king throughout his childhood would naturally result in a very strong attachment.[14] Moreover, her own children were allowed to be raised with the prince within the confines of the palace. The wife of the pharaoh Aye, who was the brother-in-law of Amenhotep III, served as wet nurse to that king's children but, unfortunately, died before her husband assumed the throne. Whether or not these women owed their position to their husbands or their fathers, a royal wet nurse's status guaranteed her children's future. Several individuals, including a chief steward of the king, a high priest of Amun, and a mayor of Thebes, honored their mother, the "Chief Nurse of the King," on the walls of their substantial tombs, boastfully pronouncing themselves to be "childhood acquaintance of the king."

More than any other, aristocratic women proudly bore the title "Mistress of the House." Modern society tends to demean the role of "housewife," but the ancients did not share that prejudice. In their world, being the mistress of the house was not of minor importance. The noblewoman who ran the manor house did not lead a sheltered life. There were times she faced famine, plague, and invasion by hostile forces, and she had to deal with such circumstances not only for the sake of her family but for her employees and their families as well. There is documented proof that many of these women supported their husbands in their jobs and took active part in carrying out their responsibilities. The influence and regard accorded the Egyptian housewife was unusual to the rest of the known world and of some repute. The Roman historian Diodorus wrote of life in Egypt: "The wife lords it over the husband . . . the men agree to obey the wife in everything." Egyptian literature substantiates the outsider's description, filled as it was with advice for the Egyptian male in his dealings with his wife. Apart from such blatantly misogynous remarks as "Do not confide in your wife; what you tell her will be on the street" and "Instructing your wife is like having a sack of sand whose side is slit open," there are warnings that have a legal ring to them: "Do not contend with her in court, keep her from power, restrain her . . ."; "Do not trust her with [household] provisions for the year"; and "Let your wife know your wealth, but do not trust her with it."

Women were not allowed into the realm of government bureaucracy. There are some recorded cases in Egyptian history of women holding an administrative position, but, considering the length of pharaonic rule, they are few and far between. A few royal women are known to have employed other women as administrators on their estates, but these managerial positions entail overseeing other women, and they in turn answered to male supervisors. There are extremely few instances of women in charge of men. Undoubtedly there were women who did not enjoy being in their husband's shadow, who longed to be something more. This is poignantly made clear by the woman who on her tombstone had written the title "vizier." She was not a vizier, nor was she ever likely to be in her life, but her belief in the efficacy of the written word gave her hope that she would be recognized as such in the next world. It is doubtful that her desire would have met with a favorable response; the overwhelming prevalence of males in positions of state confirms that ancient Egypt was, in all aspects, a male-dominated society.

Strictly speaking, as was the case with women throughout Egypt, the women of the royal harem had no political power. They held no state office and officially had no say in the operation of the government. Intimacy with the king no doubt garnered limited influence over the affairs of state, but the vast majority of harem women throughout Egyptian history were anonymous, passive observers. The few that history does record were the women elevated in status to be conduits of the kingship, to transmit the royal bloodline. Traditionally, this was the role of the *ḥmt-nsw wrt,* "the great royal wife," or the queen consort. Her eldest living son would be named heir apparent to the throne of his father. If her son or sons did not outlive their father, it sometimes remained for her eldest daughter to legitimate through marriage the succession of the new king.[15] As a result of epidemics, wars, and the high infant mortality rate, an opportunity sometimes arose for a son of a lesser wife or concubine to ascend to the throne. This was the case with the great warrior king, Thutmose III, whose mother was a harem woman of unexceptional rank. Upon his accession, the king proudly put forth the name of his mother and in earning the title *mwt-nsw* (mut-nes-u), "King's Mother," she moved to the forefront of the royal household.

Besides marrying their half sisters, there is attestation that some kings even wed their own daughters, perhaps in an attempt to keep the royal bloodline pure. It is uncertain, however, whether the title of "Great King's Wife" adopted by these princesses was honorific and the marriage a mere formality or whether in fact the title was bestowed by a consummated affair.[16]

How far a woman promoted herself politically upon gaining the queenship is another matter. Teya suffered perhaps from ill luck and poor planning in her attempted coup, but there had been queens in the past who had enjoyed success in their self-promotion. Perhaps she had been encouraged by looking back to their example. There are only a few, outstanding queens of the pharaonic age who became in effect the real power behind the throne, some even managing to wrest for themselves the absolute power of the kingship itself. And, to give credit where credit is due, it was the indomitable personalities of these individual women, not the whims of their husbands, that earned them a prominent place in their country's history. Teya and the women of her time might have felt great admiration for a queen of long ago named Nitocris, who was catapulted into the kingship by means of a regicide. Nitocris succeeded to the throne soon after the reign of Pepi II ended in about 2250 B.C. This king had the longest reign of any pharaoh, more than 90 years. Incidentally, he was only a small child when he gained the throne, and there is every indication that it was his mother who commanded the realm until he was of age. After Pepi died, a new king, Merenre-Antyemzaef, came to the throne, probably Pepi's aged son, and reigned one year before he was replaced by Nitocris, who reigned for 12 years. The little we know of her comes from a classical story written down by Herodotus, which states that she ascended to the throne after the murder of her brother by Egyptian courtiers who wished to put her in his place. According to legend, she accepted the monarchy long enough to make arrangements to avenge her brother's death. For this purpose she had a large subterranean chamber built in which she arranged a feast and invited all the people who had participated in the conspiracy against her brother. Then she had the gates of a secretly constructed channel opened and the chamber flooded, killing all in attendance. She later committed suicide to escape further revenge. Whether this story is apocryphal or not, later history records Nitocris as "the noblest and loveliest of the women of her time."

Teya's ambition could have been to mirror the memory of the queen mother extraordinaire, Ahmose-Nefertari, who lived in the latter half of the sixteenth century B.C. She was wife to King Ahmose, who had gained the throne as victor in a war of independence against a dynasty of foreign rulers. Ahmose-Nefertari was from brave stock: her mother, Ahotep, fought in the war, receiving medals of valor for her bravery, and was later buried with her battle-axes. So great became Ahmose-Nefertari's prestige and influence as queen and mother to King Amenhotep I she was deified after her death. During Teya's time the cult of Ahmose-Nefertari and her son was especially popular among the workmen of western Thebes. Their image of queen mother and son provided an obvious model for any ambitious queen.

The most famous and by far the most powerful queen in all Egyptian history is Hatshepsut. Her wonderful and unique terraced temple at Deir el Bahri, by which she is best remembered, still stands on the west bank of the Nile at Luxor and is visited by tens of thousands of tourists every year. Hatshepsut would one day secure for herself the throne, but she began her ascent as the "chief royal wife" of Thutmose II, who died after a nonillustrious reign of 18 years. At the time of his death, the only son the king had was a small boy whose mother was a harem inmate of lowly rank. Under these circumstances, Hatshepsut, being of good royal stock (for she was also the daughter of a former king), managed to take over the reigns of power from the underage heir quite easily. Unlike Teya, who could curry support from only a relatively small and questionable sector of the administration, Queen Hatshepsut enjoyed broad popular support from the outset from most of the leading families of the realm. A high-ranking official at court named Ineni reported at the time of the Thutmose II's death: "Having ascended into heaven, he (the king) became united with the gods, and his son, being arisen in his place as king of the Two Lands, ruled upon the throne of his begetter, but it was the king's sister, the god's wife, Hatshepsut, that governed the land and the Two Lands were under her control; people worked for her, and Egypt bowed the head." While in power Hatshepsut tried to promote her daughter, Neferura, as her heir to the throne over her nephew.

While no woman in Egyptian history wielded as much power in the political arena as Hatshepsut, there were others who came close. One, a commoner named Teya, so completely captured the pharaoh Amenhotep III's heart that he immediately elevated her to the rank of "Chief Royal wife" and proudly proclaimed his marriage to the entire known world. "Live King Amenhotep," the marriage announcement reads, "who is given life [and] the Chief Royal Wife, Teya, who lives. . . . She is the wife of a mighty king, whose southern boundary is as far as Nubia and northern boundary as far as Syria." With this fortuitous marriage, Teya's entire family benefited for two generations to come. The king's love and admiration for his wife is made obvious by other evidence as

The head of one of many colossal statues of the formidable Queen Hatshepsut wearing a king's crown that lined the colonnade of her magnificent mortuary temple at Deir el Bahari.

well: in Year 11 of Amenhotep's reign he commands that a large pleasure lake be dug in close proximity to the royal palace for his queen to sail her barge. This was no mean feat, for the lake measured nearly 6,500 feet in length and more than 1,200 feet in width. Moreover, Teya's name was included with the king's own titulary on all state documents of the period, and her presence is prominently recorded on state occasions. Such political kudos for a queen consort were hitherto unheard of, which underscores the king's dependence on his wife in the political affairs of state. Throughout the entire 38 years of her husband's reign, Teya dominated the royal household. The names of other wives are conspicuous by their absence: only her daughter, the royal princess, Sitamana, gained any notoriety at all.

Teya survived her husband, and as the dowager queen mother of Akhenaten she still figured prominently in the early years of her son's reign. One of the first diplomatic messages the new king received from a foreign head of state advised: "All the words I have spoken to your father, your mother, Teya, knows them. No other person knows them, so you can ask your mother Teya about them." The prospect of her namesake gaining so much power and wealth might have excited the senses of Ramesses' Teya, and since she had to share the sphere of queenly influence with Ese it would have seemed all the more important to ascend to the celebrated station of queen mother.

The strong-willed spirit of Eighteenth Dynasty queens continued with the famous Nefertiti. The famous bust of the queen's likeness has earned her the reputation of the most beautiful queen that ever lived. Beautiful she may have been, but apart from her beauty she had a strength of character that permeates the historical record. The early monuments of her husband, built at Thebes, shows that Nefertiti was depicted twice as often than the king himself. In one of the temples to the sun god erected by the king, Nefertiti is shown to the complete exclusion of her husband. The reliefs on the temple's walls are also telling. A depiction of the prow of a boat shows the queen wielding a club to smite the heads of foreign female enemies. The decoration around the dais of the queen's throne depicts women captives from the far reaches of the empire. Both these art motifs were traditionally used for illustrating the pharaoh (with male captives) but were, for Nefertiti, translated into the feminine. Depictions of her with Pharaoh in statuary and relief do not bespeak a woman in the shadow of her husband but one on a par with him in power and authority. Nefertiti was never called Pharaoh, but the art record of the period clearly demonstrates her enormous influence over the king throughout most of his reign.

Closer to Teya's time was Queen Tawosret, the dowager queen of the pharaoh Seti II, who enjoyed a brief period of sole rule. Since, however, she was swept away by the revolution that brought Ramesses III's father, Sethnakhte, to power, her name was probably anathema to the court of Ramesses III. Tawosret's likeness can be seen in her tomb, which is situated in the Valley of the Kings—she and Hatshepsut being the only females bold enough to accord themselves burial in this honored place.

In sum, these illustrious queens and harem inmates of the past would have been well known to Teya and her conspirators. Although few rose to such dizzying heights, this does not mean that less famous women of the royal harem throughout Egyptian history always meekly accepted their subordinate roles. Certainly, the incident of Ramesses III's assassination points to the king's vulnerability with regard to his harem. There was an ancient African custom of killing the king when he was no longer able to procreate, and a few scholars have speculated that, for a short time at the very dawn of pharaonic history, the ritual may have been practiced in Egypt. The royal harem would quite naturally have been the first to determine that the king's time had come. There is, however, no evidence to substantiate that this ever occurred in Egypt. The royal harem is, nonetheless, documented as a hotbed of festering discontent on more than one occasion. A biography of a high-ranking official of the Old Kingdom (ca. 2400 B.C.), named Weni, refers to a specific incident of great moment in which the pharaoh Pepi I involved him, saying:

> I acted in the name of the king for the royal harem. . . . When there was a secret charge in the royal harem against the *wrt-hts* (the harem woman's title—we are not told her name), his majesty made me go in to hear it alone. No chief judge, or vizier, no official was there, only I alone. Only I put it in writing together with just one other senior clerk. . . . Never before had one like me heard a case of the king's harem; but his majesty made me hear it because I was more trustworthy than any other official of his. . .

We are not told the crime the king's wife was alleged to have committed, but it was obviously of a very serious nature, and the king wanted the "hearing" handled in the most discreet way possible. Certainly, it would not enhance the royal persona if it were widely known that the king's wife was disloyal to him. But was there another reason for such secrecy? A second inscription from the reign indicates that, at about this time, the prime minister of the country was disgraced and ousted from office. Some scholars have speculated that he too was involved in this harem scandal.

The pharaoh Amenemhet I, who reigned ca. 1900 B.C., was also the victim of an assassination plot, which some believed was hatched in the harem. It is fairly certain that the king was murdered in his thirtieth year. In a document written up for propaganda purposes in support of the new king's right to succession, Amenemhet speaks posthumously to his son and successor, Sesostris:

> . . . hear what I tell you . . . be on your guard against all who are subordinate to you, of whose plotting one is not aware. Trust not a brother, know not a friend, make no intimates, for it is useless. When you lie down, guard your heart yourself, for in times of trouble no man has supporters. . . . It was after supper, night had come. I was taking an hour of rest, lying on my bed for I was weary. As I began to sleep, weapons meant for my protection were turned against me. I awoke at the fighting, alert, and found it was a combat of the guard. Had I quickly seized my weapons in my hand, I would have made the cowards retreat. But no one is strong at night, no one can fight alone. . . . Thus my injuries occurred when I was without you . . . before I had sat with you so as to advise you, for I had not prepared for it, had not expected it, had not foreseen the treachery. . . . Had women ever marshalled troops? Had the discord been fostered within the palace? . . . Sesostris, my son, as my feet depart, you are in my heart. . . .[17]

A popular story relevant to this incident tells of a scribe of the royal harem who is so afraid that he may be implicated in the assassination plot that he flees Egypt in fear for his life.[18] Interestingly, nearly two thousand years later, an Egyptian historian would write that Amenemhet "was murdered by his own eunuchs."

Assyrian texts also describe the royal harem as a potential powder keg. An obscure concubine in the harem of the Assyrian king Sennacherib succeeded in having her son, Esarhaddon, supplant the reigning crown prince and chief queen's son, Arad-Ninlil. In doing so, she advanced to the highest rank in the harem. A palace revolt in support of the former queen and her displaced son ensued, resulting in the assassination of Sennacherib, but Esarhaddon triumphed and gained the throne. Throughout Esarhaddon's reign, his mother was a force to be reckoned with. She outlived her son and was instrumental in gaining the throne for her younger grandson, Ashurbanipal, after forming a dislike for the firstborn.

At times, the size of a pharaoh's harem must have been remarkable. The future Ramesses II had his "fledgling" harem established while he was still crown prince, as a gift bestowed upon him by his father, pharaoh Seti I. Moreover, each king inherited the previous king's harem as well. No numbers are documented for any pharaoh's harem, and it is not possible to even guess as to the size of Ramesses III's. Turkish sources indicate that the sultans had anywhere from 300 to 1200 women. The Sassanid king Khosrau I surely had one of the largest harems ever with 12,000 women; the harem of Assyrian king Ninurta-Tukulti-Ashur, a contemporary of Ramesses III, numbered only 40.

Given the number of female inmates housed in royal palaces throughout the country, it is extremely unlikely that all or even most of them had any sexual responsibilities to the king (especially those living outside the capital city). Certainly, the pharaoh would have his favorites who would be honored by sharing his bed. Egyptian records are silent as to the protocol or procedure followed for the presence of a concubine in the king's bedchamber. Once again, Turkish records possibly shed some light. When a sultan desired the company of a particular concubine in his bedchamber, he would write the name of the lady on a label or docket and give it to an attendant, who took it to the lady in question. Once the king had retired, she was carried on a litter to his apartment, where she observed a strict procedure for bedding the king: Obliged to approach from the foot of the bed, she would lift up the coverlet and raise it to her forehead and lips and then creep in underneath, slowly working her way up until level with the sultan. Before daybreak, attendants came to rouse the lady and take her back to the women's quarters.

The occurrence is recorded in a journal noting the lady's name and date of visit. If the woman later gave birth, the book was referred to in order to substantiate the legitimacy of the child. Whether a similar procedure was followed in the Egyptian palace must remain pure speculation as there is nothing in texts or the art record that even hints at it. But, if the lowly concubine was subjected to such a routine, we know that it was not observed by the king's wife. There are inscriptions, albeit euphemistic, describing the night of the future monarch's conception:

> He (the king) found her as she slept in the beauty of her palace. She waked at the fragrance of the god, which she smelled in the presence of his majesty. He went to her immediately . . . he imposed his desire upon her, he caused that she should see him in all his glory. When he came before her, she rejoiced at the sight of his beauty, his love passed into her limbs, which the fragrance of the god flooded; all his odors were from Punt.[19] . . . Spoken by the king's wife . . . in the presence of the majesty of this august god . . . : "How great is thy fame! It is splendid to see thy front; thou hast united me with thy favors, thy sweat is in all my limbs." After this, the majesty of this god did all that he desired with her.[20]

There can be little doubt that the king paid his attentions, at least on a regular basis, to only a select few. There is considerable mention in the ancient Egyptian archives of the *ḫnrt-nsw-šmsw* (heneret nesu shemesu), the "King's-harem-in-the-following," which can only be a qualifying reference to the king's personal entourage of women who lived with him at his main place of residence. This harem must surely have consisted of women whose company the king obviously preferred to all others, and likewise those who by their standing in the harem earned this privileged place.

It was not unusual for rulers throughout the Near East to be accompanied on their hunting and military campaigns by their harem women. There were, in fact, Assyrian laws denoting orders for such travel by the king's harem. One law warned the officer of the harem to make note of the clothes the women were wearing when setting off so to be sure they were all brought back upon their return. A traveling protocol was noted by the Roman historian Quintus Curtius Rufus, concerning the harem women in the reign of the Persian king Darius. The king's mother came first on a litter, on the next his principal wife, and the women attending the queen were to follow on horseback; then followed 15 "traveling carriages" with the king's children, their governesses, and a multitude of eunuchs, who acted as bodyguards, and finally more carriages, carrying the king's 365 concubines. That such an arrangement when traveling was in effect in Egypt can be seen in the art record from the reign of Akhenaten. Reliefs show the king's principal wife, Nefertiti, first in line in the procession, being carried in a chair. Following behind on foot are six harem ladies whose titles and identities are not given, then on palanquins with hooped canopies come the three royal children, and behind them an array of bowing courtiers.

The general protocol the royal ladies followed at court is intimated to some extent by the art record. In statuary, throughout all periods of Egyptian history, women, as well as queens, are almost always situated to the left of the male.[21] This position, even today, denotes secondary importance and subservience. Certainly, the Egyptian court was well aware of the significance of where one stood in the presence of the king. The most powerful men at court such as the vizier and the first herald, as well as the king's sons, are described with honorific distinction as standing *ḥr wnm n nsw* (her wenem n nesu), "on the King's right." In the audience hall, with the king's "right-hand" men thus positioned, the queen was enthroned immediately on the king's left side, and adjacent to her assembled the king's female entourage.

The number of princesses and other harem inmates residing at royal palaces throughout the country at any one time may well have ranged in the hundreds. Almost all lived out their lives in quiet servitude to Pharaoh and then passed into oblivion. In spite of their machinations to commandeer the throne, the women of the royal-harem-in-the-following at the court of Ramesses III fared no better. There is no inkling as to the identity of these women, not simply because the court records suppress their names but because their individuality on an official level was never of any importance. That was not true of the men who participated in the conspiracy. Even though some attempts were made to disguise their identities, it is still possible to find out something of who they were.

CHAPTER FOUR

All the King's Men

Even with widespread sympathy for her cause, Teya could not hope to succeed in placing her son on the throne without the aid of some palace officials who were outside the immediate bounds of the harem apartments. In forming and setting in motion the planned coup d'état, Teya's main reliance was on several palace courtiers, no doubt men of driving ambition. Apart from the spontaneous opposition the king's ruthless character or the ineffectuality of his rule would have given rise to, the temptation to become the power behind the throne would have been overwhelming. The time was ripe, or so it must have seemed to the would-be kingmakers: the king had been on the throne more than thirty years, and the people were disillusioned by the depressed state of the economy, which may have been heightened by the prospect of a seemingly feckless old ruler.

The Names of the Conspirators

Several of the courtiers who plotted against the king were given bogus names in the official records, such as the pantry chief, Paibakamana, and at least six of the other conspirators. The name Paibakamana translates as "that blind servant" and is most certainly a corruption of the good Egyptian name of Pabakamana, which means "the servant of Amun."[1] This vilification of the criminals' names is to be expected, since most Egyptian names were theophoric, usually proclaiming the bearer to be a devout follower of one deity or another. That a convicted criminal, especially one of this magnitude, should have the protection of the deity's name, was inappropriate. Consequently, some of their names were slightly modified so as to be rendered shameful, thus removing the god's patronage. Furthermore, it was an effective form of damnatio memoriae to ensure that the real names of these criminals would not be remembered.

Paibakamana's name heads the list of accused in the trial transcripts. It was not mere chance that his name appears first. The intent was to show for posterity that Paibakamana was, indeed, the foremost of criminals in the conspiracy. His name is mentioned or directly implied by his title more times in the transcripts and supporting documents than any other. The criminal charges leveled against him, as written down in the first arraignment, name him specifically as Teya's main ally. He is, without a doubt, the man who set the plan in motion, first by contacting the relatives of the harem inmates, apprising them of the women's discontent, and probably playing on family loyalties to arouse feelings of hatred against the king. Secondly, he enlisted the aid of three of his colleagues: the butler, Mastesuria, and two administrators of the king's harem, Panouk and Pentau. Thus, the first step to seize the throne is taken: Paibakamana will rely upon the relatives of the harem inmates to win friends and neighbors to their cause and upon his colleagues to help lay the course for a revolt within the palace that involved the murder of the king.

During the course of events, Paibakamana insidiously wins the approval of a few other acquaintances within his bailiwick. Three butlers, Warona, Peluka, and Yeniny, along with Paibakamana's assistant, Ashhebsat, are incriminated because of their contact with the pantry chief. Because they fail to betray his confidence, they are tried and executed as accessories to the crime. Paibakamana's attempts to sow the seeds of discontent among palace workers were important to the success of the palace revolt set to follow the overthrow of the king. Because of the cosmopolitan nature of Ramesses III's court, his task may not have been too difficult.

During the period of the empire all classes of society felt the impact of an invasion of immigrants from abroad. Initially and principally this was due to the large numbers of prisoners of war brought back from the campaigns of conquest, who became slaves upon arrival in Egypt. But, as the empire became established, people from all over western Asia and from beyond Egypt's southern and western borders began descending upon the kingdom voluntarily, settling beside the Nile as merchants or mercenaries. The newcomers formed a sort of foreign community within Egypt. Individual "northerners" had little difficulty in climbing to high office in the administration of the state. Paibakamana's confidants, Peluka, whose name means "the Lycian," a person from southwestern Anatolia, and "the Libyan, Yeniny," are a case in point. The conspiracy texts alone document six men—two magistrates and four of the accused, including these two—who were obviously of foreign extraction. This international aspect of the court may well have compromised the hitherto unswerving allegiance accorded to the king and his appointed heir.

Paibakamana's interactions with men mentioned in the second arraignment implies that he also had a hand in the more dastardly part of the scheme. Papyrus Rifaud A states that he helped the overseer of the army, along with some others, to "go forth against the royal bark" and "overturn" it, a metaphorical description of an attack on the king. Papyrus Rollin further places Paibakamana inside the harem quarters after demobilizing the sentries by magical means. With all details seemingly taken care of, on the appointed day and time Paibakamana and a small band of men initiate the main thrust of their plan: the takeover of the palace.

While Paibakamana risked and in the event lost his life in the attempted coup, he had much to gain if the plan succeeded. His job as pantry chief was really no more than a domestic in the palace. True, he worked within the royal household, which certainly provided some advantages, but his was not a position of influence and power. There is almost no documentation on the office of pantry chief, which may mean it was of little importance in the administrative hierarchy. Much of our knowledge about Egyptian officialdom and status at court comes from information gleaned from the surviving decorated tombs of the nobility. Any Egyptian aristocrat would have held at least one, if not several, key posts in the government along with a number of honorary titles bestowed upon him by the reigning monarch. His function in life would have been proudly exposed in painted murals on the walls of his tomb. Since a tomb in ancient Egyptian society was very much a status symbol, the size and appointment would have been commensurate with the individual's wealth and status. Thus, the larger the tomb, the more important the man's office. Paibakamana's title, pantry chief, is conspicuous in its absence in both the Theban necropolis and at Saqqara, the major necropolis of Memphis. One passing textual reference to the office reveals that the function of the chief of the chamber was that of an assistant housekeeper, one specifically responsible for food inventory in the palace kitchen. Thus we can assume that Paibakamana was not a wealthy man and that the king would not have taken much notice of him, if he knew of him at all. Paibakamana's middling position, as well as his association with the overseer of the cattle of Amun, places him at home in the kitchen of the king's palace. In that regard, Paibakamana may have been a man unhappy with his station in life with little opportunity to rise in the palace echelon.

Unlike his close accomplice, the pantry chief, life held more opportunities for Mastesuria. Mastesuria's title is pronounced "web-a," (wb3) in the ancient Egyptian language and often written in this manner in the hieroglyphic script.

Commonly translated "butler" or "cupbearer," this person's basic task was to serve the king his food and wine. Because of their physical closeness to the throne, butlers sometimes became personal advisors to the king, where they could, and often did, exercise great influence. In Ramesses II's reign, one butler became an aide to a prince, another a supervisor of government work projects, and two rose to the top of the bureaucratic heap and attained the rank of prime minister. In itself, the job became further qualified and grades of butler were established. Ramesses III, himself, took credit for organizing "butlers of the palace" as a general working class of civil servants. The highest rung was that of "Royal Butler, Clean of Hands." When Ramesses III was about to deliver a speech he would address his audience by name: royal butlers were mentioned second, immediately after the king's children. Of the magistrates Ramesses III appointed to preside over his own murder trial, six were butlers. Apart from advising the king, the royal butler retained his hold over his primary responsibility, the food commissariat, which in an agricultural, "feudal" society such as ancient Egypt was enormously important. In the Theban tombs of royal butlers, they are shown inspecting produce and vintage, scrutinizing the preparation of food and drink, and presiding over the stamping and sealing of wine jars.

One cannot be certain what rank of butlership Mastesuria attained. Although Mastesuria's title is that of the unqualified "butler" in the trial transcripts, it may be that his full rank was suppressed so as to downgrade his importance. Mastesuria is listed second in the trial transcripts, following Paibakamana. Like the pantry chief, he is accused of instigating a rebellion against the throne and, like Paibakamana, is found guilty and executed. He is not mentioned in any of the surviving investigative accounts, nor in connection with the men in the second arraignment, but Mastesuria's guilty hand in the conspiracy cannot be denied. His name was anathema: "[the god] Re hates him!" One looks in vain for any surviving reference to a Maiaria, "beloved of Re," the probable true name of Mastesuria, but his name, as well as those of the other conspirators, would have been erased from any public document or personal monument. The convicts probably would have been denied a good Egyptian burial, and even their families and friends would have been obliged to scorn their memories.

Three others joined with Mastesuria and Paibakamana in making preparations for the coup d'état: Panouk, Pentau, and Panhayboni. Panouk, whose name means "the serpent," and Pentau were high-ranking officials in the harem administration. The criminal charges against the men state their involvement with the women and Paibakamana and Mastesuria in plotting a rebellion against the king. Their jobs would have placed them, at least on occasion, in the company of Teya and the other women of the royal-harem-in-the-following, who were secluded from most of the men at court. It was perhaps Teya herself who first wooed Panouk and Pentau to her cause. The two men could have easily acted as go-betweens for Teya and those accomplices who worked outside the harem proper. One can appreciate from their positions in the harem administration their usefulness in synchronizing the rebellion. Preparations and planning of the harem's day-to-day activities would fall to Panouk, assisted by the secretary, Pentau. The king's itinerary would thereby often have been known to these two, who might even have had a hand in planning it. It would have been imperative to those planning a revolt to know the king's movements and personal routine on a daily basis. Like most of the others listed in the conspiracy, there is no personal information on Pentau and Panouk, but, whatever their backgrounds and motives, their lives were ended by the death sentence.

On the other hand, Panhayboni, or "that evil Huy," as his name translates, lacks an entry anywhere in the surviving court transcripts, but there is no lack of evidence for his hand in the plot. He figures prominently in Papyrus Lee and in the Judicial Papyrus in the indictment of Pairy, the overseer of the treasury. Papyrus Lee is very clear on Panhayboni's movements: it places him at the "side of the harem" where with the aid of black magic he delivers crucial instructions to those within. As "overseer of cattle," however, Panhayboni would not be stationed inside a royal complex, and certainly he would not have been permitted near the harem apartments. Thus, he needed to gain some freedom of access to the royal grounds in a more or less legitimate way. Here Papyrus Lee sheds light: the guilty party on whom the report focuses is charged with assisting Panhayboni by supplying him with a royal document that gave him authorization to move freely within the complex. He is admitted to the grounds on the pretext of participating in a commonly held religious ceremony, specifically an oracular consultation the Egyptians referred to as the *pḥ-nṯr* ("reaching god"), at the compound's shrine. The rite was performed for the purpose of adjudicating or prophesying the outcome of matters by means of divine intervention. On public holidays, the sacred statue of the deity, which was fashioned of solid gold, would be trotted out in a portable bark in a festive procession during which the general mass of the populace would be allowed to address the god; but on private occasions within the temples' confines those who were granted an audience were probably determined by an order of precedence or honorary status.[2]

It is surprising that Panhayboni was not arraigned before the tribunal for his crimes. One would have expected his name to appear prominently in the first arraignment along with Paibakamana and Mastesuria. We are left to wonder whether Panhayboni was killed during the revolt or while escaping, or escaped altogether before being apprehended. Interestingly, the first paragraph of Papyrus Varzy gives an account of a man whose machinations could have too easily been perpetrated by the overseer of cattle. The accused of this report is guilty of embezzling the king's cattle by merely changing the branding irons to a mark of his own design. The new brand—a bowstring with a quiver in the middle—would be enough to denote ownership and transfer the cattle to Panhayboni's control. Perhaps the stolen cattle were needed to pay off bribes as a way of gaining sympathy for the rebellion. But it could well be that this accusation has nothing to do with the planned rebellion but is simply intended further to blacken the character of an accused man already deemed guilty. What is odd about the report is that, unlike the others, it does not end with the verdict and sentencing. It is reasonable to suppose that the identity of the accused of Papyrus Varzy is none other than Panhayboni, a man who was never brought to trial.

The only time Panhayboni is mentioned in the court transcripts is in the context of the incrimination of the overseer of the treasury, Pairy. Pairy's entry in the records identifies him as the son of a man called Ruma, whose name may indicate that he was a Canaanite. Thus Pairy may not have been Egyptian by birth. At the site of the ancient quarries of Gebel Silsileh, about 130 kilometers south of Thebes, Pairy left two rock inscriptions memorializing his career.[3] The shorter of the two relates that he was initially in charge of the border entry into Egypt on the Mediterranean coast.[4] The second rock inscription, which is quite lengthy, indicates that in the fifth year of the king's reign Pairy, already promoted to royal scribe and at this point a known and trusted courtier, is put in charge of acquiring stone for the king's mortuary temple, which was being erected on the west bank at Thebes. The text reveals that Pairy is responsible for an expedition of 2,000 soldiers, 1,000 officials, and 40 boats to transport the blocks.[5] It is in this context that he is made "overseer of the treasury" of this very temple. Sometime during his rise to prominence, Pairy adopts the more aristocratic name of "Sutemheb," meaning "the god Seth is in festival." Only once, in the lesser quarry inscription, are we told that Sutemheb bore the birth name "Pairy." Several deliberate abrasions occur in the longer inscription: in its first occurrence in the text Sutemheb's name has been completely erased. At the end of the text, his name is followed by the phrase "son of," but here his father's name, which would have explicitly identified Sutemheb as the traitorous Pairy of the conspiracy, has been obliterated. Pairy's fall from grace is evident. Curiously, twice in the inscription the words "life, prosperity, and health" following the king's name have also been erased.

As overseer of the treasury of the king's southern residence, Pairy no doubt became a permanent resident of Thebes. One wonders whether, after so many years working and living with his Theban colleagues, his loyalty to the Delta regime waned. As a longtime member of the Theban community, Pairy might well have become disillusioned by his royal benefactor when food and rations in the area dwindled. Pairy was indicted on the grounds that he collaborated directly with Panhayboni "in order to incite enemies to make rebellion" against the king. Since Panhayboni was responsible for facilitating communication between the harem and the people outside the palace, Pairy's support must have been enlisted for this purpose.

In Papyrus Varzy, following immediately on an entry in which Panhayboni is defamed, is the beginning of a line in which the next accused person is placed under scrutiny. This can be none other than Pairy. The line reads, "[....] is the name that Pharaoh, his lord, gave him, but it is the name of a servant of a commoner that he had." Although the actual name is not preserved, Pairy's aristocratic name of Sutemhab can be here restored with confidence based on the irrefutable evidence provided by the quarry inscriptions. The description of Pairy's offense would have followed immediately in the format in which the reports were written, but here Papyrus Varzy is torn abruptly. Significantly, Papyrus Lee A begins with the description of a deed that directly assisted Panhayboni. An official pass authorized by the seal of the king was supplied to Panhayboni by the unnamed offender. The king surrounded himself with a circle of administrators, each of whom bore the title "king's scribe," that constituted a kind of cabinet under him. The treasurer, as well as the vizier and the superintendent of granaries, were among the chief members of this council. Thus, wielding the royal seal and issuing official documents was well within the penumbra of Pairy's office. In spite of his adamant denials, the condemned man of Papyrus Lee A was executed, which, as stated in trial transcripts, was Pairy's fate. The pieces fall into place, both literally and figuratively: Papyrus Lee A joins to the bottom of Papyrus Varzy to give us a complete account on the indictment of Pairy.

The Clergy

According to the court transcripts, Paibakamana, along with the military commander Pasai and Teya's son Pentawere, were aided by the men listed in the second arraignment, whose titles leave little doubt as to their specific task in the coup d'état. Papyrus Rifaud A twice accuses these men in particular of "overturning the protections." This is said in connection with the "overturning" of the "royal bark," an implicit allusion to an attack on the king. The Egyptians believed that the kingship was in the safe custody of the gods. The king, being the one person on whom the economy and safety of the country depended, especially benefited by the magical protection afforded by the deities. Magical books housed in temple libraries were transcribed for the king's good, and rituals performed daily by priests in temples throughout the land ensured the king's safety. It was a necessary step for the conspirators to remove these protections in order to make the king vulnerable to attack. Iyroy, along with his colleague Prekamenef, the magician, had the ability to perform such sorcery, aided by two high-ranking scribes, Messui and Shotmaadje, who were able to appropriate the necessary books containing the secret spells and rituals required to carry out their nefarious deeds.

The function of the priests of Sekhmet resembled those of physicians. Sekhmet was the goddess responsible for inflicting disease and plague on Egypt's enemies. It fell to her priests to intervene in favor of those she victimized. According to surviving texts, the priests were medically qualified to diagnose diseases by "examining with the hand." Once diagnosis was done, their therapy on behalf of the patient would entail a knowledge of rituals and magical incantations to reverse the effects of the specified disease. Ranked first as overseer among the priests of Sekhmet, Iyroy performed his job specifically for the king. As royal physician, Iyroy had free access to the palace grounds. More important, he was familiar with the condition of the king's health.

Learned and well versed in the processes of magical healing, a man in Iyroy's position occupied a lofty social status in the ancient society. His affluent lifestyle is evidenced by three inscribed monuments erected to commemorate his career. The first, a limestone door lintel made for Iyroy's tomb, was discovered in the 1950s at Qantir, the site of Ramesses III's ancient Delta capital. The decoration shows Iyroy, dressed in the aristocratic garb of the time—long, pleated, linen robe, wig, and sandals—kneeling in adoration to the cartouches of Ramesses III. In front of the figure is a rather ironic inscription:

> Adoring the king . . . may he cause that I go in and out of the Palace laden with his favors (I being namely) the royal scribe, the overseer of the priests of Sekhmet, Iyroy of Bubastis . . .

There is another text behind the depiction of Iyroy, which reads:

> May the king give offering to Atum[6] (on . . . behalf of) the scribe of the king, his truly beloved one, the chief lector-priest, the overseer of the priests of Sekhmet, the one who foretells the festivals from day to day, pure of hands, Iyroy of Bubastis . . .[7]

In addition to the door lintel, two stelae that also bear Iyroy's name were found in the same vicinity. The stelae were made specifically for a man called Hori, a priest of Sekhmet and "son of Iyroy, the overseer of the priests of Sekhmet." On both these monuments the name of Iyroy was deliberately mutilated. The erasure of one's name on any and all documents and the destruction of the body would ensure that the condemned person would be deprived of a life after death. It is fortunate, indeed, that the door lintel escaped destruction, although it is apparently all that remains of Iyroy's tomb.

The monuments at Qantir provide valuable insight about a man who would otherwise, on the basis of the Judicial Papyri alone, appear rather shadowy. We now can piece together his background. Iyroy was born in Bubastis, probably grew up there, and was trained as a priest of Sekhmet. Under unknown circumstances, he came to the king's notice and was appointed overseer of all the priests of Sekhmet. He then moved to the capital to assume his duties. Besides his distinguished position and honorary title of "king's scribe," the context of the surviving inscriptions makes plain that Iyroy was not only a member of the king's inner cabinet but was a trusted friend and confidant. Mentioned no less than three times as the subject of the difficult and fragmented Papyrus Rifaud B and accomplice of the accused of Rifaud C, the testimonial afforded Iyroy for posterity is that of an ungrateful and traitorous friend upon whom the king lavished favors.

Iyroy's colleague in the medical profession, and likewise his colleague in regicide, was the magician Prekamenef. Like the priest of Sekhmet, the magician belonged to the realm of medical science. But unlike Iyroy, who was limited to diagnosis and prayerful intervention, the magician played an active role in the art of healing. The magician's knowledge of magical formulas, concoctions, and talismans, learned in childhood, made him a man who was as much feared as respected. Several preserved stories attest to the skills of the magician, which were at times awesome. One tale speaks of a magician so masterful in the art of black magic that he could rejoin a severed head. Another tells of a great magician who revenged himself on his wife's lover with the help of magical wax figures, such as a small waxen image of a crocodile, which would turn into the real animal when cast into the water. This brings us in point to Prekamenef's sinister role in the conspiracy. Both Papyrus Lee and Papyrus Rollin disclose the fact that magical wax figures were used to immobilize the watch. In particular, Papyrus Rollin records the brief of the individual responsible for making them. The magician, according to the papyrus, specifically abetted Paibakamana's actions and, when found guilty by the court, committed suicide.

The men of the second arraignment stood accused of direct collusion with the pantry chief and were allowed to take their own lives rather than face execution. The magician stands out as the obvious choice for identification as the culpable person of Papyrus Rollin. He perhaps made contact with Panhayboni at a ritual for oracular consultation, where magicians, identifiable in reliefs by a distinctive sash worn over his chest, served as "lector-priest and the master of ceremonies." If Panhayboni was admitted onto royal grounds to attend such a ceremony, it may have served as the designated rendezvous to collect the prepared waxen images deemed so necessary for the success of their plans.

We cannot be certain of Prekamenef's status at court. The magician class, like that of butler and physician, was a broad and varied one. The magician may have been a local man of no exceptional talents and fame, or, on the other hand, he may have been a professional held in high regard and a member of the king's inner conclave. Probably, the latter is true: a man of Iyroy's status would be intimate with colleagues of equal rank and would surely not cast his lot with a magician of mediocre skills. It is unlikely that further documentation of Prekamenef will ever come to light, since his real name is withheld. The name Prekamenef means "the sun blinds him," symbolically applying a punishment for his misguided conduct.

Court official censing before the king in a procession ceremony at Medinet Habu.

Of the six men indicted in the second arraignment, two were scribes of the House of Life, a national institution that held the records of religious and cultic literature. Since life, in general, was held to be under the control of the gods, the books contained therein represented a wide range of knowledge, including royal chronicles, medical and magical texts, philosophy, geographies, astronomy, ritual instructions, temple inventories, accounts and correspondence, even instructional manuals concerning painting, relief, and construction of temples. It was the scribes' job to maintain the library by recopying early manuscripts and documenting and updating current information. As scribes of these sacred and most revered writings, Messui and Shotmaadje were, in every sense, scholars of the highest academic rank.

Inscriptions from various periods of Egyptian history relate the reigning king's frequent referral to the books of this sacred library. A House of Life was established for his use within the environs of the royal residential complex. There can be no doubt that those who were in charge of it moved in court circles. Moreover, men of Iyroy's and Prekamenef's standing and profession would certainly make use of the library's services, so it is probable that Messui and Shotmaadje were not only their colleagues but perhaps their friends as well. As collaborators in the conspiracy they would have been indispensable in having access to vital magical books.

The dossier on Shotmaadje is provided in Papyrus Rifaud E, but little is related in terms of his specific role in the conspiracy. He became a very wealthy man largely owing to the good graces of the king, but, despite his sworn allegiance, he ended up betraying the king within his own palace. The words of the murdered king Amenemhat, written down centuries before, become all the more poignant: "He who ate my food raised opposition, he whom I gave my trust used it to plot against me. . . . Are rebels nurtured within the palace?"[8]

About the criminal Nibdjatfe there is scant evidence. He is listed simply as a butler without any qualifying term. Since he was arraigned in the company of the well-heeled court intelligentsia, Nibdjatfe may have been himself a man of considerable rank, perhaps a royal butler quite at home and on a par with the learned men of court. The investigative report that is Papyrus Lee 2 may pertain to him. Although an account of the crime is not preserved, it is stated that the accused was found guilty and sentenced to be executed. Facing execution, the condemned man takes advantage of a negligent bailiff and kills himself. So as to absolve themselves of any blame, the court ruled that the criminal's suicide nevertheless fulfilled the god's judgment.

The Army and the Harem Guards

The man who heads the list of the prosecuted in the second arraignment of the transcripts is the general, Pasai. Besides being specified at the trial as a close collaborator of Paibakamana and Pentawere, his central role in the rebellion is suggested by his military title. Once the king was dead, wresting the kingship away from Prince Ramesses would unquestionably require the support of the military. But how many troops would be needed? How many troops did Pasai command?

Since the time of Ramesses II, the heir apparent was named gener-
alissimo of the army. Thus, the hereditary prince Ramesses, the very
man Pasai wished to supplant, was Pasai's commanding officer. On the
other hand, Prince Pentawere was commander in chief of an elite group
of foot soldiers, and he too was Pasai's superior. In this conflict of loyalty, the latter obviously won out in garnering Pasai's support. "Overseer of the army" is another title that requires qualification in order to
distinguish rank. According to Egyptologist A. R. Schulman, who made
an in-depth study of military titles, the term overseer of the army
should be interpreted simply as "military officer." He also concluded
that it "was not a distinct rank, but rather was a title which indicated
that its bearer held a military command."[9] That Pasai was a military officer of considerable rank is intimated by the investigative report concerning his involvement (Pap. Rifaud A). More than once in the document he is referred to as "a great official of the land" and one in
command of forces stationed at local temples, a commission conferred
by the king himself.

In an ingenious piece of detective work, French Egyptologist Pierre
Grandet may have ferreted out the true identity of this military commander.[10] The name of Pasai, which can mean "the bald one," is used in
what may be a clever masking by the royal archivists. While the name
could reflect a physical attribute of the man, it could also describe any
priest, all of whom without exception were obliged to shave their
heads.[11] Pasai was not a member of the priesthood, but there was, however, an overseer of the army by the name of Pahamnata—which translates as "the priest"—known from Ramesses' reign. The general Pahamnata was one of the officials in the expedition transporting blocks
upriver for the construction of the king's mortuary temple, an expedition under the supervision of Pairy-Sutemhab.[12] If Pasai and Pahamnata
are one and the same person, it is attestation of a long-standing acquain-
tanceship between the two accused men.

The investigative report leaves no doubt that it was Pasai who was in
charge of carrying out the physical logistics of an armed revolt. Even
though it was an "uprising, which he made fierce" (Pap. Rifaud A:4), the
revolt was not successful. Pasai obviously thought that the soldiers he
could commit through his post, which may well have been the elite
troops under Pentawere's authority, coupled with Bonemwese's Nubian
unit would be enough to ensure the military takeover of the throne.
Most likely Pasai and his coconspirators, specifically Paibakamana and
Pentawere, "the one for whom Re did not allow the land to rebel" (Pap.
Rifaud A:9), reckoned that they would need only enough men to secure

the palace alone. Once Pentawere was put forward as king, the rest of the armed forces would automatically fall in line.

We can never be sure in what way their plans and calculations went awry. The reliability of the Nubian garrison under Bonemwese, whose debased name means "Evil in Thebes," would not have been doubted, for the forces and their commanders stationed in Nubia were a disaffected lot at this time. Life for the soldier in the remote outposts of the Egyptian empire was rigorous and brutal and the isolation and loneliness almost unbearable. "Come, let me describe to you his [the soldier's] going to 'damnationville' and his marching upon the hills," says one extant text. "His bread and his water are upon his shoulder like the load of an ass, his neck having formed a ridge like that of an ass. The vertebrae of his back are bent whilst he drinks of smelly water and halts only to keep watch . . . he is like a plucked bird, there being no strength in his body . . . he is like a stick which the worm has eaten. He is ill, prostration takes hold of him. . . ."[13] To be posted in Nubia in particular was likened to cruel punishment. In a judicial text of the period a tomb robber confesses to his crimes by taking an oath of god, saying: "All that I have said is true. If I change my word again tomorrow or after that may I be put in the garrison of Nubia." Under these conditions, stirring up the troops in rebellion against the crown would have been no difficult task. In fact, some 40 years after the plot against Ramesses III, another major uprising occurred among the Nubian regiments under the direction of the king's chosen commander. Interestingly enough, they were turned back and defeated by the troops in Thebes. As for the Theban contingent, perhaps Pasai and the others underestimated the respect and the loyalty of the Theban army to the memory of a king who saved the country from foreign invaders and led Egypt to victory through three wars.

Bonemwese's personal life is further elucidated by Papyrus Rifaud C. The text is extremely difficult to make much sense of or render into any connected flow; however, as in texts A and B, we are given another aspect of the career of the accused. Besides battalion commander, Bonemwese appears to have started his career as overseer of the Medjay (md3w), a paramilitary police force mainly in charge of security, and he may have been on familiar terms with some of the Medjay stationed at the palace.[14]

Bonemwese was, according to Papyrus Rifaud C, an old man at the time of the conspiracy. He led a good life, his success due largely to the good offices of the king. Apart from his obvious militant actions in the uprising, the papyrus seems to report on an assignation with the overseer of the priests of Sekhmet, Iyroy, involving the transfer of royal documents. The bits and pieces of certain lines of the reports imply that Ramesses IV caught Bonemwese and Iyroy red-handed in the House of Life.

Of the others implicated in the conspiracy, all were stationed on the grounds of the royal harem. Six men were called "agents" and were posted at the harem gate, which indicates they were in charge of security. Indeed, Papyrus Lee describes an agent at the harem gate who was responsible for carrying magical images inside to facilitate the exchange of messages. It does not seem possible that this man went unpunished, but his name as recorded in Papyrus Lee does not appear in the trial transcripts. The discrepancy can be explained: He is called Adi-ram, a name that betrays his origins in northern Canaan. It was fairly common for immigrants to adopt formal Egyptian names while continuing to be called by their birth name in everyday contexts. Of the six agents prosecuted, two, Sutempidjehuty and Sutempiamana, have names that are compounded with the names of temples. A similar phenomenon appears in American cultural history, where English place-names often provided freed slaves and American Indians with surnames. In this respect, either Sutempidjehuty or Sutempiamana could be Adi-ram's adoptive name.

The wives of the six agents were tried—and executed—along with them. Three others accused of playing a passive role in the coup, a butler, a deputy, and a secretary, held posts in the administration of the royal harem. They were merely accessories to the crime, but, more than just guilty by association, these people were all aware of the planned coup and did nothing to stop it. The security agents were privy to the discussions between the men who worked in the palace proper and the messages reaching them from the inmates of the royal harem, and were hence prosecuted in the first arraignment along with them. The three administrators in the harem actually heard the women speak of the scheme and were arraigned with Pentawere at the third trial.

Pentawere

Pentawere is the only member of the conspiracy who is not called "the great criminal," though he had direct contact with his mother and the women of the harem and was a primary player in their schemes. As in the trial transcripts, he is again coupled with Pasai in Papyrus Rifaud A, where he is called "the one for whom Re did not allow the land to rebel." Yet there is an obvious restraint in further blackening his character. No matter how dastardly the deed, it appears, one did not refer to a biological son of the reigning monarch as "a great criminal." The name Pentawere is in itself a good Egyptian name; however, the documents specify that he "bore that other name," a strong indication that Pentawere had an illustrious surname, one that would have been unthinkable to defile in a public record. Since many of Ramesses' sons bore their father's name in compound with their own, such as the princes, Ramesses-Sutakhopshaf and Ramesses-Amanakhopshaf, it may be the king's name, "Ramesses," that is here being suppressed. One the other hand, it is also possible that the name Pentawere is altogether a pseudonym. As Ramesses III was fond of naming his sons after the sons of Ramesses II, Pentawere's real name might be found among their number. The prestigious name of Seti, for one, after the father of Ramesses II, is missing from Ramesses III's roster of principal sons. It was common practice to name a son for the king's father, which could mean that Sethnakhti was the real name of Pentawere. If he had not been disgraced, Pentawere's true name and titles might now be inscribed among the procession of princes at the king's mortuary temple: "Fan bearer on the King's Right, Crown prince, King's Scribe, commander in chief of the Elite foot troops."

Nothing further can be found documenting the life of Pentawere. Apart from his full siblings, he had numerous half brothers and sisters by the queen, Isis, and quite probably by other women of the king's harem. All the king's children, whether born of the chief royal wife or not, enjoyed wealthy, aristocratic lifestyles. Certain apartments in the palace were designated as the royal nursery where the children were reared and educated. The royal children, particularly the princes, were surrounded by a multitude of retainers and servants. Reading and writing skills, history, and religious cultic tradition were given high priority, and the children's instructors were no less then the celebrated sages of the land. The children of the aristocracy were often brought in as playmates and fellow students and went through the academic paces as well as rigorous physical training along with the royal princes. First-century historian Diodorus offers a brief glimpse into the upbringing of the legendary pharaoh Sesostris: "Gathering together from all over Egypt the male children that had been born on the same day (as Sesostris), and assigning to them nurses and guardians, he (Sesostris's father) prescribed the same training and education for them all, on the basis that those who had been reared in the closest companionship and had enjoyed the same frank relationship (with the crown prince) would be most loyal, and as fellow-combatants in the wars most brave. He amply provided for their every need and then trained the youths by unremitting exercises and hardships; for no one of them was allowed to have anything to eat unless he had first run 180 stades. . . ."[15] There is further evidence that the king often was surrounded by children at the palace acting in the capacity of court pages when he conducted business in the throne room as well as on days of pageantry. Given the power and prestige of his titles, Pentawere could have made much of his high birth and career, if so inclined, but it seems he was swayed by the promise of royal greatness. As a result, he was forced into an early demise, his character sullied for all time.

In the aftermath of the king's assassination, the atmosphere at court must have been fraught with tension. All the officials at the king's court would have had, at the very least, a nodding acquaintance with each other. Apart from those who took an active part, the investigations turned up and indicted courtiers who were sympathizers. Surely, at the beginning of the investigation, most of the court fell under suspicion. Whose loyalty could the king, and especially the heir apparent, Ramesses IV, be certain of? Of those who had no prior knowledge of the plot to overthrow the king, could the king and heir know for sure whether they secretly commiserated with their colleagues? Nevertheless, Ramesses appoints twelve men as magistrates who will sit in judgment over their fellow courtiers. Five are royal butlers, two overseers of the treasury, two scribes of the archives, two standard-bearers, and the king's herald. The names of two of the butlers betray their foreign extraction: Maharbaal was a Syrian whose name means "the god Baal is a speedy warrior," and Kedendenna, the "Kedendennite," was probably named for his birthplace somewhere on the southeast coast of Asia Minor. The overseer of the treasury, Mantemtowa, appears to have served the royal family well, for he is documented as attending on Ramesses IV and later Ramesses VI. The names of three others, the standard-bearer, Kara, and the scribes, Pre-emheb and Mai, appear on a mortuary stela found in their hometown of Heliopolis, the sacred city of the sun god, Re, in the vicinity of modern Cairo. Unfortunately, the context does not give their full titles. The monument, however, does reveal the full name of Kara, given as "Amanemwia called Kara," whose military career began as a captain of a marine contingent, and proves that the three were brothers. As for the remaining judges, nothing more than their names is known. Ramesses proved to be not altogether wise in his selection of magistrates. His butler Pabasa and the Heliopolitan scribe Mai were inclined to be lenient with the culprits in spite of their crimes against the king. When their bias was discovered, another butler, Mayatas-amana, is substituted. One is tempted to view the tribunal as a representative sample of the entire court: two in twelve, one-sixth, in furtive agreement with the rebels' cause.

Mansion of Millions of Years

Two dated documents, one of Year 14 and another of Year 24, attest to Ramesses' residing in the capital city of Pi-Ramesses in the Delta for most of his reign. The city was situated on the easternmost branch of the Nile ("The water of the East," also known as the "Pelusiac" branch), in the vicinity of the ancient township of Avaris, the hometown of the family of the mighty Ramesses II. During his father's reign, Ramesses II had occasion to spend some time in the family residence at Avaris, although for the most part he was reared and groomed for the kingship in Memphis, the administrative center of the empire and royal city at the apex of the Delta just 20 kilometers south of modern Cairo. Ramesses must have delighted in his family home and had an exceptional pride in his hometown, for when he ascended the throne he transferred the court and the seat of government from Memphis to Avaris.

Expanding his father's residence, Ramesses II changed the face of the rural township of Avaris into a thriving metropolis with large and grandiose temples, administrative complexes, a substantial military installation, and an immense and ornately decorated palace. The king named the gleaming new city for himself "House of Ramesses—Beloved of Amun—Great of Victories." It must have been nothing short of spectacular, for it was spoken of by the Egyptian populace who visited it in awe-inspiring terms:

> It is a fair spot, there is nothing like it, resembling Thebes, it was the god, Re, who founded it himself. The city is pleasant to live in, its fields are full of all good things; it is furnished with abundant provisions every day; its waters are full of fish and its pools of birds; its meadows are green with herbage, the grass is a cubit and a half in height, the fruit is like the taste of honey . . . its granaries are full of wheat, they reach the sky; onions and leeks in the [fields];

clusters of flowers in the orchards; pomegranates, apples and olives; figs from the orchard; wine sweeter than honey; (many varieties of) fish from the waters of (the city) "Great-of-Victories" . . . Its ships go forth and return to port. Abundance of food is in it daily; one rejoices to dwell within it, one cannot say enough about it. The small in it are like the great![1]

The city later entered biblical tradition as the site of the Hebrews' labors until their exodus from Egypt.

Pi-Ramesses remained the capital of Egypt for a period of at least 120 years including the reign of Ramesses III. During his reign, the palace grounds were embellished, and it was renamed to include his own royal epithet: "'House-of-Ramesses-Ruler-of-Heliopolis, [....]-Great-of-Victory,' it is called forever. . . . It was furnished with large gardens and places for walking about, with all kinds of date groves and orchards, and a temple thoroughfare, brightened with the flowers of every land, plants, papyrus . . . like sand."[2] Afterward, the city was gradually dismantled block by block and carted off, mainly for use in the building of the new Delta capital at Tanis. So complete was the denudation that nothing of the monumental city remains above ground today. In fact, the exact location of Pi-Ramesses was the subject of great debate among Egyptologists for many years. However, recent excavations have all but confirmed its location with the discovery of the foundations and decorative remains (including a glazed-tiled dais) of a large palace of Ramesside date.

The site where the ancient city once stood, now occupied in part by the modern village of Qantir, shows an expanse of plowed fields as far as the eye can see. In ancient times, the royal residence rose from an island created by two channels of the Pelusiac branch of the Nile. We can only envisage the capital city in the time of Ramesses III, a magnificent show-place of gleaming white architecture and monumental gates with "door-posts of gold mounted with copper; inlay-figures of all kinds of precious stones"[3] and statuary; a city "beauteous of balconies, dazzling with halls of lapis lazuli and turquoise."[4]

Besides his palace at Pi-Ramesses, Ramesses III disposed of the royal estates in Egypt's traditional capital of Memphis and the still-flourishing harem palace at Mi-wer. Ramesses III also established at least two other royal residences: one attached to his new mortuary temple complex on the west bank of Thebes, and the other at an isolated spot some 30 kilometers north of Cairo. The site of the latter bears the modern name of Tell el-Yehudiyeh, "mound of the Jew," so called because in the second century B.C. Onias, an emigrant Jew, built a temple there. The site today is rather remote, situated alongside a two-lane paved road with no town in sight for miles. Its location in what was the floodplain near the banks of the Pelusiac branch of the Nile in the eastern Delta region explains its choice as the site of a royal residence for Ramesses III. His capital city of Pi-Ramesses was approximately 85 kilometers to the northeast along the same Nile branch. To the south of Tell el-Yehudiyeh at a distance of about 20 kilometers lay the important religious center of Heliopolis, home of the sun god, Re, the protector of the kingship in the Egyptian pantheon. Heliopolis was a place to which the king would make regular visits—usually, by river—to discharge his obligations as the earthly son of the deity. If the king were in residence at the capital and required to travel to Heliopolis, he would board his royal barge and sail south. Considering the relative slowness of ancient river travel, relying as it did on wind and strong currents, the probable stopping point after a long day's journey would be the immediate vicinity of Tell el-Yehudiyeh. The trip itself would not have proved to be of any hardship for the king considering the size and appointment of the royal barge. Ramesses III described it in these terms: "I had built thy[5] majestic ship [called] 'Washi' of 130 cubits in length upon the river, made of great cedars of the royal domain, of remarkable size, overlaid with fine gold to the water line. . . . a great cabin was in the midst of it, of fine gold, with inlay of every precious stone, [finials in the shape of] rams heads of gold from front to rear, and [fitted] with uraeus-serpents wearing atef-crowns."[6]

The Hyksos invaders of Egypt in the seventeenth century B.C. had fortified the town at Tell el-Yehudiyeh, by means of an enormous earthwork functioning as an enclosure wall. The pharaoh Ramesses II later took advantage of having a standing fortification within a day's travel of his new capital city and built a rest house within its guarded confines. Ramesses III followed suit and had his own pleasure resort erected to the immediate west of his predecessor's. Archaeology documents the opulence of this king's lifestyle. From the decorative fixtures recovered from the excavation of the building, it proves to have been an exquisite dwelling, elegant and finely crafted. Brightly colored glazed tiles in the form of lotus blossoms and rosettes embellished limestone-veneered chambers and porticos. Tiles depicting bound, foreign captives from the far reaches of the empire were appropriately placed beneath Pharaoh's feet in flooring throughout the structure. Inlays of gleaming alabaster engraved with the king's name lined the palace balconies.

The king may have spent many days luxuriating in the comforts of the palaces of Memphis, Tell el-Yehudiyah, and Mi-wer, but when not at home in Pi-Ramesses it is likely that Ramesses bestowed his company on the people of Thebes far more often than all the others combined. The impetus for the city's initial rise had come from the Eighteenth Dynasty of pharaohs native to Thebes in the south. Thebes was the seat of the most prominent god of the Egyptian pantheon, Amun, "the hidden one." Amun was perceived by the royal house to have guaranteed and promoted Egypt's imperialistic forays, and when the empire proved a success it was to this god above all others that pharaohs turned in thanks and gratitude. "You have certainly let every country and foreign parts know," declared Ramesses III, "that you are the champion of Pharaoh—may he live, be prosperous and healthy!—your fair child! . . . you it is that has made Egypt strong, it is solely your land. And that is not due to the power of any army, but your great might (alone)!" As a reward for his backing, Amun received the majority of the booty from foreign wars and was catapulted to the pinnacle of the pantheon, where he received the title "king of the gods," a heavenly counterpart to Pharaoh. By the time of the reign of Ramesses III his main temple at Thebes had grown to be the largest in Egypt, the temple estates nine times as wealthy as all other temples combined. As a result, Amun's priesthood was powerful and far-reaching, and it behooved the king to make regular visits to the god's seat.

Moreover, the salubrious climate of Upper Egypt made Thebes the ideal escape from the Delta's cold and rainy winter season for many royals throughout the New Kingdom and Ramesside Age. Amenhotep III, for one, moved his entire court permanently to Thebes from Memphis in the latter part of his reign. The perennial sunshine of the south was a strong attraction for the aged king who was suffering from ill health.

A dated text from the reign documents that Ramesses was still living in Pi-Ramesses in Year 30. During that year, an age-old festival called the Heb-sed, celebrated by every pharaoh who attained 30 years on the throne, was celebrated at the capital. Soon after, the king relocated to Thebes. Ramesses III might not have particularly desired living in Thebes, especially in the latter years of his reign, when discontent among the people of the area was overt, but failing health may well have demanded it. Whatever his reason, the king was already residing in Thebes when he celebrated the thirty-second anniversary of his accession.

The Great Papyrus Harris records that this coronation anniversary was the last festival observed by the king before his death. The papyrus specifically inventories the king's gifts and annual endowments to the various temples of the gods throughout Egypt. It records that Year 31 was the last year that these obligations were met, with one exception. Ramesses III's coronation day, inscribed on a wall at his mortuary complex as being the first month of Shomu (third season), day 26, is recorded in the Great Papyrus Harris as being celebrated in Year 32. It further states that, in the twenty-second year of his reign, the king made the anniversary of his accession a festive celebration 20 days in length. Officially the feast was named "Making-Thebes-Festive-for-Amun," which leaves no doubt as to where the celebration was to take place.[7]

Wherever the king decided to locate, his extensive coterie of upper-echelon administrators, priests, domestics, army commanders, and, of course, his family would have followed. Iyroy was born in the eastern Delta region and expected to be buried there, but he relocated to Thebes with the royal family. Pairy, who may also have been born in the vicinity of the eastern Delta, spent the early part of his career there before overseeing the construction of the king's Theban residence and mortuary temple. Of the appointed judges in the trial, the standard-bearer, Kara, and his brothers, the scribes Pre-emheb and the disgraced Mai, were a Heliopolitan family who as members of the king's court made the necessary move to the south. Another judge, the overseer of the treasury, Mantemtowa, is known to be at Thebes from an ostracon dated to the reign of Ramesses IV that identifies him as the official responsible for work carried out in the king's tomb in the Valley of the Kings, the great royal necropolis of Thebes. Certainly, all of the magistrates would have been selected from officials residing in the immediate vicinity.

Teya and the other women, as members of the royal-harem-in-the-following, may well have lived part of their lives in Pi-Ramesses, but the texts of the harem conspiracy strongly indicate that they were of Theban origins. In the indictment of Paibakamana it is emphatically stated that messages were being delivered outside to the women's families urging them to stand ready to assemble for the revolt. As for the others listed in the conspiracy, there is no indication as to their city of origin, or whether they had previously resided at Pi-Ramesses. Most were civil servants: butlers, scribes, food preparers, overseers, inspectors, and bearers of these titles could be found on staff at any royal palace throughout Egypt. It is certain, though, that the men planning the overthrow of the king proceeded as if sure of local support, in particular for Teya and her son Pentawere.

As the place to stage a regicide, Thebes makes eminent sense. The king was a northerner by birth: there were no special bonds of kinship with the people of the south, and in Thebes the king was more than 600 miles from his most loyal subjects. Indeed, in the later part of his reign, it was the people of Thebes that were his most vocal critics. The commander of the Nubian battalion, induced by his sister to bring his troops north to serve as a military backup for the coup, was confident that the men of his outfit would follow his lead. In spite of the fact that Ramesses III's heir apparent was the commander in chief of the army, they were sanguine that with the general Pasai's involvement there would be little resistance.

Ramesses III's Theban residence was a palace built within the confines of his famous mortuary temple located on the west bank of the Nile, opposite the city of Thebes, which was on the east bank.[8] Ramesses III's compound was built on the edge of the ancient floodplain some four miles south of the royal necropolis on a venerated tract of land the ancients called "Djame." It is a magnificent edifice that has withstood the test of time and is one of the highlights on any tourist's visit to the Luxor area. Today known by the Arabic name of "Medinet Habu," it was to the subjects of Ramesses III "the Mansion of Millions of Years of the King of Upper and Lower Egypt Wasmuaria-Miamana, 'United with Eternity.'" This was the building project put in the hands of Pairy-Sutemheb, the king's minister who would later be convicted of treason. Pairy's official record of the event states that the building project began in Year 5. When it was completed, Ramesses took great pride in recording its specifications for posterity: "abiding upon the mountain of the West, built of sandstone, gritstone, and black granite; the doors of electrum[9] and beaten copper. Its towers were of stone, towering to heaven adorned and carved with the engraver's tool in the great name of [the god's] majesty. I built a wall around it, established with labor, having ramps and towers of sandstone. I dug a lake before it, flooded with the celestial waters, planted with trees and vegetation like the Delta."[10]

As Ramesses aptly described, the temple complex was a veritable fortress surrounded by two enclosure walls. In ancient times the outer temenos, a four-meter-high crenellated wall, was approached by a canal now silted up leading from the Nile. Fronting the central gate of the outer enclosure a stone landing dock, more than 10 meters wide, extended into a turning basin into which the canal flowed. The temple itself stood on land slightly elevated above the surrounding floodplain in an attempt to protect its foundations from the annual inundation of the Nile.[11] The canal leading to the temple served irrigation purposes and provided a means of transportation direct to the temple from the Nile for goods and visiting foreign dignitaries. In years of extreme flooding, the lower outer enclosure wall was intended to prevent waters from eroding the inner girdle wall of the complex, which was made from unfired mud brick.

Proceeding a short distance from the waterfront entry to the compound, visitors reached the impressive inner girdle wall, which in antiquity was 10 meters thick and rose to about 18 meters in height. Within this massive circumvallation rose the twin towers of the high-gate. The fortified entry on the east was undoubtedly the official main entrance of the temple complex and is today the only entrance into Medinet Habu. In antiquity there existed an identical high-gate on the west, at the op-

View from the western cliffs of Ramesses III's temple complex
on the edge of the Nile floodplain.

posite end of the complex, which faced the rugged desert cliffs encompassing the royal necropolises and was not far from the village that housed the stonecutters, artists, and general workers who serviced the temple and labored on the royal tombs. The workmen and staff entering the temple daily probably passed through the west gate, which perhaps can be quaintly viewed as "the service entrance at the rear." At both east and west entrances security would not have been lax. Sentries guarded granite doorways that were once provided with enormous double-leaved doors of thick cedar wood with heavy copper and bronze fittings and mammoth sliding-bar bolts attached on the inside.

The towers of the eastern high-gate were constructed both of sandstone and mud brick. Those sections of the two towers erected of mud brick provided living quarters. Unfortunately, they have not survived, but the central stone structure that connected the two wings still stands. The ground floor of the towers was built as a solid structure without

The eastern high-gate as it appears today. The windows and some of the rooms
of the harem apartments where the women resided in seclusion
from the rest of the court are still intact.

rooms, but occupying the upper stories is a block of rooms identified as
the harem apartments. Both the second and third floors contained such
rooms within each of the twin towers, which were joined by a room in
the central block with two large viewing windows on opposite walls.

The windows facing east afforded a view of the canal; those facing
west looked out over the grounds and buildings of the temple complex.
The positioning of the two windows also provided a cross breeze essential
for cooling the rooms in the torrid afternoons of the Theban summer. Today only the second-story central room, located above the gate passageway, is preserved to an extent that one can still enter. The ceiling of the
room is missing, making visible the walls of the room directly above it.

The walls of both these central rooms are decorated in relief with
scenes of the king in the company of his harem. The king is shown in the
various vignettes seated on a chair while the women of the harem entertain him with musical instruments, present floral bouquets and fruit, offer wine, play games of senet with the king, and anoint him with scented
oils. The king is four times shown chucking a girl under the chin and in
one scene has his arm around another. In other poses, the women stand
before the king with hand gestures that denote conversation, although a

RAMSES III PLAYING DRAUGHTS WITH A PRINCESS AND ATTENDED BY ANOTHER
THIRD-FLOOR ROOM IN NORTH TOWER, NORTH WALL

Pictured on the walls of the harem apartments at the king's mortuary temple are the
women of the royal harem playing a game of senet with Ramesses III.
(Courtesy of The Oriental Institute of The University of Chicago.)

few are shown with an extended clenched fist, which has sexual over-
tones and may suggest sexual stimulation. Apart from large borders inscribed with the royal epithets and cartouches, there are few textual regis-
ters and the focus is strictly on the king. In the scene showing the girls
musically entertaining the pharaoh, the words to their song appears:
"[To] your ka Sesi,[12] the divine king, [the] sun of every land. May you re-
peat coronation anniversaries like Atum, your limbs being like Khepri.
May many years and a lifetime of the sun in the sky be ordained for
[you]." Accompanying a scene in which a senet match is underway between the king and one of the girls, the caption relates the girl's praise as
to how flawlessly the king plays. No doubt the king always won.

The reliefs appear to represent the women without clothes. On close
inspection, however, there are a few subtle outlines on some of the female figures implying the deliberately vague depiction of sheer
garments.[13] Even by the formal standards of Egyptian art, the intimacy of
the scenes and the sexuality of the harem women are blatantly conveyed.

The carvings of most of the female figures in the harem rooms suggest
young maidenhood, but two of the female faces, one drawn with a labial
fold and another with a downward crease at the mouth line, indicate
that some of the women were not in their first bloom. Also present are
the king's little daughters. These little girls, drawn not much larger in
scale than the king's knees, are identified in a caption that begins:
"Words spoken by the king's children . . ." The words put in their
mouths eulogize the king's facial features as resembling precious stones.

It is easy to imagine the harem apartments at Medinet Habu as the
focus of the conspiracy against the king. A significant passage in Papyrus
Lee appears to be describing the layout of the eastern gate. One line in
the text relates that the unnamed conspirator, upon whom the report is
focused, arrived at the "side entry of the harem" of "that other very expansive place."[14] A sobering note: when clearing the gate area, excavators found evidence that the main entrances to the harem quarters had
doors that bolted on the outside by means of cords and metal fastenings.

The high gate overlooks an expanse of land within the great girdle wall
that stretches some 80 meters to the majestic pylons of the main temple
structure. Today the ground here is almost devoid of features, except for
three small chapels built later by ruling priestesses between the eighth and
sixth centuries B.C. But the king himself described a beautiful garden that
once grew here: "It was surrounded with vineyards and orchards, abun-
dant with fruit and flowers in honor of the serpent goddesses. I built their

kiosks; I dug a pool before them, filled with lotus flowers."15 Standing below in the dry, dusty grounds that was once a lush garden where the women of the harem dallied, one can still envisage the girls peering out from the windows of the tower over the verdant green to the Nile watching the approach of foreign dignitaries and messengers or the arrival of tribute from far-off lands. Beside the garden to the immediate south, archaeological excavations have also uncovered the remains of buildings identified as the royal stables and living quarters for the king's bodyguard.

The gigantic pylons of the temple are almost completely intact, rising nearly 30 meters high and covering an expanse of more than 50 meters. They front the temple edifice, which consists of two columned processional courts, a multicolumned inner sanctum with an attached block of shrines, and storerooms at the rear. This structure extends along a main axis for more than 140 meters. Officially, the temple is dedicated to the cult of Amun as the god's "palace," but most of the walls, especially those in the first court and on the exterior, were utilized to extol the might and majesty of Pharaoh.

Though the reliefs present a historical narrative of Ramesses' military campaigns, they, in essence, attest also to his enormous ego. Pharaoh was portrayed on a gigantic scale with superhuman abilities routing Egypt's enemies. A punitive raid into Nubia, skirmishes with the Libyans and Hittites, and the watershed battles with the Peoples of the Sea are featured, subjects intended to show his invincibility. No one escapes Pharaoh's vengeance. The scenes are executed with stereotypical poses of the king charging in his chariot discharging his arrows with infallible accuracy. With his troops before him, the encounter results in mass chaos and annihilation for the enemy. Accompanying texts use locutions that are word pictures of what is graphically being presented: the king "slays hundreds of thousands on the spot under his horses"; a fallen Libyan chief is "slit wide open on the ground"; the king's attackers "are thrown down on their ass." But within these rather monotonous renderings are poignant images of the suffering being visited on these people.

One illustration shows a Nubian village apparently being caught unaware: a woman with her basket by a date palm stops in her task of picking fruit to watch the slaughter of the village men; a child runs in fright among the melee; one Nubian, perhaps a female, holds up a wounded man while an Egyptian soldier stands beside them with raised battle-ax ready to deliver the deathblow to them both. In the encounter with the Libyans, a man is shown cupping the face of his wife as she falls forward with Pharaoh's arrow in her back as her child looks helplessly on; an Egyptian soldier grabs hold of the beard of a kneeling Libyan to slit his throat while another soldier cuts off the hand of his still-alive nemesis. In the aftermath of the battle, Pharaoh is seen leisurely sitting on the back of his chariot watching Egyptian scribes tallying the body count by means of the removed phalluses of the enemy dead. The scribes are also shown tabulating piles of right hands assuring that those enemy warriors left alive will give Pharaoh no more trouble. Bound prisoners of war, their hands intact, are also paraded before the king and branded with hot irons by their captors to be deported to Egypt for slave service. As they are led away, Pharaoh speaks: "Listen and pay attention to my words that you may understand my measures for keeping you alive."

The reliefs were in no way meant to excite compassion for the enemy. In the world of the ancients, military victory meant increased prosperity and wealth and secure borders. God was on their side. He condoned and divinely facilitated Egypt's triumph over its enemies. The ancient Egyptians would have viewed the fallen foes as pathetic losers and considered their suffering apt punishment for those who would foolishly attempt to defy Egypt's sovereignty.

The first and second courts at the temple were designed for processions and large gatherings of people and were open to the sky. It was in the first court that crowds would be assembled to hear the king's many speeches, which he delivered from a royal balcony built into the court's south wall. In the second court of the temple, wherein the revealing and much-debated scene of the procession of princes is engraved, religious ritual takes precedence over military campaigns in wall decoration. It is in this section of the temple that the grand religious festival of the god Min is portrayed with scenes in which the king is brought in his litter on the shoulders of his sons. The entire court appears in attendance: the queen, the king's children, his cabinet, high priests, and military officers.

The second court leads to the halls of the sacred shrine of the god at the back of the temple. Only the king and a select few would be allowed in this part of the temple. The sanctuary was hallowed ground, a mock-up of the mound of creation. It was flanked by storerooms, the wall decor of which reveals the gold, silver, and other precious items of the king's treasury housed within.

Situated at right angles to the southern exterior wall of the first court of the temple proper are the remains of the royal palace. The front of the palace abuts this exterior wall, so that the main entries to the palace are made through the first court via two rather narrow doorways. The relief on the left wall of the entryway shows the king entering his palace; the opposite wall shows him going out. Except for doorways and columns, the royal residence was made of mud brick, as were other living and

A view of the first court with the window of appearances from which
the king addressed his court.

working quarters in the compound. As a result, the walls of the palace
along with whatever painted murals were on them have long since disappeared. The ground plan, however, was excavated and restored in the
early 1900s, revealing a building of modest size and interesting layout.[16]

The design centers upon a six-columned audience hall at the rear of
which once stood the stone dais for the king's throne. Patterns of discol-
oration left on the external temple wall where it met the palace walls
show that the audience hall had vaulted ceilings—another device
against heat. A single doorway in the back wall leads to the king's private apartments. A short passage connects to three rooms: on the left is a
small, two-columned throne room with the stone dais still in situ. It
might be assumed that this room was used for private sessions with the
king or, perhaps, cabinet meetings. To the right of the passage, a few
steps from the throne room dais, is a small bathroom for the king's con-
venience. At the far side of the throne room a door gives entry to what
the excavator designated as the king's bedroom. A restored stepped plat-
form may have served as a pedestal for the king's bed.

To the west of the king's quarters, though inaccessible to them and the
main audience hall, is another small throne room, with the dais still preserved. The smaller scale of this throne room in comparison to the king's

Ground plan of the royal palace as restored by excavators.

A reconstructive drawing of the palace audience hall as it was in the days of Ramesses III.
(Courtesy of The Oriental Institute of The University of Chicago.)

quarters possibly suggests that it was meant for the queen. A recessed entry to the left of the dais hides another bathroom while to the right of the dais is a doorway to a long block of rooms at the back of the palace spanning its entire width. These rooms were identified by the excavator as living quarters of the king's immediate household. There are three suites, each suite consisting of a small anteroom, a larger square room, and two small adjoining rooms, one of which was a bathroom. A long passageway provided direct access out of the palace on the east side to the garden and hence a pleasant walk to the harem quarters at the high-gate.

At the far end of the audience hall is a double stairway leading to a large viewing window with a wooden balcony that opened onto the temple's first court. The reliefs on the court wall surrounding the "window of appearances," as it was called, indicate that, besides delivering speeches, the king would watch temple ceremonies from here, including wrestling matches, and preside over the handing out of rewards to his courtiers. A mural on one of the temple's walls shows that the balcony was decorated with depictions of bound captives from the empire and cushioned for Pharaoh's comfort. The king further boasts in an inventory document that the balcony was lined in fine gold, and the doors, their frames, and columns in the palace were of electrum.

Walking around what remains of the palace today, it is striking that one must enter the audience hall from a side entry at the opposite end of the room from the dais. Moreover, it would have been impossible to see the throne upon entry because of the large columns blocking the view. So one would have to proceed to the middle of the room and approach the king straight on. This certainly makes sense in terms of court protocol: one would surely have to wait to be announced before being allowed to approach the throne. In addition, it was a useful security measure. In fact, archaeological excavations revealed that the palace underwent renovation in the latter part of Ramesses' reign in what appears to be an attempt to make the palace and the king himself less accessible to outsiders. For one thing, the main audience hall was made smaller by the addition of closet-sized side chambers, which the excavator surmised to be sentry boxes. There was also evidence that a lightweight screen, probably made of wood, was erected running the width of the audience hall, cutting the room in two and thus effectively blocking the throne from the view of anyone entering the hall. While a double-sided stairway replaced a single one leading to the window of appearances, access to both sides was made more restrictive, allowing for the passage of only one individual at a time. Last, the royal sleeping quarters at the back of the palace were only accessible through two doorways, both situated within a few steps of the king's dais. One wonders whether the civil strikes and the general feeling of discontent among his subjects at this time made the king more concerned about the matter of his personal safety.

Abutting the palace on the west and running the length of the second court to the end of the edifice were the administrative offices of the king's southern court. Within these myriad rooms would have been located the king's scribal pool, the office of the treasury, the taxation department, and the state archives. It was probably here that Pairy, Peluka, and the scribes and overseers implicated in the conspiracy came to work each day. Evidence of a well that probably provided water to palace and temple residents and staff was also found within this area, as was a nilometer that officially recorded the height of the Nile at various times of the year.

The temple complex of Medinet Habu was a visual testimony to the majestic presence of Ramesses III. Its estates were manned by 62,626 men, which included thousands of prisoners of war. It was stocked with products from all over the empire. Its treasury groaned with gold, silver, and precious stones, which in the king's words numbered "by the hundred thousand." The temple granaries overflowed with grain, and the crops of its fields and herds were as bountiful "as the sand of the shore." Its walls served to illustrate all that the king had done for the glory and prosperity of Egypt. In spite of the many standing temples of previous reigns and those that would come after, the preeminence of Ramesses III's monument would be recognized by the people of ancient Egypt, who would forevermore refer to it as simply "the temple."[17]

Both before and after the reign of Ramesses III, however, Thebans were never quite content to be ruled by families from the north. Consequently it was no doubt politically prudent to hold coronation ceremonies and anniversary festivities in the Thebaid. On more than one occasion throughout the long course of pharaonic rule, the people of Thebes showed contempt for the ruling family from the northern part of the country through civil disobedience, out-and-out civil wars, and even instances of crowning their own king. One cannot shake the impression that the conspiracy against Ramesses III was a Theban plot: Teya and her female accomplices, daughters of the Theban aristocracy, were handpicked by the king to become members of his household in the hopes of strengthening the bonds of kinship. But Teya's offspring, a son of the pharaoh's, is overlooked as heir apparent. Returning home in the royal entourage, the women are greeted by the local palace staff—doorkeepers, pantry chiefs, butlers, military officers—men who were perhaps distant relatives or old family friends. They had bided their time, but now the king was on their soil. Soon, a son of Thebes would rule Egypt.

CHAPTER SIX

"The Hawk Has Flown to Heaven"

The succession of the kingship from Ramesses III to his son was duly noted by the court scribes in Papyrus Harris. The document begins:

> Year 32, third month of Shomu (third season), day six, under the majesty of the King of Upper and Lower Egypt, Wasmuaria-Miamana, life, prosperity, and health; son of Re, Ramesses (III), Ruler of Heliopolis, life, prosperity, and health, beloved of all gods and goddesses; king, shining in the White Crown like Osiris; ruler, who brightens the Netherworld like Atum; [ruler] of [...] of the great house in the midst of the necropolis, traversing eternity forever as king of the Netherworld; the King of Upper and Lower Egypt; Wasmuaria-Miamana; son of Re, Ramesses, Ruler of Heliopolis, life, prosperity, and health, the great god.[1]

In unmistakable terms, the passage bespeaks the death of the king. The document was therefore being prepared on what was the last day of the king's reign—or at least what was expected to be the king's final day. News of the king's death was further documented on an ostracon found in the worker's village at Deir el Medineh, located less than a kilometer from Medinet Habu. It reads: "Year 32, third month of Shomu, day 16, it has been announced, the hawk has flown to heaven. The king, Wasmuaria-Satepnamana (Ramesses IV), life, prosperity, and health, the sovereign, sits upon the throne of the sun god in his place." The obvious discrepancy—the day the king died is recorded as "day 6" on the state document and as "day 16" on a public document—is resolved by an ostracon found at Deir el Medineh, which establishes the accession date of Ramesses IV unequivocally as "third month of Shomu, day 15." As in all monarchical systems, the heir apparent, in this case, Ramesses IV, acceded to the throne immediately upon the death of his father, and "day 15" can be postulated without reservation as the date of Ramesses III's passing.[2]

The people of Thebes were told of the king's death the very next day. Messengers carrying news of the king's death would have also been dispatched to cities and townships throughout Egypt and in particular to Pi-Ramesses, a journey which would have taken at least 10 days. As for the date given on Papyrus Harris, two possible explanations present themselves. The royal document was written in the "hieratic" script, a cursive form of hieroglyphics that allowed the scribe to write more quickly. In this hand, the difference in writing the number 6 as opposed to 16 is the omission of a single stroke, | . In other words, it may simply be a case of a scribal error. Alternatively, the king may not yet have been dead on the day the papyrus roll was being written but death appeared imminent and preparations were already underway. It can be ascertained, by computing from the Sothic cycle, the day of the king's death, the third month of Shomu (third season), day 15, fell on April 18.[3]

Nowhere in the texts does it state unequivocally that the revolt against the crown resulted in the king's death. Taken metaphorically, the passage in Papyrus Rifaud that refers to the overturning of "the royal bark" comes closest to an admission that the dastardly act had been accomplished. Such a metaphorical acknowledgment of regicide is understandable given the Egyptians' strong religious beliefs. The reports are very careful to anathematize the conspirators, reporting that the gods did not support their actions. They even go so far as to assert that the god Re never really affirmed two of the criminals' tenure in office.

The king's mummy, which was recovered in an excellent state of preservation, shows a considerably obese man with no wounds on his body. Before indulging in speculation that the king was drowned, poisoned, suffocated, or strangled, it must be admitted that in the absence of an autopsy the evidence militates in favor of a natural death. There are, however, problems concerning the king's mummy, specifically the estimated age at death. In his book *An X-Ray Atlas of the Royal Mummies*, James Harris contends, after a detailed x-ray examination of the body, that Ramesses III was no more than 35 years old at the time of his death.[4] It is conceivable that Ramesses came to the throne as a toddler, but then the king's claims of engaging in warfare as early as Year 5 would defy explanation. Equally problematic is the dating of the mummy of Ramesses' son and successor, Ramesses IV. At the time of his death, he is estimated by Harris and his associates to have been near 40 years of age.

Ramesses IV reigned only six and a half years following the death of his father. Moreover, Ramesses IV was not the king's eldest son. Ramesses III buried three of his heirs during his lifetime.

There has been much dispute and questioning of Harris's age estimates not only for the mummy of Ramesses III but for most of the royal mummies. Indeed, the historical record for many of the pharaohs examined by Harris suggests that, overall, the age estimates given in the pathology report are far too low.[5] Considering the war reliefs of Year 5, which portray Ramesses III as an adult; the length of his reign; and the age of his middle son when he inherited the throne, a more reasonable estimate is that Ramesses III lived 60 years or longer.

If, on the other hand, Harris's age estimates are to be taken seriously, then we must entertain the possibility that the mummy thought to be Ramesses III is not really he. The wrapped mummy of Ramesses III was found in the great royal cache at Deir el Bahri in the late 1800s.[6] Owing to the indignities suffered by the royal mummies from tomb robbers, the necropolis priests of the Twenty-first Dynasty collected and rewrapped them for a common burial. The king's mummy was first thought by the discoverers of the royal cache to be that of Queen Ahmose-Nefertari, as it was in her coffin that the king's body rested. Upon closer inspection, the restoration docket painted on the bandages of the mummy identified it as Ramesses III and indicated that it had been rewrapped three times. Since some of the royal mummies showed no label of identification on the wrappings and others were placed in coffins that did not belong to them (Ramesses III's coffin was reused for Amenhotep III), it is certainly within the realm of possibility that those responsible for reburying the bodies confused their identities. But, until some hard evidence surfaces to the contrary, it must be assumed that the mummy rewrapped and labeled as Ramesses III is indeed the king.

Papyrus Harris gives evidence that the king was alive to enjoy the entire 20-day festivities commemorating his thirty-second anniversary on the throne. The celebrations began on "the first month of Shomu (third season), day 26" (February 28) and continued until "the second month of Shomu (third season), day 15" (March 19). By "the third month of Shomu (third season), day 16" (April 19), it was announced to the public that the king had died. Sometime within this 30-day period the overthrow of the king was attempted. There is evidence that something was amiss on the second month of the third season, day 29 (April 2). The daybook of the royal necropolis workmen asserts that, on that day, the men again crossed over the security wall of their Deir el Medineh village, as they had done in Year 29 to march on nearby Medinet Habu in order

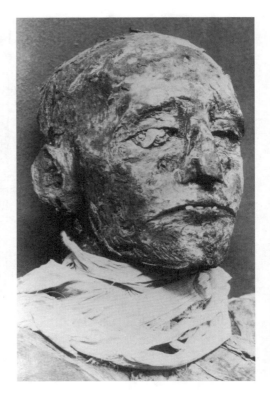

More than three millennia after his
death, one can still gaze at the face
of Ramesses III on display in the
Cairo Museum. From G. Elliot Smith,
The Royal Mummies (Cairo: Institut
Français d'Archéologie Orientale, 1912).

to demand their wages. The entry, however, gives no indication of a labor strike. The commotion continued throughout the next day, the last
day of the second month; by the day after, the first day of the third
month, things had settled down and the men were back to work. This
uprising, occurring within two and a half weeks of the king's death, is
too suspicious to be mere coincidence. It is plausible that the log entry
coincides with the coup d'état, set in motion on the twenty-ninth day of
the second month of the third season.

A tantalizing bit of information concerning this particular day of the
month appears in a hemerology of New Kingdom date and is worth considering with regard to this event. As many people do today, the ancient
Egyptians sometimes consulted their daily horoscope for lucky and un-
lucky days in making decisions and planning events. Their premonitory
listing of dates was based not on the stars but on religious mythology,
and it carried great weight with them. Some "daily horoscope guides"
have survived from the New Kingdom, and one of these is referred to as
the Cairo Calendar.[7] Those scheming the overthrow of the king would

The ruins of the workers' village at Deir el Medineh.

have undoubtedly consulted a copy of such a book-roll in planning the exact day to make their move. According to the Cairo Calendar, anything acted upon on the twenty-ninth day of the second month of the third season will have a good outcome.

Evidence, then, militates in favor of the assumption that the king did not die immediately from the assassination attempt but survived for 16 days before passing away, helping to explain the discrepancy concerning the king's date of death found in the Papyrus Harris. The scribes documenting the transition of the kingship were perhaps predicting that the old king would be dead by day 6, while in fact he hung on for nine more days. Consequently, the passage in Papyrus Rifaud concerning overturning the royal bark cannot be taken literally to mean an attempt by the conspirators to drown the king. Strangulation or suffocation can also be ruled out as the modus operandi, and the lack of obvious wounds on the body indicate the pharaoh was not attacked with a metal weapon.

Poison, Snakes, and Magic

Death by poisoning has been put forth by some as a reasonable supposition. The ancient Egyptian pharmacopoeia was well stocked with lethal poisons, and there are several obvious choices that would have provided an effective means for murdering the king. Mandrake, for one, commonly depicted in painting of Egyptian gardens, is a poisonous plant associated with magic through the ages. It was administered in wine as a cure for sleeplessness, but an overdose would ensure a sleep from which the victim would never wake. The mandrake plant produces a fruit that can be eaten safely, but eating the plant itself is fatal within 30 minutes. The properties of the common poppy, from which morphine is derived, were known and well utilized throughout the ancient world, and it too was often depicted in garden scenes growing alongside the mandrake plant. A morphine overdose is fatal within two to three hours of ingestion, death being preceded by paralysis and coma. The medicinal properties of the indigenous castor-oil plant was known to the Egyptians as far back as prehistoric times. Every part of the plant, especially the seeds, contain the highly poisonous ricin. Just a few would be needed to cause acute respiratory failure. Paralysis and death can occur from within hours to up to 12 days. Nightshade, a deadly plant from which two potent alkaloids, atropine and scopolamine, are extracted, still grows wild in the Egyptian Delta today. The raw berries and stems are highly toxic, and ingestion can damage the nervous system. All of the above plants were utilized for medicinal purposes by the ancient Egyptians. Egyptian medical books reveal that liquid vehicles such as beer, wine, and milk were sweetened with honey to which was added the "corrective." The poisons were, therefore, easy to procure, especially by a physician, and could as easily have been put into the king's food or wine. Both Paibakamana, the chief of the chamber, and Mastesuria, the king's butler, were responsible for the king's food and drink. The unsuspecting king would have readily accepted his meals and beverages from these courtiers, and certainly those served at the hands of his harem women.

With the armed revolt to take over the palace undoubtedly set to coincide with the king's death, the conspirators intended the king to have a reasonably quick demise with no chance of recovery. They would have known that the effect of some poisons was unpredictable. For one thing, most would have an extremely bitter taste, and the king would have to have been forced to ingest enough to kill him.

Quicker and more precise than poison administered in a drink would be death by an attack by a venomous snake. There are some reasons death from a snakebite should be given equal consideration. First and foremost is the fact that, posthumously, Ramesses III was appealed to for protection against snakebites. The intriguing spell is known from a small statuette of the king portrayed as a lion. It is a prophylactic, with a magical incantation on the reverse of the statue to be used against snakes and scorpions:

> King Wasmuaria-Miamana is a lion who spreads astonishment by his force. He is Shesemu-Matai whose arms Re coated when he, the one in his hole, fell on his face. Do not bite the son of Re, Ramesses, ruler of Heliopolis—he is Re! Do not sting him—he is Khepry! Do not bring the flame of your mouth against him—he is Spaciousness, he is the Great Eternity whose form is present in every god. He is the Lion who protects himself, he is the great god who fights on behalf of his brother. The one who would bite him will not survive. The one who would rage against him, his head will not be fastened. For he is a lion who wards off gods and spirits when he has stricken all male snakes and all female snakes who bite with their mouth, who sting with their tail on this day, in this month, in this year, and its addendum!
>
> Words to be said over a lion of faience, threaded to red linen. To be applied to a man's hand. It is to be given as a protection of the bedroom.[8]

Adding to the evidence is a group statue set up in a chapel on an eastern desert route near Heliopolis that depicts Ramesses III seated alongside the goddess Ese on a throne inscribed with spells against venomous snakes. The purpose and choice of locale for such a shrine is obvious. One of the real hazards of expeditions into the eastern desert was the presence of aggressive and deadly vipers. What is not readily obvious and is indeed highly unusual, however, is why a king, specifically Ramesses III, should be prayed to as the protector against poisonous bites rather than the god Horus, whose role this was in the Egyptian pantheon. In Egyptian mythology, the goddess Ese saves her son, Horus, from the bite of a snake. In one myth, she and Horus are sailing in the "bark of the sun god Re," and the exposed vertebra of Apophis, the serpent god, threatens to "overturn it." (One is tempted to see symbolic reference in the passage of Papyrus Rifaud in which the accused is said to be responsible for helping the others "to go forth against the royal bark and it was overturned.") The role of the patron saint in the Christian religion might be somewhat comparable. A Christian saint or martyr who had suffered some physical mutilation or handicap or had died in a specific fashion became the person to beseech for relief or protection from similar circumstances or from a like fate. For example, St. Lucy, blinded as punishment for her beliefs, became patroness of eyes and eyesight; St. Apollonia, who as part of her torture suffered her teeth to be wrenched from her mouth, is invoked by those who suffer from tooth ailments. If Ramesses was bitten by a deadly snake, that he survived sixteen days might appear to be nothing short of miraculous.

There are no treatments for snakebites in the medical compendia of Ancient Egypt, since they were considered to be incurable by practical means. Deliverance of the victim would depend on magical spells, potions, and appeals to the gods. The lethal venom of the Egyptian cobra is famous in myth and legend. The Roman historian Galen reported that a bite in the breast from this snake was used as a means of giving a merciful death to condemned prisoners. The Egyptian cobra is the most likely identity of Cleopatra's asp. If enough venom is injected in a bite from a cobra, death would occur within two hours. The carpet viper, considered by some herpetologists to be the most dangerous snake in the world, is another possibility. A venomous bite from this reptile will cause death from massive internal bleeding. While symptoms will appear within an hour of being bitten, death may not occur for one to twelve days. An unusually toxic type of venom from one of Egypt's most deadly snakes, the saw-scaled viper, can cause both external and internal hemorrhages that are fatal within 12 to 16 days after the bite. The venom of other poisonous vipers known from this part of the world can cause a victim to suffer irreversible liver damage and kidney failure and die up to several months after being bitten.

Procuring the reptile and conveying it into the king's presence would not have posed any difficulty. Snake charmers are a fixture of every village in Egypt still today, and the men are quite adept at handling these venomous creatures. They are able to make them as rigid as a stick by applying pressure on the neck and thus to transport them up their sleeves. If we were to look for the snake charmer among the accused, two men by name are glaringly conspicuous. One is Panouk, whose name translates as "the serpent," who as overseer of the king's harem had access to their private apartments. The other is a butler in the company of those men responsible for making the king vulnerable to attack by magical means—the magician, the overseer of the priests of Sekhmet, and the scribe from the House of Life—whose name is given an Nibdjatfe, a corruption meaning "lord of snakes."

A third possible cause of Ramesses' demise should not be overlooked. Although it is alien to Western beliefs, we must consider that the king died simply because the magic worked. It cannot be stressed too strongly that the belief in and use of magic was endemic in Egyptian religion and ingrained in the Egyptian way of life. As an agricultural society at the mercy of the elements, magic provided a means of controlling their environment. Papyrus Lee and Rollin state emphatically that magical incantations and waxen images were relied upon to bring the plan to fruition. It has been suggested that incapacitating the guards could have been accomplished by adding a narcotic to the waxen figures that, when lit, produced a smoke capable of sedating those nearby.[9] But the practical measures taken in the guise of waxen images and potions only worked, the Egyptians believed, by means of the magical spells and incantations invoking the gods' powers. In every aspect of their daily lives, the people of ancient Egypt surrounded themselves with magico-religious beliefs in an effort to protect themselves from danger, to cure themselves of any maladies that afflicted them.[10]

The king, like his subjects, had every confidence in the effectiveness of magic. The realization that his court magician and his chief lector-priest, in possession of sacred magical books written specifically for the king's protection, had used sorcery to bring about his demise would alone have been detrimental to the king's well-being. Egyptologist Barbara Mertz speculated that perhaps the waxen images were akin to voodoo dolls and "that one of the figures may have been that of Ramesses III, animated by means of a magical roll and thus a puppet in the hands of the conspirators."[11] The king was a man well into his sixties, seriously overweight, and his move to Thebes suggests he was in failing health. He was not a likely candidate to survive being seriously traumatized. It is documented that, in certain parts of Africa and the Caribbean, persons believed by their fellow villagers to have magical abilities can simply "point their finger" to kill someone. The doomed person lies down and waits for death while others prepare for his funeral. Papyrus Rifaud thrice accuses the conspirators of "overturning the (magical) protections," perhaps analogous in ancient Egyptian society to pointing the finger.

Several scenarios present themselves in terms of the actual delivery of the lethal stroke. Whether by snakebite, poison, or magical confrontation, the presence of Teya and the women of the harem is strongly implied. The fact that the king was not attacked with a weapon argues that the plan of action involved doing away with the king, or at least making sure of his imminent demise, in rather surreptitious fashion. Such an assassination attempt would have to be planned for a time and place at which the victim would least expect such an attack, especially a man as well guarded as a king. Teya and the women of the harem, household members in the king's secluded apartments, were best in a position to carry such a scheme forward. Moreover, it is evident from the surviving documents that none of the men implicated in the conspiracy had a direct hand in killing the king. Only Pasai, in Papyrus Rifaud A, is accused of aiding and abetting those that did.

It may be coincidental that any statement concerning the assassination of the king and the prosecution of Teya and the women of the harem is missing elements of the record, but it may not. It stands to reason that, if the throne were to be wrested from the heir apparent and Pentawere proclaimed king, his supporters would have to be ready and in position physically to secure the palace when it was believed the king was about to die. If timed properly, the establishment of a new king on the throne would be uncontested by the rest of the country. While their male accomplices were preparing to take up arms against the heir apparent, it fell to Teya and the women of the harem to make sure the death-blow found its mark. Since the overthrow of the king was Teya's idea, she may well have done so with relish.

Burying a King

Written nine days before the king's passing and speaking of Ramesses III in terms of an already deceased monarch, the Great Harris Papyrus is proof that either directly or indirectly the attempted assassination had seriously compromised the king's health and that death was imminent. Undoubtedly, preparations for the royal funeral were under way.

In a desolate valley in the desert northwest of the royal palace at Medinet Habu, a short distance from the Nile, the king's tomb lay ready to receive him. For the three and a half centuries since the beginning of the Empire period, the rulers of Egypt carved out their complex hypogea in this area famously known as the Valley of the Kings. Excavation of Ramesses' tomb commenced before his ascension to the throne, and since Ramesses reigned for more than thirty years the royal sepulchre was very near completion by the time of the king's death. Seen today by thousands of tourists every year, the king's tomb reveals no secrets as to its owner's untimely end.

Located in what is now the main thoroughfare through the Valley of the Kings, not far distant from the famous tomb of Tutankhamun, Ramesses III's final resting place is in most respects typical in style and decoration to others of the Nineteenth and Twentieth Dynasties. The cavernous and multiroomed tomb proceeds in an unsteady descent almost in a straight line for about 430 feet from the entrance to the back wall of the final passage. Construction of the tomb, numbered KV11, was begun by permission of Ramesses' father, the reigning king, Sethnakhte, for his son who would succeed him. By the time Ramesses gained the throne, three corridors of the tomb had been completed and, as he himself had insisted in the tombs he gave his sons, the likeness of the father adorned the walls.[12] After his father's death, Ramesses III was in full command to show his own image. The theme of the decoration is mainly religiofunerary texts and vignettes deemed essential for salvation. In small antechambers off the central axis, however, depictions of the royal accoutrements and other luxury items, such as furniture, vases, and weaponry, grace the walls, suggesting that these items were stockpiled here.

Work on funerary equipment, the elaborately decorated coffin, shrines, statuary, and chests for papyrus scrolls so necessary to the Egyptians' life in the netherworld, might have been started nearly as early on as the tomb itself. Besides ritualistic items, such as baskets of food, flowers, perfumes and oils, personal effects belonging to the king, his favorite chariot and hunting bows, his throne and bed, his jewelry, clothes, even his sandals, would be buried with him. A daybook entry kept by the workmen of the royal necropolis states that on the fiftieth day following the king's death funerary goods were taken to the tomb: "First month of Inundation, day 4 . . . (various funerary goods) . . . on this day arrived at the tomb from the great river."

On the day of his death, the body of Ramesses III was taken from the palace to the embalming house to undergo mummification, a process that traditionally took 70 days. The brain of the king was extracted through his left nostril and the cavity packed with resin-impregnated linen. His eyes were removed as well and the orbits also packed with linen. His stomach was emptied of its contents and his vital organs, except for his heart, were likewise removed through a long incision made in the left side of his torso. The viscera were then wrapped in linen bundles and placed in canopic jars of carved alabaster. His stomach was packed with more resin and amulets and the incision sewn up. This initial stage took about four days to complete. His entire body was then immersed in dry natron to dry up all bodily fluids, a procedure that usually lasted for about 52 days. During the final 19 days, the king's body was wrapped with linen strips a few hundred meters in length and then covered with several shrouds of fine linen. It was finally wreathed with garlands of flowers and placed in the coffin. Thus wrapped for eternity, the king was ready for his final journey to his tomb.

The day of the king's interment is routinely noted in the daybook of the necropolis workmen on the twenty-fourth day of the first month of the inundation season, exactly 70 days after the king's death. A large funeral procession involving priests, professional mourners, and servants carrying a great variety of burial goods, as well as the king's family and courtiers, would have accompanied the king's coffin from the gates of Medinet Habu north through an impressive wadi walled by the rugged cliffs of western Thebes to the king's tomb in the ḥr-ḫnw-ḫnỉ, the burial ground reserved for pharaohs. Thus witnessed by his subjects, pharaoh was there laid to rest under the lid of a stone sarcophagus decorated with a depiction of a slithering viper.[13]

His tomb in the Valley of the Kings, however, would not be Ramesses' final resting place. About two generations after the labor strikes that his regime endured, the descendants of these workmen took to robbing graves, and for decades nothing the authorities did could abate the wholesale pillaging of the royal tombs. Ramesses III and several of his illustrious predecessors were disturbed in their eternal slumber by profane hands carting off their valuables en masse. At length the local priesthood was driven to trying to outwit the robbers by moving the royal mummies from tomb to tomb. But it was not until the coffins were secreted in a deep shaft in the area of Queen Hatshepsut's temple at Deir el-Bahari that the royal corpses finally found rest. There the body of Ramesses III lay forgotten until accidentally discovered toward the close of the nineteenth century. He now lies in the Cairo Museum.

CHAPTER SEVEN

"United with Eternity"

Amid the sophisticated trappings of art and literature that made up the glorious culture of ancient Egypt is an aspect of that society that causes sober reflection. Sanctions for what society and the state defined as criminal behavior were severe and rigorously applied. Everyone indicted in the Juridical Papyrus found guilty of treason was given the death sentence, carried out either by execution or suicide. Although the texts are not explicit about "the great punishments of death" that befell those convicted, there is ample evidence of the forms of capital punishment utilized throughout pharaonic history.

Unlike other areas of the ancient Near East, no complete book containing an Egyptian law code of pharaonic time has survived, although we know for certain that collections of legal punishments did exist. The Greek writer Diodorus refers to such a collection of laws, which filled eight volumes, compiled from as far back as the First Dynasty. Bits and pieces of what was the standardized law of the land can be gleaned from royal and civil archives as well as from religious and literary texts. For instance, besides the Judicial Papyrus of Turin, a papyrus dating from the Twelfth Dynasty attests to the laws for disciplining fugitives, and another, known as Papyrus Mayer, cites the criminal prosecution of tomb robbers in the late Ramesside period.

For less serious offenses against the state and civil wrongdoing that involved such things as petty thieving, minor cases of assault, tax evasion, or false accusation against a colleague or superior, the common punishment was a severe beating, forced labor, and restitution to the aggrieved party. Some texts indicate an immediate and spontaneous chastisement of the miscreant: "They (the tax collectors) beat him furiously. He is bound and thrown into the well; he is soused in a headlong dipping.

His wife has been bound in his presence, his children are in fetters. . . ."[1] For official, state-decided cases, a penalty of "100 blows" or "200 blows and the opening of five wounds" was often exacted as the specific corporal punishment; it is ambiguous, however, as to whether the open wounds were a result of the blows or separately inflicted. The administration of the bastinado is pictured on many tomb walls depicting scenes from everyday life. In the tomb of Mereruka, a vizier of the Old Kingdom, a man is shown seated on the ground straddling a broad post atop which are two carved heads. One official holds the man's arms about the post while two others stand opposite ready to strike with their upraised sticks. In another tomb, a man is depicted stretched out on his stomach with one official holding his arms, another his legs, and a third standing over him meting out his thrashing with two cudgels in the shape of human hands. Captions that are to the point and sometimes even sarcastic in tone often accompany the scenes of punishment: "Tie him to the whipping post"; "Causing that he come in steps of his evil"; "He is evil"; "Beating is its name; it produces pleasure of heart"; "May your heart be happy!"

Mutilation was also very much a part of the Egyptian system of sanctions. Cutting off a person's nose and ears was deemed appropriate punishment for certain crimes. It was the penalty suffered by the corrupt magistrates in the harem conspiracy trials. Interestingly, the Greeks found a settlement in the Sinai whose name perpetuates this barbarity: "Amputated-Nose Town [Rhinocolura]." Documentation from as far back as the First Intermediate Period, circa the twenty-second and the twenty-first centuries B.C., states that persons caught desecrating tombs were punished by having their arm cut off. There was an obvious community of perception in terms of what was believed to be acceptable sanctions for lawbreakers throughout the ancient Near East. Corporal punishment and mutilation were measures employed not only by Egypt but by Babylon, Assyria, Canaan, and other neighboring states. In particular, preserved portions of Hammurabi's Law Code and the Laws of the Middle Assyrian Empire are quite graphic about the penalty for unlawful conduct: "they shall cut out his tongue," "they shall pluck out his eye," "they shall cut off her breast," "they shall break his bone," "beaten 60 times with an oxtail," "they shall cut off his ear," "they shall draw his lower lip across the blade of an axe and cut it off."

Even unintentional negligence entailed a fierce punishment in Assyria: a physician who botched an operation was liable to have his hand cut off. The harsh penalties adopted in this part of the ancient world were based on a simple logic that satisfied the human feelings for re-

venge. Hammurabi's Law Code states: "If a citizen destroys the eye of another, his eye shall be destroyed. If he broke another citizen's bone, his
bone shall be broken. If he knocked out the tooth of a citizen, his tooth
shall be knocked out."[2] The Bible puts it more succinctly as "an eye for
an eye, and a tooth for a tooth." In their world such retribution was
morally justifiable. Of all the peoples of the Near East only the Hittites of
central Anatolia did not subscribe to this brutal form of justice. To judge
from their laws, the Hittites were the most humane of the ancient peoples of the region. Capital punishment was scarcely known among
them; for all crimes, including premeditated murder, the penalty was a
fine: for major crimes a substantial fine, for minor crimes a lesser one.
Deliberate bodily mutilation of the guilty party is entirely absent from
the corpus of Hittite law.

Beatings and mutilation were practiced in Egypt not only as punishment for those convicted of a crime but as part of a regular and accepted
procedure for legal interrogation carried out by the state. Once suspects
were in the custody of the Medjay, they were repeatedly interrogated by
such means. As one would expect, torture often led to the extraction of a
confession and facilitated the arrest and prosecution of accomplices.[3] In
addition to undergoing a thrashing, the suspect was obliged to swear an
oath to the king or sometimes to the god with respect to any statement
he was to make concerning the crime. The procedure is very much akin
to being sworn in on taking the witness stand in a court of law today;
where we would say "As god is my witness" or "I do solemnly swear before God," the Egyptians recited "As truly as god or King x lives . . ." or
"As truly as King x endures!" Because perjuring oneself to a god was believed by the Egyptians to have far more serious spiritual ramifications
than we believe today, administering an oath was a great inducement for
speaking the truth.

The accused of Papyrus Lee began his testimony by swearing such an
oath as to his innocence, but he was not believed. In addition to its spiritual significance, perjury was also a serious crime. In the ancient Near East
a person being interrogated was strictly warned not to give false testimony on penalty of mutilation. The "Tomb Robbery Papyrus" (Papyrus
Mayer) and others relate the usual police routine for examining a suspect:
"He was examined by beating. The Oath of the Lord was given to him not
to speak falsely . . . He was examined again and said: 'I did not see anything.' He was examined with the stick and placed under arrest"; "Examination was made of [the accused's name], under the authority of [the official in charge], by beating with a stick, the bastinado being thoroughly
applied to his feet. An oath on penalty of mutilation was given to him

not to speak falsely. He said: 'What I said is exactly what I did!'"[4] The same brutal methods of interrogation were applied to women. Severe beatings, the bastinado applied to the feet, mutilation, and imprisonment are all documented as penalties meted out to females in individual cases. A painted depiction of one case in a tomb at Beni Hassan shows a crouching female with an infant in arms about to be delivered a whipping by a male official; curiously, however, it is a female official holding a switch who holds her down. Tomb scenes such as these, showing the close proximity of the whipping post and flogging to the presiding court magistrate, prove that these were summary beatings dealt out on the spot.

Once the police had elicited a confession or were at least satisfied they had gotten to the truth, the suspect was then brought to trial. A painted mural in one tomb of early New Kingdom date actually depicts a criminal trial in progress. The tomb owner, the king's vizier, named Rekhmire, presides as judge sitting at the far end of a long columned hall. This scene and other textual references show that cases heard by the state took place in an actual building designated as a law court called the ḥwt-wr (the Great Hall). The accused is shown being brought forward, held down by a bailiff's hand on the back of his neck; another strikes a respectful salute while being roughly grasped by the wrist by a second bailiff who brandishes a stick. A third court official blocks the entrance from other spectators and litigants awaiting their turn. Rows of magistrates are also present. Before them are leather rods spread out on four reed mats. The caption refers to them as "šsm." These were perhaps to be used as instruments of the sentencing or perhaps to make sure there was no retraction of a confession. There were no lawyers or persons appointed to represent the plaintiff or the accused in ancient Egypt; a person argued his or her own case and could bring forward witnesses and submit sworn depositions. An often-copied tale from the Middle Kingdom, entitled "The Eloquent Peasant," tells of a man who presents his argument in such an articulate and entertaining manner that he is obliged to continue his pleadings over several court appearances simply to entertain the magistrate by his eloquence. Although intermittently beaten by court bailiffs, he eventually attains the justice he seeks.

Of course, there were bound to be cases in which the guilt or innocence of a person could not be determined by ordinary means in a court of law. In such instances, one accepted and well-established procedure followed by many states in the region for resolving the issue was the "water ordeal" or "ordeal by river." It involved the accused being obliged to throw himself into the river. If he drowned, then he was guilty; if, on the other hand, the river did not overwhelm him, he was proven innocent and all charges were dropped. In compensation the survivor of the water ordeal was given the entire estate of his accuser. This practice was also a well-established means for deciding on charges of sorcery and adultery, where tangible proof was difficult to procure.

While the water ordeal is explicitly described in the Law Code of Hammurabi and the Middle Assyrian Laws as a means of deciding one's innocence, Egyptian records make no reference to it. Sources only allude to the punishment of being "thrown to the crocodiles" as a means of settling accusations of adultery. What means were employed to determine guilt or innocence in such matters is not known for certain: surviving an attack by a Nile crocodile was unlikely.

Crimes against the Gods

In Egyptian society, there was no distinction made between the sacred and the secular, for they were one. Treason, the use of sorcery against the throne, tomb robbery, disposing of royal or temple property, or encroaching on temple estates could, therefore, be construed as crimes of sacrilegious intent, which warranted the sentence of capital punishment. A revolt against the throne was, in effect, opposition to the god in a legal context. Accordingly, there is every indication that the verdict and sentencing, most notably for treasonous acts, were ascribed to the jurisdiction of the gods. Tomb inscriptions from Middle Egypt refer to the execution of "criminals whom the god has cursed." In studying legal texts of the Old Kingdom, one scholar observed that the term used for the "guilty" verdict was "it is what the king hates, truly, truly."[5] By Ramesside times the phrase had long since passed out of use, but did another stock phrase take its place? Throughout the various documents of the harem conspiracy, there is a similarly worded phrase, which is repeatedly employed in summation to the crimes of the individuals: "the [great] abomination of all [the gods of] the land." Although the phrase does not carry the same connotation as "guilty as charged," the expression implies the delivery of a verdict. What follows is the passing of the death sentence, emphatically stated to be carried out by order of the gods. This was truly divine justice at its most literal! The Egyptians, and in particular the Egyptian king, absolved themselves of any introspection or nagging conscience due to the possibility of putting an innocent person to death. It was the gods that found the accused guilty; it was the gods' pronouncement that the guilty be executed.

In appointing the court, Ramesses III adamantly asserted that the judgment and punishment of those accused would not be on his head.

No moral sensibility can be accredited to Ramesses III in making such statements: they point rather to a "politically correct" tradition long held by pharaohs of the distant past. A famous literary piece surviving from the Tenth Dynasty adumbrates guidelines for the then monarch, Merikare, to rule by. Included among the many instructions are: "Beware of punishing wrongfully. Do not kill, for it will not benefit you. Punish with beatings and with detention, for thus will the land be set in order; Except for the rebel whose plans are found out, for god knows the traitors, god will punish his evil doing with blood. . . ."[6]

The operating mechanism for divine intervention in adjudicating criminal cases, as well as settling civil complaints, was oracular consultation. The Egyptian expression for conducting an audience with the divine was called the ph-ntr, which literally means "to reach god." The procedure consisted of a specific ritual performed before the sacred image of the god whereby questions would be posed and the image would deliver a response. This was the same type of ceremony Panhayboni was allowed to attend in order to gain him entry into the royal residence. When the god's bark went forth in procession, eight priests were chosen to carry out the rite, and they were required to undergo a ten-day "purification" process that, among other things, involved chewing natron. A gold or gilded statue of the god would be carried aloft on a model bark held by these priests, fronted by one or more lector-priests or magicians with incense burner in hand. Suddenly, the bark would stop, the question would be asked, and the response given. The ancients speak unequivocally of the deity uttering his responses, but both physical and textual evidence points to a nonvocal response to a yes-or-no question. Specifically, it appears that a physical movement of the statue or the entire litter such as a "nodding," "trembling," or forward or backward thrust would be deemed an affirmative or negative answer. In some cases, it seems the statue nodded or pointed toward a response written on a label or ostracon, which would in effect provide the god with a worded reply.

As rationalists we must consider that a physical stimulus was needed to make the apparatus tremble or move. One naturally thinks of physical manipulation provided by the priests themselves, but we should not be too quick to explain it away as some fraudulent machination of the priesthood. The oracular response was referred to by the Egyptians as the *bi3yt*, or "miracle." Here was a community of ardent believers, and it is extremely unlikely that any deliberate prompting would be tolerated by either the priesthood or the laity. It has been suggested that the purification process might have had some toxic effect on the priests, thereby causing involuntary movements when carrying the litter, but

The sacred bark being carried on the shoulders of priests around the halls and courtyards of the king's mortuary temple.

there is no solid evidence to back the theory. From this distance in time, there is no way to explain the phenomenon of a shaking litter. The priests who performed the ritual and those who witnessed it could not have described it in terms other than the supernatural, nor would they have wished to. Sincere in their beliefs, it was to them a miraculous event, a physical manifestation of the god's will. The voice of god was speaking to them.

Textual sources imply that a specific form of capital punishment was utilized for a particular crime and that certain methods were more popular than others at one time or another. For instance, tomb robbery in Egypt of the twenty-first and twenty-second centuries B.C. was punishable by decapitation. Several texts refer to the violators' neck being "severed like that of a bird"; another cites dying at "the king's execution block." The executioner's block and knife is well represented in the hieroglyphic script. By late Ramesside times (twelfth century B.C.), convicted tomb robbers were put to death by impalement. Recorded statements given under duress by suspects imply that impalement was also the mode of execution meted out to those absconding with state property. Elsewhere it is specifically stated that a person caught in the act of stealing property belonging to the state was given "100 blows," the implication being that the stolen property was recovered; if that person disposed of the stolen goods, he was "placed upon the stick." "Putting upon the stick" was the idiom for impalement and was literally illustrated by the hieroglyph

Impalement appears to have come into vogue in the New Kingdom. The pharaoh Akhenaten of the fourteenth century B.C., history's first monotheist, utilized impalement against foreign captives. (So much for religious devotees who wish to see him as a pacifist.) It was also a "popular" mode of execution of other peoples of the Near East, particularly the Assyrians. Assyrian war reliefs depicting their fierce military campaigning include vignettes of impaled prisoners on public display immediately outside the walls of the captured city. It appears that women were not spared this gruesome method of execution. According to Assyrian law, a woman found guilty of deliberately aborting her pregnancy was impaled on stakes.

References abound affirming that death by fire was the punishment in Egypt dealt to rebels. In a letter to a recalcitrant vassal, Akhenaten threatens death by fire if he continues on his treasonous course. On a temple wall in Upper Egypt, the pharaoh Sesostris I sentences unspecified rebels to the flames. Persons found guilty of insurrection were sentenced to be bound and cast upon the brazier." Specifically, it is the brazier of a certain god that is cited in various contexts as the implement of death. Death by fire, then, can be interpreted as the divine mode of execution. A large, flaming cauldron was used, a veritable "fiery furnace." Braziers used for burnt offerings of sacrificial animals have been recovered from temple sites, but one in particular found at Edfu is decorated with reliefs of bound, nude men and priests brandishing knives and torches. An important historical text from the ninth century B.C., called "The Chronicle of the High Priest Osorkon," makes the analogy between the animal sacrifices and human immolations. In this account of a Theban rebellion, it was decided that the captured rebels "perish like goats on the night of offerings under which braziers are lit . . . like the braziers at the (festival) of the Going Forth of Sothis, all of them were burned with fire in the place of [his] crime. . . ." Moreover, a religious book of the Late Period refers to human sacrificial victims as "cattle people," which one scholar interprets as "people who revolted" and as a result "were sacrificed like cattle on the brazier of the local temple."[7]

Temple altar for burnt offerings at Karnak. Through the doorway a short staircase
ascends to the elevated brazier stone.

Criminals were executed in public, perhaps as a deterrent to would-be
lawbreakers and, quite possibly, as a gruesome social event. The impalement of prisoners outside the gate of the city or great temple enclosure
wall is well illustrated in the ancient Near Eastern art record. Public execu-
tions were carried out in Greco-Roman times throughout the Near East as
well, with crucifixion as the modus operandi. Like other political prisoners and petty thieves, Christ was crucified just outside the city gates of
Jerusalem; at the ancient city of Mendes, in the eastern Nile Delta region,
the remains of crucified individuals were excavated outside the main eastern gate of the great temple temenos wall; the Assyrians were fond of
putting their captives on display on the slopes of the captured city's wall.

Incinerating people was at times carried out in a religious, ritualistic
venue. Braziers would have been set up immediately outside the temple
precincts, as they were for religious festivals. A fictitious literary piece of
Ptolemaic date called *The Instructions of Ankhsheshonq*, which relates a
tale of a conspiracy against a king's life, tells of an earthen furnace

erected "at the door of the royal palace" into which the ringleader "together with all the conspirators" were tossed. Another tale tells of the adulterous wife of a favored courtier who by incurring the wrath of Pharaoh was consigned to the flames in an area to the north of the king's residence. The king's son, Osorkon, informs us that the rebel Theban magistrates were sacrificed, not at a designated place of execution, but "in the place of their crime," the location of which we can surmise to be an administrative building in the area of the Great Temple of Amun at Karnak. Interestingly, archaeological excavations outside the southeast corner of the Karnak enclosure wall uncovered a columned hall that was destroyed by an intentional and confined firing. Carbon dating tests done on ashes from that layer proved the conflagration to date to the time of the Theban uprising.[8]

Putting an end to the criminal's life on earth was not enough to satisfy Egyptian sensibilities. Truth and justice in their society demanded eternal damnation. Just as retributive as the death warrant, if not more so, was the denial of a proper burial. The Egyptians believed that the preservation of the physical body was necessary for the individual to "live on" in the next world, hence their elaborate embalming methods. Capital punishment, especially death by fire, not only served to end the prisoner's life but destroyed the body in the process. The condemned's ashes were said to be scattered about on the ground. As for those suffering impalement or beheading there are references to their corpses being thrown in the river or their remains simply being put in a hole in the ground, or "smelling the earth."[9] The underworld, graphically depicted on funerary papyri and on royal tomb walls such as Ramesses VI's and Ramesses IX's, visualize divine jurisdiction over burial. The punishments inflicted in life are extended and prolonged in the realm of the gods. Illustrations include the flaming braziers upon which the condemned souls burn for eternity (a precursor to the Christian hell); the decapitation of the bound figures; and an allusion to the ordeal by water, the river in which the guilty have drowned.

A wisdom text set around the Twenty-sixth Dynasty, entitled *The Instructions of Ankhsheshonq*, provides a fictitious account of a planned conspiracy to overthrow the king by the king's own chief physician. Though unrelated to the events of Ramesses III's reign, it provides an imaginative scenario as to how a part of the harem conspiracy might have played itself out:

> Harsiese, son of Ramose, the chief physician, consulted Ankhsheshonq, son of Tjainufi about it. Then said Ankhsheshonq to him: "[How can you]

agree to the misfortune of Pharaoh? Pharaoh has done for you many good things, [more than to] all [the courtiers] of the palace. You were brought to the palace when you had nothing in the world. He appointed you chief physician. He let you be given everything that belonged to the chief physician entirely. . . . Is what you are doing in return to have him killed?" Said he: "Let go of me, Ankhsheshonq! . . . There is nothing to the words you have said. The councillors, the generals, the grandees of the palace are all agreed to do it." Now it happened that everything Harsiese was saying to Ankhsheshonq and that Ankhsheshonq said to him in reply was overheard by a man of the household inside who was called Wahibre-makhy, son of Ptahertais. . . . When night came [this same man] lay down in the vestibule of the private chamber where Pharaoh was. . . . He related to Pharaoh everything he had overheard . . . without altering a single word. Pharaoh was unable to sleep till morning. . . ."[10]

Four men indicted in the harem conspiracy, Yeniny, Peluka, Warona (all butlers), and Ashhebsat (assistant to Paibakamana) were accused of being told directly of the plot by the perpetrators and executed for not revealing it. They in fact could have played a role similar to that of Ankhsheshonq. Although perhaps not willing accomplices, the men had loyalties to their friends that prevented them from informing the king in spite of whatever sympathy they might have had for him. As for the role of Wahibre-makhy, the man in the narrative who warned Pharaoh of the impending plot, no such person stepped forward in the real conspiracy to save Ramesses from his demise. There were certainly enough men who had overheard the plans of the conspirators—six agents at the harem gate who in turn told their wives, and three administrators stationed within the harem who were privy to the women's conversations—but for whatever reason they did not feel compelled to give the conspirators away.

Through their own actions, the plot was revealed by the perpetrators themselves and carried out as far as they were able before the king's guard and those at the palace loyal to the heir apparent won control of the situation. Papyrus Rifaud A speaks of a fierce uprising. Bonemwese with his battalion of archers, the general Pasai, undoubtedly with men loyal to his command, as well as the king's workmen from the nearby village of Deir el Medina, who scaled the walls, were all part of the melee. How long the uprising went on is unclear, but finally all were apprehended save one. Panhayboni, the notorious overseer of cattle, managed somehow to escape. His indictment is absent from the trial transcripts, and no sentencing is adumbrated in the investigative report on him found in Papyrus Varzy. It is possible that he fled to the inaccessible marshes of the Nile Delta like other fugitives before him.

Capture and Execution

Back at Medinet Habu, Panhayboni's accomplices were taken into custody. One by one they were tied to the whipping post where police issued a severe beating in order to make them more susceptible to interrogation. Court scribes were on hand to take down every word of their sworn statements. On pain of mutilation the bailiffs were finally able to illicit a confession. The investigation proceeded further with the arrest of those who were accessories to the crime—those men and women who were aware that the coup d'état was to be attempted but did nothing to prevent it. They too were brutally questioned and coerced into admitting that they had failed their king.

During the investigation Ramesses III passed away, but not before he appointed 12 judges to preside over the criminal proceedings. In every respect they are a jury of their peers: two overseers of the treasury; two standard-bearers of the army; the king's herald; two librarians; and five butlers. On the appointed day the court assembled at the Hall of Judgment for the first session.[11] Six of the 12 appointed judges—Mantemtowa, Pafrawa, Kara, Pabasa, Mai, and Hori—presided over the arraignment of the pantry chief, Paibakamana, and his four partners, Pentau, Mastesuria, Panouk, and Pairy. Seated at the far end of the hall, the magistrates were fronted by a row of court scribes as, one at a time, the men were ushered in by bailiffs bending them forward by the scruff of their neck. Their depositions were given and the guilty verdict rendered: "The great abominations of the land." The same procedure was carried out that day for their four passive colleagues, Ashhebsat, Warona, Peluka, and Yeniny, along with the gatekeepers and their wives. A sentence of execution was then sanctioned by a *ph-ntr* ceremony in which the sacred statue of the deity, brought in on a litter, "nodded" his affirmation. This particular cult statue, enshrined at Medinet Habu, had been requisitioned by Ramesses himself and bore the name "Amun-Endowed-with-Eternity." The convicted men and women were then taken from the court hall to the area just outside the temple gate where a blazing furnace had been erected. And there, in front of their children, their relatives, and crowds of curious onlookers, they were burned alive.

One other man stood trial that day: Bonemwese, the battalion captain who was induced by his sister to join the rebellion. But he would not face the same judges as the others. Four butlers—Kedendenna, Paerswana,

Maharbaal, and Djehuty-rekh-nafa—decided Bonemwese's fate in what was probably a private hearing. The same magistrates would sit in judgment over the accused of the third arraignment, the trial of Ramesses' son, Pentawere, and the three administrators posted within the confines of the royal harem. The reason some of the defendants were judged separately is clear: the testimony of those five men was directly related to the crimes of the harem women and would reveal in the women's own words the discussions about the king and their desire to overthrow him. Pentawere and the harem women were members of the king's extended family and the family's "dirty laundry" was not a matter for public knowledge. Like Weni of 1,200 years earlier, who boasted that only he and a single scribe were allowed by Pharaoh to hear the charges against the royal harem, it would be these high-ranking butlers, confidants of the king, who would be entrusted with hearing the sensitive evidence.[12]

That Bonemwese's hearing was scheduled with the first arraignment (and recorded thus) rather than with the third may be indicative of the part social status played in the legal system of ancient Egypt. All the persons indicted in the first arraignment including Bonemwese were executed regardless of the role each played in the conspiracy. The crime committed by the six agents at the harem gate was no different than that of the three officials listed in the third arraignment, yet the former are executed while the latter are mercifully allowed suicide. The agents, who were probably nothing more than doorkeepers, and their wives were obviously of a low social class; in fact all who are convicted in the first arraignment appear to have been of a lower administrative rank (butlership could easily fall within this lower echelon as well) than the other convicted members of the conspiracy, except perhaps for the overseer of the treasury, Pairy. But Pairy was of foreign extraction, as were eight others listed in this grouping. Whether or not "low birth" or "racism" had anything to do with the sentencing, certainly the day of the first arraignment was scheduled to be a day of public execution. The flaming brazier was made ready and whoever was included in this group, if convicted, would be incinerated. When his private hearing was over, Bonemwese was led with the others to a fiery death.

The prosecution of the general Pasai, the magician Prekamenef, the infamous chief physician Iyroy, and the two scribes of the House of Life and a serpent-named butler, followed in a second court arraignment. Although the magistrates were not specifically named in the transcripts for the session, it is evident that Pasai had information as to who were slated to sit in judgment of him and his compatriots. Sometime before the court session, two of the judges, Mai and Pabasa, were caught in a rendezvous with the general and the women of the harem; a third judge, Hori, was implicated. With these three removed, it probably remained for Parennuta, the king's herald, and Pre-emhab, another librarian, the only two appointees whose seating is otherwise unnoted, to decide the fate of the six. Perhaps owing to their high social rank or because four of these six aristocrats possessed an expertise in the art of black magic, they were prosecuted with some trepidation. They were found guilty, but the court transcripts make it very clear that no one laid a hand on them. With the court adjourned, the disgraced men were left alone to take their own lives. They were brought into the Hall of Judgment for their trial. Whether by metal weapon or fast-acting poison, they did not leave alive.

The four butlers who had condemned Bonemwese sat in judgment over Pentawere and his harem colleagues, with the addition of a newly appointed judge, a man named Mertisiamun, who was perhaps a replacement for the doomed Pabasa. The tragic prince, Pentawere, could offer no defense that would save his life. He and the other three officials, Amanakhau, Hnetenamana, and Pairy, were spared the final degradation of a public execution and allowed to commit suicide in private.

The fate of Teya and the women of the harem is unknown. No extant document sheds light on the specific nature of their punishment. Since the women were implicated in the prosecution of the disreputable judges and the security officers, it is evident that they too were remanded into custody for a time. The public would not have been allowed to hear their inflammatory testimony, and the proceeding, it seems, was not recorded on paper. The legal system of the day had no sensitivities about exacting severe corporal penalties on women, and it is unlikely given the seriousness of their crime that the harem women escaped execution. Whether by flaming brazier or Nile crocodile, one can be certain that Teya and her cohorts were put to death. Whatever personal effects belonged to them would have been claimed and perhaps even fought over by their successors, who would from then on shun the mention of their name.

For their perfidy, the king's two appointed magistrates, Pabasa and Mai; the police chief Naneu; and the bailiff Taynakhte were sentenced to endure the mutilation of their nose and ears. With the discharge of the penalty, they would never be able to live down the public humiliation of their actions. For Pabasa, a man used to moving within the inner circles of the royal court, it was too much to bear, and he soon ended his misery by killing himself. A third magistrate, a military officer named Hori, falsely accused of duplicity, was exonerated by the court. With that, the files on the harem conspiracy were closed.

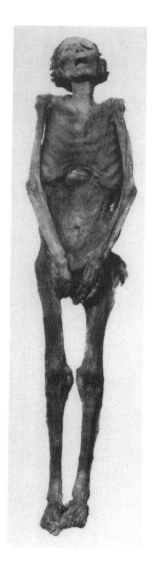

An unidentified young man discovered among the royal cache at Deir el Bahari in the late 1800s. Like the mummies of Egyptian royalty, including that of Ramesses III, which had been removed from their tombs in the Valley of the Kings for safekeeping, he too was stored in a deep shaft high in the western cliffs overlooking the temple of Queen Hatshepsut.

There is every indication that this person died in disgrace. The corpse was naturally desiccated, with internal organs still intact. Apart from a small amount of natron sprinkled over the body, none of the usual embalming procedures had been carried out. His contorted facial features indicate that he had died in agony, possibly from poison, as there are no wounds to the body. Moreover, his hands and feet had been bound and the body wrapped in a sheepskin and placed in a plain, white, wooden coffin. Neither those who had overseen his burial nor the later necropolis priests had allowed him to be identified, and yet, when unearthed, he lay among kings. Given his presence in the cache, there is reason to suspect that he too was a member of the royal house. Could it be possible that this unfortunate young man is none other than the ill-fated Pentawere? From G. Elliot Smith, *The Royal Mummies* (Cairo: Institut Français d'Archéologie Orientale, 1912). That this unfortunate could be the body of prince Pentawere was first mooted by G. Maspero, *Les Momies royales de Dèir el-Bahari* (Paris: E. Leroux, 1889).

After the flaming brazier had cooled, whatever bodily remains were left were scattered over the dirt roads for donkeys to tread on. The tombs the condemned individuals had prepared for themselves in life were desecrated, their coffins and grave goods seized, and the door lintel bearing their name dismantled by orders of the crown. The families of those who committed suicide may have been allowed to remove their bodies for burial under authorized supervision. The burial allotted those condemned for all eternity would have been one anathema to all Egyptians. The body would not be embalmed; it would not be placed in a wooden coffin decorated with protective spells but wrapped in a reed mat or animal skin; there would be no grave goods for them to take with them to the next world. Instead, they would be placed in the ground to "smell the earth" forever.

The records of the trial and investigative reports concerning the conspiracy against Ramesses III are blatantly and deliberately one-sided. Whatever testimony the condemned men gave in their own defense would not be recorded; a written record of their remarks for future generations to ponder would not be a forum allowed to them. Not even after millenia would they be able to garner sympathy for their cause. We can only surmise what their motives were. We can only wonder at their course of action.

"Of Whom Is Pharaoh Still Master?"

With the trials of the conspiracy over and the perpetrators dead, the new pharaoh, Wasmuaria-Satepnamana Ramesses IV, would have sought to put the whole affair to rest and proceed with the expectancy of a long, prosperous, and secure reign. The Papyrus Harris, written upon the death of his father, ends with a demand that the people give the new king their absolute devotion:

> Be attached to his sandals, kiss the earth in his presence, bow down to him, follow him at all times, adore him, praise him, magnify his beauty as you do to the sun god, Re, every morning. Present your tribute to him in his palace, bring to him the gifts of the lands and countries. . . . Obey his orders . . . labor for him . . .; drag his monuments, dig canals for him, do for him the work of your hands. . . .[1]

Any pharaoh might expect such subservience, even that it be given with a fair degree of willingness, but for one who had benefited from an incident that devastated so many families it was, perhaps, too much to hope for. That the heir apparent was not a popular choice is perhaps apparent from his father's dying prayers. Ramesses III beseeched the gods of Egypt to "put the love of him in the hearts of the people" and "to cause the whole land to rejoice at the sight of him."

Thirty-two men and women had been put to death, not including Teya and an unknown number of harem inmates. Moreover, the law confiscated not only the family tombs but the entire estates of the condemned, leaving many of the families destitute. The extended family was—and still is—the foundation of Egyptian society, and the wealth and status of a family rested upon its most successful member. Having a position at the pharaoh's court, whether in the upper or lower echelons—gatekeeper, pantry chief, scribe, or royal harem inmate—was lucrative. It would have not only provided for the acquisition of goods but ensured jobs for other family members, and sons could count on succeeding their fathers in those positions in never-ending succession. The dishonorable demise of the family provider would irrevocably end all that. The economic repercussions for the family after the murder of Ramesses III would have been felt by family members for generations. The loss of wealth notwithstanding, the grief and disgrace felt by the families at seeing their loved ones—son, daughter, father, mother, or sibling—die an agonizing death, or the sight of a lifeless body being carried from the court hall, could not but reverberate in a groundswell of animosity against the Ramesside house that would rankle for years to come. The king, in an encomium avowing himself to be a champion of justice, absolved himself with the declaration that certain misdeeds fell "upon the heads of those who committed them." He further had inscribed on the walls of his tomb a statement in his defense: "King Ramesses has not killed, nor has he ever given orders to kill anyone wrongly." Nevertheless, this was the legacy Ramesses IV inherited and, to some extent, had been responsible for creating.

Ramesses IV had waited more than 10 years to claim the kingship. The examinations of his mummy coupled with a historical and chronological evaluation estimate the age at death to be in his fifties. If the estimate is correct, Ramesses, a man in his mid- to late thirties at a time when smallpox was rampant and 50 years was considered a long life, would have been waiting, perhaps even eagerly, for his father's passing. In retrospect, it forcibly strikes one that the only person to have gained from the assassination of the king was the crown prince and future king Ramesses IV. During his tenure as heir apparent, the future Ramesses IV's residence was in the north, either at Memphis or Pi-Ramesses, and he would have remained there even after his father's move to Thebes to continue in his official duties. Thebes was probably not well acquainted with the heir to the throne, but Papyrus Rifaud C places him there, surprising Bonemwese in the House of Life. As heir apparent Ramesses IV's primary duty was as "commander in chief of the army," and as such he would have been prepared to quell an uprising, especially if he were aware in advance that one was about to occur.

If the crown prince had been informed of the plot, certainly the Theban contingent was not aware of it. There is nothing to suggest they had not genuinely hoped to aid Pentawere gain the throne. The government investigation discloses that Paibakamana and his cronies were largely responsible for the uprising. That a lowly pantry chief, however, would attempt a coup d'état or try personally to become a kingmaker even with the backing of the king's harem is nothing short of astonishing. It is

Sometime after the death of his father, Ramesses IV had his name inscribed to identify the figure of the "king's son and commander in chief of the army" here beneath the window of appearances and elsewhere in the temple of Medinet Habu. Note the name of Ramesses is not as deeply carved as the original relief.

conceivable that Paibakamana was an unwitting pawn in an internal power struggle. The legal heir to the throne was not only on hand to squash the revolt but to bear witness to his father's passing. Within 24 hours of the king's death, the local population was informed that the reins of kingship had been assumed by his son, the new pharaoh

Ramesses IV. He further asserts that by means of divine oracle it was Amun himself, the god of Thebes, that selected him to rule.[2] In what may be a passing reference to the uprising, Ramesses IV declares that he had dealt with the rebels who stood in his way.

The new king immediately set out to model himself after his illustrious predecessor, Ramesses the Great (II), and planned a building agenda to equal his. To carry out such an ambitious strategy, Ramesses ordered one of the largest expeditions to the stone quarries of the Wady Hammamat that Egypt had ever seen.[3] Besides the king himself, 9,263 men were requisitioned for the campaign into the desert to the east of Thebes, including high-ranking administrators, priests, stonecutters, military contingents and their officers, mercenaries, and the king's own personal slaves, who numbered 2,000. Although a stela set up at the quarry boasts of its success, it also records that 900 men died during the gruelling mission. This, the only real achievement of his reign, could not have endeared Pharaoh to his subjects, particularly those in the southern half of the country.

The curious thing about the affair is that an expedition of such grand scale should have produced enough stone to erect a temple the size of the Great Temple of Amun, which still stands at Karnak. But no colossal monument or structure of any size was ever erected during Ramesses IV's reign. What therefore happened to all the stone that would have been quarried from this gigantic undertaking? It provokes some suspicion that Ramesses would send off so many officials and underlings to the quarries soon after he took over the reins of kingship. Being sent to the mines or the quarries was considered a sentence of punishment throughout most of Egyptian history. It was a hazardous journey from which not all would be expected to survive. The pharaoh Akhenaten sent his nemesis, the high priest of Amun, to the quarries when he decided to worship the sun disk to the exclusion of all others. Perhaps the Hammamat expedition was a way of "cleaning house." It would have been certain to clear out the court and the townspeople of any suspected supporters of his dead half brother's scheme to deny him the crown.

Ramesses IV protests throughout his reign that he was indeed the eldest surviving son and rightful heir to the throne of Egypt, and there is no good reason not to believe him. As the firstborn son of the pharaoh and the great king's wife, Ramesses IV had expectation of gaining the throne; nevertheless, as a prince of Egypt a tomb was prepared for him in the Valley of the Queens in the event of an early demise. By Year 28 of his father's reign, it might have appeared more likely that the crown prince would indeed survive his father and one day become Pharaoh, and to that end Ramesses III, like his father had done for him, allowed the prince to prepare a new tomb more befitting his station in the Valley of the Kings.[4] The size and appointment of the new tomb, however, still deferred to the reigning king, and the remnants of decoration show that representations of Ramesses III along with his cartouches were mandated. When the prince became king, he abandoned this tomb for one of more majestic size and one in which he and only he would appear.

In spite of his repeated entreaties to the deities that appear on his monuments for a reign double that of any other pharaoh, Ramesses IV lived only slightly more than seven years after his accession.[5] There is a suspicion of ill health in his prayers to the gods asking for "strength to my limbs, sight to my eyes." Moreover, in the second year of his reign, Ramesses IV doubled the necropolis labor force to number 120 men in what may have been an effort to hasten completion of his royal tomb and mortuary temple.[6] His body was laid to rest in a gigantic sarcophagus carved from a single block of rose-colored granite, deposited in his tomb in the Valley of the Kings.

Rumblings heard in subsequent reigns reveal that Pentawere was not the only brother who was dissatisfied with the ordering of the royal line of succession and, more to the point, with the succession of Ramesses IV. The triumph of Ramesses IV over Pentawere that occasioned his death and the execution of his supporters did nothing to lessen the enmity within the family and may have even served to exacerbate it. Certainly, the traumatic events at the end of his father's reign had their effect on him; throughout his reign, Ramesses IV is at pains to assert over and over again, on stelae, temple walls, and documents, that he is the legitimate ruler of Egypt, not a usurper, and that his offspring are the rightful heirs to the kingship. Whatever his fears were to the contrary, his son, Amanakhopshaf, did succeed him to become Ramesses V without any overt acts of dissension from collateral lines of the family. In the second year of Ramesses V's reign an official tribute to him issued for the masses claimed everyone in Egypt was pleased to see him on the throne. With the accession of Ramesses VI four years later after the untimely death of the king from smallpox, however, there is a suspicion that tensions and discord within the family continued to run deep.

The younger full brother of Ramesses IV, Ramesses-Amanakhopshaf VI, became king when his nephew died without issue. He was named at birth after his deceased elder brother and former crown prince, who had passed away during their father's reign. The first Amanakhopshaf was undoubtedly held in great esteem not only by his parents, who named another child after him, but also by his brother, Ramesses IV, who in turn named his own son after this most beloved prince. But, seemingly, this brotherly love did not exist between the others. In fact, Ramesses VI's resentment of his brother is palpable. Once on the throne, Ramesses VI ordered the erasure of Ramesses IV's name from many of the monuments his predecessor had erected and had his own name put in its place. It does not appear that the rancor Ramesses VI had toward his brother spilled over to include his son. Ramesses VI did complete the tomb of his nephew in the Valley of the Kings for himself, but the first four corridors, which were excavated and decorated for Ramesses V, were allowed to remain in his name. The body of Ramesses V, however, waited two years for interment while a small side chamber in the tomb was prepared to receive it.

Ramesses VI was responsible for inscribing the names and titles of himself and his brothers on the princely processional scene on the wall of his father's mortuary temple at Medinet Habu. Here he claims that he held the position of crown prince, second in line to his brother, Ramesses IV. One wonders whether the situation can be likened to what transpired in the modern kingdom of Jordan. There, throughout King Hussein's reign, his brother Crown Prince Mohammed was the family's designated successor, but just before the king passed away he displaced his brother in favor of his own son.

During his years on the throne Ramesses VI managed to continue to exert some control over Egypt's waning empire in the north, although he was probably the last pharaoh to retain any real influence there. As was said of his immediate predecessors, official pronouncements state that all's right in Egypt, everyone is well fed and delighted with their sovereign. It might be that Ramesses-Amanakhopshaf should be given credit for at least the attempt to reconcile with his family, particularly his half brothers, after the discord produced by the harem conspiracy and the succession of his brother, Ramesses IV. That he commanded their names and titles be carved for posterity at Medinet Habu can only be viewed as acknowledgment of their legitimate birthright. The king further honored his mother, Queen Ese Ta-Habadzillatu, with the decoration of her tomb in the Valley of the Queens.

Ramesses VI's queen was a woman named Nubkhesbed, who gave birth to at least one daughter. This girl, named for the king's mother, Ese, is regaled on a stela as "the great hereditary princess" and high priestess of Amun. Perhaps also by this wife, the king had two sons, Panibenkeme and It-Amana, to whom the kingship passed.[7]

It-Amana ascended the throne as Ramesses VII and, like his father, reigned into his seventh year. Even with that short reign, he may have exceeded expectations for his survival, for there are subtle signs that the king would not be long-lived. At one point Ramesses VII commissioned one of his personal secretaries to travel to the cult temple of Osiris, the god of the dead, at Abydos in Middle Egypt to beseech the god for a long reign. In itself that plea could mean nothing out of the ordinary, but the king's tomb in the Valley of the Kings has all the earmarks of a construction planned to be completed in a relatively short space of time.[8] Even so, the tomb was not yet ready when the king passed away, and the unfinished stone sarcophagus that was intended to hold his coffin was instead used to cover a pit carved into the floor of the burial chamber that received his mummy.

The king could have been the victim of a plague that was rampant at the time. Certainly something was decimating the royal line. The pharaoh Siptah suffered from poliomyelitis, and tuberculosis is well documented in the Nile Valley. Perhaps more likely is an epidemic of smallpox, a disease to which his cousin Ramesses V succumbed. Ramesses VII's own son might also have shared this fate. That boy, entitled "the commander in chief of the army and the king's foremost son," was obviously meant to succeed his father, but he predeceased him.

With the death of Ramesses-It-Amana VII and his heir apparent, the throne reverted once again and for the last time to a son of Ramesses III. Quite ironically it would be Queen Teya's progeny who would carry on the dynasty. Sutakhopshaf, the eldest surviving son of the royal family and full brother of Pentawere, was an old man when unexpectedly his turn came, but Teya's son managed to wear the crown of Egypt as Ramesses VIII for one brief year before passing away. In his youth a tomb had been made for him in the Valley of the Queens, but later, while still a prince, Sutakhopshaf was given the right of burial in the Valley of the Kings, no doubt as a royal favor from one of his brothers or nephews who reigned as king. Excavation of the tomb did not proceed very far before it was abandoned, in all likelihood when the aged prince became king, but neither the final resting place nor the mummy of Ramesses-Sutakhopshaf VIII has ever been found.[9]

The next person to claim the throne ruled as Ramesses IX for a credible eighteen years. Given his lengthy tenure, it is unlikely that this king was himself a son of Ramesses III. Although his bloodline cannot be confirmed, Ramesses IX's birth name of Khaemwese (and the names he gave his two sons) suggests he was a grandson of Ramesses III. Upon gaining the throne, the king named his eldest son, Manthikhopshaf, as his intended successor, bestowing on him the rank of "commander in chief of the army." It has been hypothesized that Ramesses IX named the crown prince after his own father, the sixth-born son of Ramesses III,

A relief of Ramesses IX at Karnak depicting the king rewarding his high priest.
Note that the figure of the high priest is as large as that of the king's, indicative
of the royal family's loss of prestige.

Manthikhopshaf.[10] A tomb in the Valley of the Kings, one begun for
Prince Sutakhopshaf, was completed for the crown prince, whose por-
trait on the walls indicate that he had reached adulthood during his
father's reign. But the prince would not survive his father, and the
throne would instead pass to his younger brother, Amanakhopshaf. As
Ramesses X, this man would in turn name his son after his father and
appoint him the heir apparent. After son succeeded father once more,
the Ramesside line ended with Ramesses-Khaemwese XI.

Ramesses XI's regnal years numbered 27, a long but somewhat ineffectual tenure. Like his seven relatives who preceded him, Ramesses would
reside in the Delta, taking care to stay out of the Thebaid. Southern
Egypt had never been a welcoming place for his family, and over the 70-
plus years since the death of Ramesses III the people of Thebes became
increasingly independent of the Delta regime, even contemptuous of it.
The laxness of government authority and security in Upper Egypt is ap-

parent at various times throughout this entire period: marauding bands of Libyans wrought havoc in the region of Thebes, terrifying its inhabitants and disrupting work schedules all during the reign of Ramesses V, who did or could do little to stop it. Things settled down upon occasion, but the raids continued into the reign of Ramesses XI, who left it up to southern military forces finally to take control of the situation. Large-scale embezzling by government administrators in the southern reaches of the country went unnoticed for ten years before being exposed. The pillaging of royal tombs in the Valley of the Kings, an act once thought sacrilegious, became rampant toward the end of Ramesses IX's reign and would continue for several generations. Moreover, royal building projects continued to diminish in number and there are strong indications that foodstuffs, in particular grain, was in devastatingly short supply since the days of Ramesses IV. Indeed, under the successors of Ramesses III prices shot up to five times what they had been during his reign. Although the famine was relieved during the reigns of Ramesses VII through IX, rations again became seriously deficient by the time of Ramesses XI.

During the last half of the dynasty a powerful Theban family in possession of the high priesthood of Amun gradually gained complete political and military control of the southern region of the country and did all but adopt the title of king in defiance of the Ramesside house. By this time even the northern half of the country had lost confidence in the royal line, and as a result an able administrator by the name of Smendes was able to assume the reins of leadership over most of the Delta. Smendes united politically with the Amun priesthood and divided control of the country between them, effectively squeezing out Ramesses XI. A letter written by the son of the high priest sums up the situation: "As for Pharaoh, how shall he reach this land? Of whom is Pharaoh still master?" The snide comment marks a fitting end to the Ramesside family that constituted the Twentieth Egyptian Dynasty. They would be remembered in history in the words of Diodorus: "After Remphis (Ramesses III) died kings succeeded to the throne . . . who were confirmed sluggards and devoted only to indulgence and luxury. Consequently in the priestly record no costly building of theirs nor any deed worthy of historical record is handed down in connection with them. . . ."[11]

Ramesses III and his progeny, which included three sons, three grandsons, one great-grandson and one great-great-grandson, held the throne of Egypt for more than 100 years. Teya and her cohorts tried and failed to change to course of that succession and paid with their lives, but their machinations may well have set in motion the beginning of the end. With the death of Ramesses III, Egypt's imperial age drew to a close.

Dramatis Personae

Ramesses III the reigning pharaoh of Egypt and against whom the conspiracy was directed.

Ramesses IV (Prince Ramesses) the pharaoh's son and appointed heir to the throne whom the conspirators hoped to displace.

Teya a chief wife of Ramesses III and instigator of the plot to overthrow Pharaoh.

Pentawere the son of Teya and Ramesses III whom the conspirators meant to place on the throne.

Paibakamana pantry chief and Teya's main ally in the coup d'état.

Mastesuria a court butler and colleague of Paibakamana who took an active part in the planned coup.

Panouk overseer of the royal harem and colleague of Paibakamana and Mastesuria who joined them in planning the coup.

Pentau a scribe of the royal harem and colleague of Paibakamana, Mastesuria, and Panouk who joined them in planning the coup.

Panhayboni overseer of cattle and a prime mover of the conspiracy who somehow managed to escape trial.

Pairy, Son of Ruma overseer of the king's treasury who collaborated with Panhayboni

Bonemwese battalion commander of Nubian bowmen and brother of one of the harem women, who persuaded him to help spearhead an armed rebellion.

Pasai general of the army who together with Bonemwese initiated an armed rebellion.

Iyroy the king's physician responsible for the king's spiritual welfare.

Prekamenef court magician and colleague of Iyroy who was adept in the art of black magic.

**Messui
Shotmaadje** both librarians of the House of Life who safeguarded the king's magical books.

Nibdjatfe royal butler, magician, and colleague of Iyroy.

Hnetenamana butler serving in the royal harem who was privy to the plotting of the harem women.

Amankhau second in command of the royal harem who was privy to the plotting of the harem women.

Pairy scribe of the royal harem who was privy to the plotting of the harem women.

Ashhebsat assistant to the pantry chief who was privy to the plot to overthrow the king.

Warona court butler and colleague of the pantry chief who was privy to the plot to overthrow the king.

Yeniny a court butler of Libyan descent and colleague of the pantry chief who was privy to the plot to overthrow the king.

Peluka court butler and scribe of the king's treasury who was informed of the plot to overthrow the king by the pantry chief.

**Petewentamana
Karpusa
Khaemope
Khaemmalu
Sutempidjehuty
Sutempiamana** six security agents of the harem gate who were convicted as sympathizers.

Unnamed the wives of the six security agent who were likewise convicted as sympathizers.

Naneu police chief indicted for corruption.

Taynakhte court bailiff indicted for corruption.

Pabasa royal butler and appointed judge indicted for corruption.

Mai librarian and appointed judge indicted for corruption.

Hori	standard-bearer of the army and appointed judge indicted for corruption.
Mantemtowa	overseer of the king's treasury and appointed judge.
Pefrawa	overseer of the king's treasury and appointed judge.
Kara	standard-bearer of the army and appointed judge.
Parennuta	the king's herald and appointed judge.
Pre-emheb	the scribe of the archives and appointed judge.
Kedendenna	royal butler and appointed judge.
Maharbaal	royal butler and appointed judge.
Paerswana	royal butler and appointed judge.
Djehuty-rekh-nafa	royal butler and appointed judge.
Mayatas-amana	royal butler and replacement for the disgraced judge, Pabasa.
Ese-Ta-Habizallatu	chief wife of Ramesses III and mother of Ramesses IV.
Amanakhopshaf **Sutakhopshaf** **Manthikhopshaf** **Prehiwomnef** **Khamwese** **Mayatum** **Maiamana**	principle sons of Ramesses III.
Unnamed	the women of the royal-harem-in-the-following.

The Calendar

A singular accomplishment of pharaonic Egypt and one of its many lega-
cies to the modern world was the invention of the solar calendar. Prehistoric Egypt had known a calendar, but it had been a lunar one, based
upon the phases of the moon. The first day of the lunar month for the
prehistoric Egyptians began on the morning when the diminishing crescent was no longer visible in the east just before dawn. Each month consisted of 29 or 30 days, all named; but larger divisions of time, whether
sensed or not, were apparently not a practical necessity in the neolithic
farming communities.

The needs of business life in pharaonic times, however, demanded a
calendar founded with accuracy upon the year, not merely the month.
The Egyptians were early impressed with the regularity of the agricultural year in their land. The annual flooding of the Nile, the inundation,
was followed in turn by the sprouting of the crops, and the harvest.
Those three broad divisions constituted the seasons of the Egyptian year,
called by them respectively *Akhet, Proyet,* and *Shomu.* Why not begin the
calendar with the first sign that the river was rising? The only difficulty
was that the coming of the inundation was not as regular as it first appeared, occurring sometimes as early as mid-April or as late as the end of
June. Thus the difference between consecutive inundations, in terms of
days, might in a given instance be as few as 336 or as many as 415. In
other words, the lunar calendar controlled by the rising of the river
would vary between 11 and 14 months.

A more fixed phenomenon had to be chosen to begin the calendar
year, and this was found in the heliacal rising of the dog star, Sirius, a
phenomenon, the Egyptians were quick to note, that coincided roughly
with the rising of the waters. For many months of the year Sirius is absent from the night sky, since it shines above us unseen in the daytime.
It reappears just before dawn on July 19 or 20, and from this date on for
several months it is visible at night. The Egyptians called the star's rising
"the going forth of Sothis," named after the cow goddess in whose image Sirius took form in a constellation. It was this event that marked the
morning of the Egyptian New Year's Day. The 365-day period from one
rising to the next was divided into 12 months of 30 days each, each season lasting 4 months, with 5 epagomenal days tacked on at the end.

The modern calendar has descended indirectly from the Egyptians, but they did not yet realize that the year was one quarter day longer than 365 days. After 4 years, the rising of Sirius came one day later than expected; after 8 years had passed, it came two days late. After 120 years, the star delayed one whole month in rising! After 1,460 years the rising was 365 days late, and Sirius appeared once again on New Year's Day. This full rotation of the calendar is referred to as the Sothic Cycle. If the Egyptians had found some method, as we today have, of adjusting the calendar regularly, the ever-growing discrepancy would not have plagued them. But they did nothing about it: better to suffer the slight inconvenience of a topsy-turvy calendar than to break with tradition. But the Roman scholar Censorinus noted in the third century that in A.D. 139 the rising of Sirius once again coincided with New Year's Day, and from this scholars are able to extrapolate the actual dates of events in Egyptian history.

Notes

Introduction

1. Th. Devéria, *Le Papyrus Judiciaire de Turin et Les Papyrus Lee et Rollin* (Paris: Ernest Leroux, 1897), 2; S. Groll, "The Stenographic Style of Papyrus Lee, Papyrus Rollin, Papyrus Varzy, and the Judicial Papyrus of Turin," in G. Rendsburg, R. Adler, M. Arfa, and N. H. Winter, eds., *The Bible World: Essays in Honor of Cyrus H. Gordon* (New York: Ktav, 1980), 67ff. On papyrus documents in general, see J. Černý, *Paper and Books in Ancient Egypt* (London: H. K. Lewis, 1952); R. Parkinson, S. Quirke, and U. Wartenberg, *Papyrus* (Austin: University of Texas Press, 1995).

2. See chapter 3. See also Groll, "Stenographic Style," 76n.6.

3. J. J. Rifaud, *Voyage en Égypte, et en Nubie, et lieux circonvoisins: depuis 1805 jusqu'en 1827* (Paris: Bibliographie de la France, 1834), pl. 187.

4. J. Vercoutter, *The Search for Ancient Egypt* (New York: H. N. Abrams, 1992), 62ff.

5. D. Jankuhn, *Bibliographie Der Hieratischen und Hieroglyphischen Papyri*, Göttinger Orientforschungen, IV, band 2 (Wiesbaden: Harrassowitz, 1974).

Chapter 1: Murder at Court

1. Senet is an ancient Egyptian board game. For more information, see R. H. Wilkinson, *Reading Egyptian Art: A Hieroglyphic Guide to Ancient Egyptian Painting and Sculpture* (London: Thames and Hudson, 1992), 210–11; W. Decker, *Sports and Games of Ancient Egypt*, trans. A. Guttman (New Haven, Conn.: Yale University Press, 1992), 124ff.

2. For another interpretation, see H. Goedicke, "Was Magic Used in the Harem Conspiracy against Ramesses III?" *Journal of Egyptian Archaeology* 49 (1963): 71–92. Goedicke therein states: "The conspirators were in too risky a situation to entrust the outcome of their plot to magical procedures." As his view depends largely on the mistranslation of well-documented Egyptian magical terminology, it has been widely discounted. That the conspirators relied on magical procedures to carry out their deed is accepted by most scholars. See, among others, J. H. Breasted, *The History of Egypt: From the Earliest Times to the Persian Conquest* (New York: C. Scribner's Sons, 1905), 209, 220ff.; R. O. Faulkner, *Life in Ancient Egypt*, trans. H. M. Tirard (1894; rpt., New York: Dover, 1966), 33; G. Pinch, *Magic in Ancient Egypt* (Austin: University of Texas Press, 1994), 94–95; A. Dodson, *Monarchs of the Nile* (London: Rubicon, 1995); and, in particular, R. Ritner,

The Mechanics of Ancient Egyptian Magical Practice (Chicago: Oriental Institute of the University of Chicago, 1993), 192–98.

3. See P. Grandet, *Ramsès III: Histoire d'un Règne* (Paris: Pygmalion/G. Watelet, 1993), 336.

4. What follows is the Judicial Papyrus of Turin. For other translations, see J. H. Breasted, *Ancient Records of Egypt: Historical Documents from the Earliest Times to the Persian Conquest,* vol. IV, *The Twentieth to the Twenty-sixth Dynasties* (Chicago: University of Chicago Press, 1906), 421; A. deBuck, "The Judicial Papyrus of Turin," *Journal of Egyptian Archaeology* 23 (1937): 152–64. For transliteration of the hieratic text, see K. A. Kitchen, *Ramesside Inscriptions: Historical and Biographical,* 7 vols. (Oxford: Blackwell, 1968–1990) V:350, 148.

5. Ritner, *Mechanics,* 193–94n.893.

6. For other translations of this document and Papyrus Lee, see Breasted, *Ancient Records,* IV:454–56; Goedicke, "Was Magic Used in the Harem Conspiracy?" 71–92; Ritner, *Mechanics,* 193–98.

7. On restoration, see chapter 3.

8. For other transliterations and translations, see F. Chabas, "Lettre de Mr. F. Chabas à Mr. Lepsius," *Zeitschrift für Ägyptische Sprache und Altertumskund* 5 (1867): 76ff.; A. Gardiner, *Ramesside Administrative Documents* (London: Oxford University Press, 1948), 59–60.

9. Literally, "the place I am in."

10. The Egyptian called the ritual the *pḥ-nṯr,* which literally means "to reach god."

11. I.e., perhaps the military command of troops attached to local temples.

12. A term for a military policing force.

13. Having to do with ruling powers.

14. For other transcriptions and translations of Papyrus Rifaud A, B, and C, see S. Sauneron and J. Yoyotte, "Le Texte Hieratique Rifaud," *Bulletin de l' Institut Français d'Archéologie Orientale* 50 (1952): 107–15; Kitchen, *Ramesside Inscriptions,* V:9, 150.

15. Transcription and translation after Y. Koenig, "Nouveaux textes Rifaud II (document E)," *Cahier de Recherches l'Institut de Papyrologie et d'Égyptologie de Lille* 11 (1989): 53–58.

Chapter 2: A House Divided

1. A literal translation, "the one who gave the orders."

2. The preceding passage describes Sethnakhte's funeral procession and his interment in the Valley of the Kings.

3. These three gods represent the three most powerful priesthoods in the country at this time: the cult of Amun-Re centered at Thebes, Ptah at Memphis, and the sun-god, Re-Atum, at Heliopolis.

4. Translation after Breasted, *Ancient Records,* IV:401.

5. The Egyptian god of war.

6. For further reading, see E. Oren, *The Sea Peoples and Their World: A Reassessment* (Philadelphia: University Museum, University of Pennsylvania, 2000).

7. Translation by D. B. Redford

8. Statue of Ramesses III at the temple of Mut; see Kitchen, *Ramesside Inscriptions*, V:367.

9. On tomb 51 in the Valley of the Queens, see C. Leblanc, *Ta Set Neferou: Une nécropole de Thèbes-ouest et son histoire*, vol. I (Cairo: C. Leblanc, 1989). On the statue of king at Karnak, see Kitchen, *Ramesside Inscriptions*, VI:287. On the block from Deir el-Bakhit, see Kitchen, *Ramesside Inscriptions*, VI:322.

10. For more information, see Leblanc, *Ta Set Neferou;* S. Redford, "The Valley of the Queens," in D. B. Redford, ed., *The Oxford Encyclopedia of Ancient Egypt* (New York: Oxford University Press, 2000), 474–76.

11. Decoration of these tombs may well have proceeded in stages, thus accommodating changes and additions to the individuals titles. There is evidence also of redecoration, as in QV53, the tomb of Prince Ramesses. See J. Yoyotte, "The Tomb of a Prince Ramesses in the Valley of the Queens (No. 53)," *Journal of Egyptian Archaeology* 44 (1958): 26ff. For other interpretations as to Tyti's identity, see J. Grist, "The Identity of the Ramesside Queen Tyti," *Journal of Egyptian Archaeology* 71 (1982): 71ff.; K. A. Kitchen, "Family Relationships of Ramesses IX and the Late Twentieth Dynasty," *Studien Zur Altägyptischen Kultur* 11 (1984): 127ff.

12. Immediately adjacent to QV41 is QV40. This tomb, decorated for a "great king's wife" and "king's daughter," may also be presented as the one meant for Ramesses III's unnamed queen. The cartouches have been left blank, and the one instance in the tomb where a name appeared was erased. There is also no evidence that the tomb was ever used. However, the tomb is situated next to QV38, one made for the queen of Ramesses I. Architecturally, QV40 is more similar to QV38 and others in the immediate vicinity to the north. Thus QV40 may represent the southernmost of this group of tombs excavated in the early Nineteenth Dynasty. There is still the possibility that QV40 was later usurped and decorated for our elusive queen. For a study on the architectural grouping of these tombs, see C. Leblanc, "Architecture et Évolution Chronologique Des Tombs De La Vallée Des Reines," *Bulletin de l'Institut Français D'Archéologie Orientaledu Caire* 89 (1989): 227ff.

13. Identification of the king's mother, Teya-Maienese, as the Teya of the conspiracy is not worthy of serious consideration. Great store cannot be set by the similarities of the name. The name "Teya" was often a diminutive or shortened version of a longer appellative and by this time was as common and undistinguished a female's name as "Mary" is in our society. Moreover, if the king were well beyond middle age at the time of his death, his mother would have been in her dotage, and since there is no mention of her throughout his reign we must assume that she had been deceased for a long time.

14. A textual inscription in QV55, the tomb of prince Amanakhopshaf (LeBlanc, *Ta Set Neferou*, pl. CXXXIII).

15. The cartouche of the last reigning king to appear on the wall is that of Ramesses VIII. However, the awkward placement of this king's cartouche outside

the register lines indicate that they had been inscribed earlier. As it is unlikely that Ramesses VII would have bothered to inscribe the names on a series of reliefs in which he does not appear, Ramesses VI remains the only possible choice.

16. For other views, see K. C. Seele, "Ramesses VI and the Medinet Habu Procession of the Princes," *Journal of Near Eastern Studies* 19 (1960): 184ff.; K. A. Kitchen, "Ramessses VII and the Twentieth Dynasty," *Journal of Egyptian Archaeology* 58 (1972): 182ff.

17. The Egyptian forces that fought in Asia under the Ramessides comprised four divisions named after the gods Amun, Re, Ptah, and Sutekh, with each division numbering roughly 5,000 infantry supported by chariots and archers. When large expeditionary forces were required, one man in every ten from the personnel of the vast temple estates might be recruited.

18. The immediate successor of Ramesses IV was that king's own, who assumed the throne as Ramesses V. Consequently, his name was not inscribed before any of the figures meant to depict his uncles.

19. See Epigraphic Survey, Oriental Institute, University of Chicago, *Medinet Habu,* 8 vols. (Chicago: University of Chicago Press, 1930–1970), V, pt. 1, pl. 339.

20. Of particular note is the hieroglyphic writing of both titles: the word "foot soldier" *(mnf3t)* is denoted by a long-skirted figure, either standing or kneeling, holding a staff; the word "army" *(mš3)* is expressed by a kneeling, short-kilted man holding a bow. Inscriptions of Prince Ramesses made during the reign of his father depict his title of commander in chief of the army using only the kneeling bowman; however, his title in the procession reliefs, inscribed in the aftermath of his father's death and Pentawere's demise, is shown depicting both the bowman and foot soldier side by side.

21. Ramesses V and Ramesses VII are not named in the processional scene for a very good reason: they were not sons of Ramesses III (see also Kitchen "Ramesses VII and the Twentieth Dynasty," 183–84). Whether or not the scene was originally carved using likenesses of the individual princes, it was well known that it represented the actual sons of Ramesses III in some intended order of rank. The sculptors in the service of Ramesses VI would certainly not have inscribed one of the figures for Ramesses V, a man who was not of their number. It is even more telling in terms of the seriousness with which the identification of these figures was taken that Ramesses VII did not bother to apply his cartouche to any of the figures. By affixing his cartouche to the fourth figure, Ramesses VIII is in effect saying: "that's me."

22. This term has frequently been taken to mean "King's Eldest (surviving) Son." Since it is inexplicable that Sutakhopshaf was the eldest sibling at any time during the king's reign, it is more likely that a less literal meaning is correct. For use of this more general translation, see K. A. Kitchen, *Pharaoh Triumphant: The Life and Times of Ramesses II, King of Egypt* (Warminster: Aris & Phillips, 1982), 102.

23. Though often accepted to mean "firstborn" son, the fact that two of the king's sons were given the title contradicts that translation. It is interpreted here as a purely honorific designation for ranking among the principle sons. For

a debate on the meaning of this term, see Kitchen, "Ramesses VII and the Twentieth Dynasty," 186; Kitchen, "The Twentieth Dynasty Revisited," *Journal of Egyptian Archaeology* 68 (1982): 121.

24. For more on this, see the epilogue.

25. Heliopolis was located in an area that is now a suburb of Cairo, still bearing the same name.

Chapter 3: The Royal Harem

1. See A. Malamat, "Is There A Word for the Royal Harem in the Bible?" in D. Freedman, A. Hurvitz, and D. Wright, eds., *Pomegranates and Golden Bells: Studies in Biblical, Jewish, and Near Eastern Ritual, Law, and Literature in Honor of Jacob Milgrom* (Winona Lake, Ind.: Eisenbrauns, 1995), 785ff.

2. An oasis located some 70 kilometers south of Cairo to the west of the Nile.

3. The site is today known as Medinet el-Ghurab, some 125 kilometers south of Cairo on the south side of the entrance to the Fayum. For identification of this site as a harem estate, see B. J. Kemp, "The Harim-Palace at Medinet el-Ghurab," *Zeitschrift für Ägyptische Sprache und Altertumskunde* 105 (1978): 122ff.

4. This particular Teya lived during the reign of the pharaoh Amenhotep III, ca. 1412–1375 B.C.

5. Translation after N. Scott, *The Daily Life of the Ancient Egyptians* (New York: Metropolitan Museum of Art, 1976).

6. Avesta, Yast. 17, 10, p. 278.

7. This title has also been arguably translated to mean "decorated by the king." See D. Nord, "*hkrt-nsw* = king's concubine?" *Serapis* 2 (1970): 1–16.

8. P. Insinger 32.20. Translation by M. Lichtheim, *Ancient Egyptian Literature: A Book of Readings*, 3 vols. (Berkeley: University of California Press, 1980), 3:211.

9. The king of Siam was similarly limited by law to only four wives. See A. Leonowens, *The Romance of the Harem*, edited and introduced by S. Morgan (1873; rpt., Charlottesville: University Press of Virginia, 1991).

10. One is tempted to draw another parallel from the court of Siam where "some of the women were or would be concubines (a title, complete with a decoration, gained by sharing the king's bed at least once) or had been concubines for a night or a week or longer. . . . A few women were or had been the king's 'favorite'" (S. Morgan, "Introduction" to Leonowens, *Romance of the Harem,* xviii).

11. Leonowens, *Romance of the Harem,* xxxi.

12. A canopic jar is a vessel made to receive one of the organs of the deceased. A set of four jars, one each for the heart, lungs, kidneys, and liver, was supplied as standard funerary equipment.

13. Translation of passages after Lichtheim, *Ancient Egyptian Literature,* 1:216–17.

14. As a Roman writer of the second century after Christ, Aulus Gellius, noted: "the child's own feelings of affection, fondness, and intimacy are centered wholly in the one by whom it is nursed and therefore just as happens in the case

who are exposed at birth it has no feeling for the mother who bore it and no regret for her loss." J. Rolfe, trans., *Aulus Gellius: Attic Nights,* Loeb Classical Library Series (Cambridge, Mass.: Harvard University Press, 1998), XII:1.21–23.

15. The brother–(half) sister marriages gave rise to a theory that the right of succession to the throne descended directly through the eldest daughter of the king and his principal queen, in a role as "royal heiress," but as there is no evidence that this was carried through by all the idea has been largely discarded. See G. Robins, "A Critical Examination of the Theory that the Right to the Throne of Ancient Egypt Passed through the Female Line in the 18th Dynasty," *Göttinger Miszellen* 62 (1983): 67ff.; L. Troy, *Patterns of Queenship in Ancient Egyptian Myth and History* (Uppsala: Almquist & Wiksell, 1986), 103ff.

16. See G. Robins, "*ḥmt-nsw wrt* Meritaton," *Gottinger Miszellen* 52 (1981): 75ff. It has been suggested that besides the title "Great King's Wife," a peculiar headdress consisting of a modius topped by a floral arrangement can identify a "daughter-wife" of a pharaoh (C. Van Siclen, "A Ramesside Ostracon of Queen Isis," *Journal of Near Eastern Studies* 33 [1974]: 150ff.). This same headdress is depicted on Isis and Tyti in their tombs and is used as evidence that Tyti was the daughter-wife of Ramesses III (Grist, "Identity of the Ramesside Queen Tyti"). For contradiction of this theory, see A. Dodson, "The Takhats and Some Other Royal Ladies of the Ramesside Period," *Journal of Egyptian Archaeology* 73 (1987): 227ff.; A. J. Peden, *The Reign of Ramesses IV* (Warminster: Aris & Phillips, 1994), 5.

17. Translation after Lichtheim, *Ancient Egyptian Literature,* 1:136–38; W. K. Simpson, *The Literature of Ancient Egypt: An Anthology of Stories, Instructions, and Poetry,* with translations by R. O. Faulkner, W. K. Simpson, and E. F. Wente, Jr. (New Haven, Conn.: Yale University Press, 1972), 193–97.

18. See "The Story of Sinuhe," in Simpson, *Literature of Ancient Egypt,* 57ff.

19. Punt is a land (identified by some as Ethiopia) whence the Egyptians imported fragrant trees and plants that produced precious oils and perfumes.

20. Translation after Breasted, *Ancient Records,* II:196–97.

21. One famous exception is a surviving statue of the royal couple, Akhenaten and Nefertiti, in which the powerful queen is placed shoulder-to-shoulder on the king's right.

Chapter 4: All the King's Men

1. The name of the god would have been pronounced as "Amana" by the ancient Egyptians. There is documentation for the name of "Paikamen," which means "the blind one," though this may well indicate the individual's actual physical disability. The ancient Egyptians had no compunction about applying nicknames to people for any obvious physical attribute or for even their ethnic background. Such Egyptian names as "beautiful one," "big nose," "the Amorite," "dark one," "shortie," etc., abound.

2. For a description of the mechanics of this ritual, see chapter 6.

3. Kitchen, *Ramesside Inscriptions,* V:419, 227–29.

4. It may have been that Pairy's birthplace, or possibly his family's foreign origins, suited him for the post (ibid., V:419).

5. Ibid., V:227–29.

6. One of the chief sun gods of the Egyptian pantheon.

7. Ibid., V:425.

8. Translation after Lichtheim, *Ancient Egyptian Literature,* 1:136–37.

9. See A. R. Schulman, *Military Rank, Title, and Organization in the Egyptian New Kingdom* (Berlin: B. Hessling, 1964), 43–44.

10. Grandet, *Ramsès III,* 103–4, 333.

11. See chapter 3, n. 1.

12. Kitchen, *Ramesside Inscriptions,* V:341.

13. See R. A. Caminos, *Late-Egyptian Miscellanies* (London: Oxford University Press, 1954), 91ff.

14. With the great influx of immigrants during the empire period, foreign peoples from the south often gravitated into the police force. They became so numerous in this profession that long before 1200 B.C. the name of the principal Nubian tribe, Medjay, had become a generic term meaning "policeman."

15. C. H. Oldfather, trans., *Diodorus Siculus: The Library of History,* Loeb Classical Library Series (Cambridge, Mass.: Harvard University Press, 1968), I.53.1–4.

Chapter 5: Mansion of Millions of Years

1. Translation of Papyrus Erzherzog Rainer after A. Gardiner, "The Delta Residence of the Ramessides," *Journal of Egyptian Archaeology* 5 (1918): 185.

2. Translation after Breasted, *Ancient Records,* IV:121–22.

3. Gardiner, "Delta Residence of the Ramessides," 194.

4. Ibid., 186ff.

5. Dedicated to the god Amun.

6. Translation after Breasted, *Ancient Records,* IV:120.

7. Postulated by J. Černý, "Datum des Todes Ramesses III und er Thronbesteigung Ramesses IV," *Zeitschrift für Ägyptische Sprache und Altertumskunde* 72 (1936): 112.

8. Each king built a large temple for the worship of himself after death, but no shrine or tumulus could be erected outside the entrance to the royal tombs for security reasons.

9. An alloy of silver and gold.

10. Translation after Breasted, *Ancient Records,* IV:113–14.

11. Every year since the height of the Ice Age the melting snows of the Abyssinian highlands, whence the Nile takes its rise, caused the river to overflow its banks in the spring. The Egyptians had long since learned how to irrigate their fields utilizing this natural phenomenon by a network of canals and catch basins over the floor of the valley. Each year the waters of the inundation could be trapped within this maze, to be let out slowly to water the fields when the river reached its lowest level during the heat of the summer.

12. Short for Ramesses.

13. The figure of the king shows an angled line running across his stomach and another just above the knee suggesting the presence of a kilt, possibly once illustrated in paint.

14. The word "other" indicates that there were two such structures (i.e., eastern and western high gates) and that the eastern gate was unfamiliar, utilized less frequently by temple personnel.

15. The kiosks were small garden pavilions the king had erected and named for these goddesses. The translation of this passage is after Breasted, *Ancient Records,* IV:115–16.

16. Hölscher, "Architectural Survey of the Great Temple and Palace of Medinet Habu (Seasons 1927–28)," *University of Chicago, Oriental Institute Communications* (Chicago, 1929), 37ff.

17. J. Černý, "'The Temple,' as an Abbreviated Name for the Temple of Medinet Habu," *Journal of Egyptian Archaeology* 26 (1941): 127ff.

Chapter 6: "The Hawk Has Flown to Heaven"

1. Translation after Breasted, *Ancient Records,* IV:182.

2. This view was expressed by J. Černý, "Datum des Todes Ramesses III," 109ff.

3. On the Sothic cycle, see appendix B.

4. J. Harris and E. Wente, *An X-Ray Atlas of the Royal Mummies* (Chicago: University of Chicago Press, 1980).

5. An attempted explanation for the lack of synchronism between the inscriptional evidence and Harris's findings is given by E. Wente in a chapter on historical chronology in Harris's book. See also G. Robins, "The value of the estimated ages of the royal mummies at death as historical evidence," *Göttinger Miszelle* 45 (1981): 63ff., who concludes that there is "a lack of precision in defining higher ages in mummies" (64).

6. G. Maspero, *Les Momies royales de Dèir el-Bahari* (Paris: E. Leroux, 1889); G. E. Smith, *The Royal Mummies* (Cairo: Institut Français d'Archéologie Orientale, 1912).

7. A. M. Bakir, *The Cairo Calendar, No. 86637* (Cairo: General Organisation for Government Printing Offices, 1966).

8. Translation by J. F. Borghouts, *Ancient Egyptian Magical Texts* (Leiden: Brill, 1978), spell 142.

9. Groll, "Stenographic Style," 77n.11

10. For an in-depth study on the use of magic in ancient Egyptian society, see Ritner, *Mechanics*.

11. B. Mertz, *Temples, Tombs, and Hieroglyphs: The Story of Egyptology* (New York: Coward-McCann, 1964), 264.

12. That the tomb was begun and the first three corridors decorated under Sethnakhte was detected by C. N. Reeves and R. H. Wilkinson, *The Complete Valley of the Kings: Tombs and Treasures of Egypt's Greatest Pharaohs* (London: Thames and Hudson, 1996), 159ff. However, the authors' interpretation differs from my

own in that they see KV11 as being started for Sethnakhte before he later abandoned it in favor of usurping the tomb of Tawosret (KV14).

13. The sarcophagus of Ramesses III has been the subject of some debate. A. Dodson has suggested that the sarcophagus may have been initially carved for the pharaoh Seti II of the Nineteenth Dynasty and later appropriated by Ramesses III (Dodson, "Was the Sarcophagus of Ramesses III Begun for Sethos II?" *Journal of Egyptian Archaeology* 72 [1986]: 196ff.). On the other hand, B. Mojsov sees the sarcophagus as possibly having been taken over from Amenmesse (Mojsov, *The Sculpture and Relief of Ramesses III* [Ph.D. diss., New York University, 1992]).

Chapter 7: "United with Eternity"

1. Translation after Caminos, *Late-Egyptian Miscellanies*, 247.

2. Translation of Hammurabi's code and the laws of Middle Assyria after T. J. Meek, "The Code of Hammurabi" and "Middle Assyrian Laws," in J. B. Pritchard, ed., *Ancient Near Eastern Texts: Relating to the Old Testament* (Princeton, N.J.: Princeton University Press, 1969), 163–80, 180–88.

3. Indeed, torture has survived as a means of interrogation in this part of the world. While on an archaeological survey, encamped next to a police station, the author witnessed the interrogation of a suspect by police, who had him tied to a tree and whipped him with a switch while repeatedly asking the suspect where his accomplice was. Later in the afternoon, the suspect sat under the same tree, unfettered, along with his erstwhile tormentors, smiling and enjoying a cup of tea.

4. J. A. Wilson, "The Oath in Ancient Egypt," *Journal of Near Eastern Studies* 7 (1948): 136, 137.

5. D. Lorton, "The Treatment of Criminals in Ancient Egypt," *Journal of the Economic and Social History of the Orient* 20 (1978): 8.

6. Translation after Lichtheim, *Ancient Egyptian Literature*, 1:99–107.

7. H. Willems, "Crime, Cult, and Capital Punishment (Mo'alla Inscription 8)," *Journal of Egyptian Archaeology* 76 (1990): 50.

8. See D. B. Redford, *The Akhenaten Temple Project*, vol. 3, *The Excavation of Kom el-Ahmar and Environs* (Toronto: Akhenaten Temple Project, 1994), 14–15.

9. Willems, "Crime, Cult, and Capital Punishment," 34.

10. Translation after Lichtheim, *Ancient Egyptian Literature*, 3:161.

11. For this, the "trial of the century," only one of two places would have most surely served as a designated judgment hall: within the temple complex at Medinet Habu, or the environs of the great temple of Amun at Karnak on the east bank. The pillared courtyards of both these temples are documented as the sites of court hearings.

12. See the biography of Weni in chapter 3.

Epilogue

1. Translation after Breasted, *Ancient Records*, IV:412.

2. See A. Gardiner, "A Pharaonic Encomium," *Journal of Egyptian Archaeology*

42 (1955): 30; K. Jansen-Winkeln, "Die Wahl Des Königs Durch Orakel in Der 20. Dynastie," *Bulletin Société D'Égyptologie Genève* 23 (1999): 54.

3. The Wady Hammamat, a well-traveled route that connected the Nile Valley, 35 miles north of modern Luxor, with the Red Sea coast, was a major source of black granite.

4. KV3. See Reeves and Wilkinson, *Complete Valley of the Kings,* 161.

5. See Peden, *Reign of Ramesses IV,* 76.

6. See C. A. Keller, "Speculations concerning Interconnections between the Royal Policy and Reputation of Ramesses IV," in D. P Silverman, ed., *For His Ka: Essays Offered in Memory of Klaus Baer* (Chicago: Oriental Institute of the University of Chicago, 1994), 145ff.

7. The relationship of It-Amana Ramesses VII to Ramesses VI is not clearly established, although it is generally accepted that they were father and son. See the argument of Kitchen, "Ramessses VII and the Twentieth Dynasty," 182ff.

8. See Reeves and Wilkinson, *Complete Valley of the Kings,* 106.

9. Study and analysis of this prince's tomb in the Valley of the Kings is currently being undertaken by Edwin Brock.

10. See Kitchen, "Family Relationships of Ramesses IX," 127ff.

11. Oldfather, trans., *Diodorus Siculus,* I.63.1.

Bibliography

Aldred, C.

1963   The Parentage of King Siptah. *Journal of Egyptian Archaeology* 49:41ff.

Badawy, A.

1956   About Three Egyptian Hieroglyphs. *Journal of Near Eastern Studies* 15:75.

Bakir, A. M.

1966   *The Cairo Calendar, No. 86637.* General Organisation for Government Printing Offices, Cairo.

Batto, B. F.

1974   *Studies on Women at Mari.* Johns Hopkins University Press, Baltimore.

Berg, D.

1988   *The Genre of Non-Juridical Oracles (ḫrtw) in Ancient Egypt.* Unpublished Ph.D. dissertation, University of Toronto.

Berman, L. M.

1988   Overview of Amenhotep III and His Reign. In *Amenhotep III: Perspectives on His Reign,* edited by D. O'Connor and E. Cline, pp. 1ff. University of Michigan Press, Ann Arbor.

Bierbrier, M.

1972   A Second High Priest Ramessesnakht? *Journal of Egyptian Archaeology* 58:195ff.

Blackman, A. M.

1921   On the Position of Women in the Ancient Egyptian Hierarchy. *Journal of Egyptian Archaeology* 7:8ff.

Borghouts, J. F.

1978   *Ancient Egyptian Magical Texts.* Brill, Leiden.

Breasted, J. H.

1905   *The History of Egypt: From the Earliest Times to the Persian Conquest.* C. Scribner's Sons, New York.

1906   *Ancient Records of Egypt: Historical Documents from the Earliest Times to the Persian Conquest,* vol. IV, *The Twentieth to the Twenty-sixth Dynasties.* University of Chicago Press, Chicago.

Brier, B.

1994   *Egyptian Mummies: Unraveling the Secrets of an Ancient Art.* W. Morrow, New York.

Bryan, B.

1991   *The Reign of Thutmose IV.* Johns Hopkins University Press, Baltimore.

Caminos, R. A.

1954   *Late-Egyptian Miscellanies.* Oxford University Press, London.

Carter, H., and A. Gardiner.
  1917   The Tomb of Ramesses IV and the Turin Plan of a Royal Tomb. *Journal of Egyptian Archaeology* 4:130ff.
Černý, J.
  1935   *Catalogue des ostraca hiératiques non littéraires de Deir el Médineh,* vol. III. Institut Français d'Archéologie Orientale, Cairo.
  1936   Datum des Todes Ramesses III und er Thronbesteigung Ramesses IV. *Zeitschrift für Ägyptische Sprache und Altertumskunde* 72:109ff.
  1941   "The Temple," as an Abbreviated Name for the Temple of Medinet Habu. *Journal of Egyptian Archaeology* 26:127ff.
  1952   *Paper and Books in Ancient Egypt.* H. K. Lewis, London.
  1958   Queen Ēse of the Twentieth Dynasty and Her Mother. *Journal of Egyptian Archaeology* 44:31ff.
  1962   Egyptian Oracles. In *A Saite Oracle Papyrus from Thebes in the Brooklyn Museum (Papyrus Brooklyn 47.218.3),* edited by R. A. Parker, pp. 35ff. Brown University Press, Providence, R.I.
  1965   Egypt: From the Death of Ramesses III to the End of the Twenty-first Dynasty. In *The Cambridge Ancient History,* vol. II, pt. 2, chap. XXXV. Cambridge University Press, Cambridge.
Chabas, F.
  1867   Lettre de Mr. F. Chabas à Mr. Lepsius. *Zeitschrift für Ägyptische Sprache und Altertumskund* 5:76ff.
Champollion, J-F.
  1973[1844]   *Monuments de l'Egypte et de la Nubie: Notices Descriptives,* vol. I. Reprint. Éditions des Belles Lettres, Geneva.
D'Abbadie, J. V.
  1950   Un Monument Inédit de Ramsès VII au Musée du Louvre. *Journal of Near Eastern Studies* 9:134ff.
deBuck, A.
  1937   The Judicial Papyrus of Turin. *Journal of Egyptian Archaeology* 23:152ff.
Decker, W.
  1992   *Sports and Games of Ancient Egypt,* translated by A. Guttman. Yale University Press, New Haven, Conn.
Devéria, Th.
  1897   *Le Papyrus Judiciaire de Turin et Les Papyrus Lee et Rollin.* Ernest Leroux, Paris.
Dodson, A.
  1986   Was the Sarcophagus of Ramesses III Begun for Sethos II? *Journal of Egyptian Archaeology* 72:196ff.
  1987   The Takhats and Some Other Royal Ladies of the Ramesside Period. *Journal of Egyptian Archaeology* 73:224ff.
  1995   *Monarchs of the Nile.* Rubicon, London.
Drenkhahn, R.
  1976   Bemerkungen zu dem Titel ẖkrt-nsw. *Studien zur Altägyptischen Kultur* 4:57ff.

Drioton, E.

1939   Une statue prophylactique de Ramesses III. *Annales du Service des Antiquities de l'Egypte* 39:57ff.

Edgerton, W. F.

1951   The Strikes in Ramses III's Twenty-ninth Year. *Journal of Near Eastern Studies* 10:137ff.

El Mahdy, C.

1989   *Mummies, Myth, and Magic in Ancient Egypt.* Thames and Hudson, London.

Epigraphic Survey, Oriental Institute, University of Chicago

1930–1970   *Medinet Habu.* Vols. I–VIII. University of Chicago Press, Chicago.

1980   *The Tomb of Kheruef: Theban Tomb 192.* Oriental Institute of the University of Chicago, Chicago.

Erman, A.

1966   *The Ancient Egyptians: A Sourcebook of Their Writings,* translated by A. M. Blackman. Harper and Row, New York.

1971[1894]   *Life in Ancient Egypt,* translated by H. M. Tirard. Reprint. Dover, New York.

Faulkner, R. O.

1966   Egypt: From the Inception of the Nineteenth Dynasty to the Death of Ramesses III. In *The Cambridge Ancient History,* vol. II, pt. 2, chap. XXIII. Cambridge University Press, Cambridge.

Fèvre, F.

1992   *Le Dernier Pharaon: Ramsès III, ou, le crépuscule d'une civilisation.* Presses de la Renaissance, Paris.

Gaballa, G. A.

1973   Three Documents from the Reign of Ramesses III. *Journal of Egyptian Archaeology* 59:109ff.

Gardiner, A.

1918   The Delta Residence of the Ramessides. *Journal of Egyptian Archaeology* 5:179ff.

1948   *Ramesside Administrative Documents.* Oxford University Press, London.

1954   The Tomb of Queen Twosre. *Journal of Egyptian Archaeology* 40:40ff.

1955   A Pharaonic Encomium. *Journal of Egyptian Archaeology* 42:8ff.

1958   Only One King Siptah and Twosre Not His Wife. *Journal of Egyptian Archaeology* 44:12ff.

Gauthier, M. H.

1914   *Le Livre Des Rois D'Égypte,* vol. III, *De la XIXe à XXIVe dynastie.* Institut Français d'Archéologie Orientale 19, Cairo.

Ghalioungui, P.

1963   *Magic and Medical Science in Ancient Egypt.* Hodder and Stoughton, London.

Goedicke, H.

1963   Was Magic Used in the Harem Conspiracy against Ramesses III? *Journal of Egyptian Archaeology* 49:71ff.

Grandet, P.
1993   *Ramsès III: Histoire d'un Règne.* Pygmalion/G. Watelet, Paris.
1994   *Papyrus Harris I: BM9999.* Vols. 1–2. Institut Français d'Archéologie Orientale, Cairo.

Grayson, A. K.
1976   *Assyrian Royal Inscriptions,* vol. I, pt. 2. Harrassowitz, Wiesbaden.

Griffith, F.
1927   The Abydo Decree of Seti I at Nauri. *Journal of Egyptian Archaeology* 13:193ff.

Grist, J.
1982   The Identity of the Ramesside Queen Tyti. *Journal of Egyptian Archaeology* 71:71ff.

Groll, S.
1980   The Stenographic Style of Papyrus Lee, Papyrus Rollin, Papyrus Varzy, and the Judicial Papyrus of Turin. In *The Bible World: Essays in Honor of Cyrus H. Gordon,* edited by G. Rendsburg, R. Adler, M. Arfa, and N. H. Winter, pp. 77ff. Ktav, New York.

Green, L.
1988   *Queens and Princesses of the Amarna Period: The Social, Political, Religious, and Cultic role of the Women of the Royal Family at the End of the Eighteenth Dynasty.* Unpublished Ph.D. dissertation, University of Toronto.

Harris, J., and E. Wente.
1980   *An X-Ray Atlas of the Royal Mummies.* University of Chicago Press, Chicago.

Helck, W.
1957   *Urkunden der 18. Dynastie,* vol. IV:1738. Akademie-Verlag, Berlin.

Hölscher, U.
1929   Architectural Survey of the Great Temple and Palace of Medinet Habu (Seasons 1927–28). *University of Chicago, Oriental Institute Communications.* Chicago.
1941   *The Excavation of Medinet Habu,* vol. III, *The Mortuary Temple of Ramses III, part I,* translated by K. C. Seele. Oriental Institute of the University of Chicago, Chicago.
1951   *The Excavation of Medinet Habu,* vol. IV, *The Mortuary Temple of Ramses III, part II,* translated by E. B. Hauser. Oriental Institute of the University of Chicago, Chicago.

Jankuhn, D.
1974   *Bibliographie Der Hieratischen und Hieroglyphischen Papyri.* Göttinger Orientforschungen, IV, band 2. Harrassowitz, Wiesbaden.

Jansen-Winkeln, K.
1999   Die Wahl Des Königs Durch Orakel in Der 20. Dynastie. *Bulletin Société D'Égyptologie Genève* 23:51ff.

Kadish, G.
1969   Eunuchs in Ancient Egypt? In *Studies in Honor of John A. Wilson,* intro-

duced by G. Kadish, pp. 55ff. University of Chicago Press, Chicago.

Keller, C. A.
1994   Speculations concerning Interconnections between the Royal Policy and Reputation of Ramesses IV. In *For His Ka: Essays Offered in Memory of Klaus Baer*, edited by D. P. Silverman, pp. 145ff. Oriental Institute of the University of Chicago, Chicago.

Kemp, B. J.
1978   The Harim-Palace at Medinet el-Ghurab. *Zeitschrift für Ägyptische Sprache und Altertumskunde* 105:122ff.

Kieckhefer, R.
1989   *Magic in the Middle Ages.* Cambridge University Press, Cambridge.

Kitchen, K. A.
1968–1990   *Ramesside Inscriptions: Historical and Biographical.* 7 vols. Blackwell, Oxford.
1972   Ramessses VII and the Twentieth Dynasty. *Journal of Egyptian Archaeology* 58:182ff.
1982a   *Pharaoh Triumphant: The Life and Times of Ramesses II, King of Egypt.* Aris & Phillips, Warminster.
1982b   The Twentieth Dynasty Revisited. *Journal of Egyptian Archaeology* 68:116ff.
1984   Family Relationships of Ramesses IX and the Late Twentieth Dynasty. *Studien Zur Altägyptischen Kultur* 11:127ff.
1985   Review of J. Harris and E. Wente, *An X-Ray Atlas of the Royal Mummies. Journal of Near Eastern Studies* 14:235ff.

Koenig, Y.
1989   Nouveaux textes Rifaud II (document E). *Cahier de Recherches l'Institut de Papyrologie et d'Égyptologie de Lille* 11:53ff.

Leblanc, C.
1989a   *Ta Set Neferou: Une nécropole de Thèbes-ouest et son histoire,* vol. I. C. Leblanc, Cairo.
1989b   Architecture et Évolution Chronologique Des Tombs De La Vallée Des Reines. *Bulletin de l'Institut Français D'Archéologie Orientaledu Caire* 89:227ff.

Leahy, A.
1984   Death by Fire in Ancient Egypt. *Journal of the Economic and Social History of the Orient* 27:199ff.

Leonowens, A.
1991[1873]   *The Romance of the Harem,* edited and introduced by S. Morgan. University Press of Virginia, Charlottesville.

Lichtheim, M.
1973–1980   *Ancient Egyptian Literature: A Book of Readings.* 3 vols. University of California Press, Berkeley.

Lorton, D.
1974   The Treatment of Criminals in Ancient Egypt. *Journal of the Economic and Social History of the Orient* 20:2ff.

1995   Legal and Social Institutions of Pharaonic Egypt. In *Civilizations of the Ancient Near East,* vol. 1, edited by J. M. Sasson, pp. 355ff. Scribner, New York.

McDowell, A. G.
1990   *Jurisdiction in the Workmen's Community of Deir el-Medina.* Nederlands Instituut voor het Nabije Oosten, Leiden.

Malamat, A.
1995   Is There A Word for the Royal Harem in the Bible? In *Pomegranates and Golden Bells: Studies in Biblical, Jewish, and Near Eastern Ritual, Law, and Literature in Honor of Jacob Milgrom,* edited by D. Freedman, A. Hurvitz, and D. Wright, pp. 785ff. Eisenbrauns, Winona Lake, Ind.

Maspero, G.
1889   *Les Momies royales de Dèir el-Bahari.* E. Leroux, Paris.

Manniche, L.
1989   *An Ancient Egyptian Herbal.* University of Texas Press, Austin.

Meek, T. J.
1969a   The Code of Hammurabi. In *Ancient Near Eastern Texts: Relating to the Old Testament,* edited by J. B. Pritchard, pp. 163ff. Princeton University Press, Princeton, N.J.
1969b   Middle Assyrian Laws. In *Ancient Near Eastern Texts: Relating to the Old Testament,* edited by J. B. Pritchard, pp. 180ff. Princeton University Press, Princeton, N.J.

Mertz, B.
1964   *Temples, Tombs, and Hieroglyphs: The Story of Egyptology.* Coward-McCann, New York.

Mojsov, B.
1992   *The Sculpture and Relief of Ramesses III.* Unpublished Ph.D. dissertation, New York University.

Monnet, J.
1965   Remarques sur la famille et les successeurs de Rameses III. *Bulletin de l' Institut Français d'Archéologie Orientale* 63:209ff.

Moran, W.
1992   *The Amarna Letters.* Johns Hopkins University Press, Baltimore.

Murnane, W.
1971–1972   The "King Ramesses" of the Medinet Habu Procession of Princes. *Journal of the American Research Center in Egypt* 9:121ff.
1980   *United with Eternity: A Concise Guide to the Monuments of Medinet Habu.* University of Chicago Press, Chicago.

Nord, D.
1970   *ḥkrt-nsw* = king's concubine? *Serapis* 2:1ff.

Oldfather, C. H., trans.
1968   *Diodorus Siculus: The Library of History.* Vol. 1. Loeb Classical Library Series, Harvard University Press, Cambridge, Mass.

Oren, E.
2000   *The Sea Peoples and Their World: A Reassessment.* University Museum, University of Pennsylvania, Philadelphia.

Parker, R. A.

1962   *A Saite Oracle Papyrus from Thebes in the Brookleyn Museum (Papyrus Brooklyn 47.218.3).* Brown University Press, Providence, R.I.

Parkinson, R., S. Quirke, and U. Wartenberg.

1995   *Papyrus.* University of Texas Press, Austin.

Partridge, R.

1994   *Faces of Pharaohs: Royal Mummies and Coffins from Ancient Thebes.* Rubicon, London.

Peden, A. J.

1994   *The Reign of Ramesses IV.* Aris & Phillips, Warminster.

Peet, T. E.

1928   The Chronological Problems of the Twentieth Dynasty. *Journal of Egyptian Archaeology* 14:52ff.

1930   *The Great Tomb-Robberies of the Twentieth Dynasty: Being a Critical Study, with Translations and Commentaries, of the Papyri in Which These Are Recorded.* 2 vols. Clarendon Press, Oxford.

Penzer, N. M.

1974[1937]   *The Harēm: An Account of the Institution as It Existed in the Palace of the Turkish Sultans of the Grand Seraglio from Its Foundation to the Present Time.* Reprint. AMS Press, New York.

Pleyte, W., and F. Rossi

1981[1869–1876]   *Papyrus de Turin.* Reprint. LTR-Verlag, Wiesbaden.

Pinch, G.

1994   *Magic in Ancient Egypt.* University of Texas Press, Austin.

Porter, B., and R. Moss

1964   *Topographical Bibliography of Ancient Egyptian Hieroglyphic Texts, Reliefs, and Paintings,* vol. I, *The Theban Necropolis.* Clarendon Press, Oxford.

1972   *Topographical Bibliography of Ancient Egyptian Hieroglyphic Texts, Reliefs, and Paintings,* vol. II, *The Theban Temples.* Clarendon Press, Oxford.

Quirke, S.

1992   *Ancient Egyptian Religion.* British Museum Press, London.

Ranke, H.

1935   *Die Ägyptischen Personennamen,* vol. I. J. J. Augustin, Glückstadt.

Redford, D. B.

1984   *Akhenaten, the Heretic King.* Princeton University Press, Princeton, N.J.

1994   *The Akhenaten Temple Project,* vol. 3, *The Excavation of Kom el-Ahmar and Environs.* Akhenaten Temple Project, Toronto.

1997   The War Reliefs at Medinet Habu. *Akhenaten Temple Project Newsletter,* no. 2 (May).

2000   New Kingdom History: Overview. In *The Sea Peoples and Their World: A Reassessment,* edited by E. Oren, pp. 1ff. University Musuem, University of Pennsylvania, Philadelphia.

Redford, S.

1992   The Women of the Royal Harim. *Bulletin of the Canadian Mediterranean Institute* 12:7.

1993   Ramesses III and the Women of the Royal Harim. *Bulletin of the Cana-dian Society for Mesopotamian Studies* 26:39ff.

2000   The Valley of the Queens. In *The Oxford Encyclopedia of Ancient Egypt,* edited by D. B. Redford, pp. 474ff. Oxford University Press, New York.

Reeves, C. N., and R. H. Wilkinson

1996   *The Complete Valley of the Kings: Tombs and Treasures of Egypt's Greatest Pharaohs.* Thames and Hudson, London.

Reiser-Haslauer, E.

1972   *Der königliche Harim im alten Ägypten und seine Verwaltung.* Verl. Notring, Vienna.

Rifaud, J. J.

1834   *Voyage en Égypte, et en Nubie, et lieux circonvoisins: depuis 1805 jusqu'en 1827.* Bibliographie de la France, Paris.

Ritner, R.

1993   *The Mechanics of Ancient Egyptian Magical Practice.* Oriental Institute of the University of Chicago, Chicago.

Robins, G.

1981a   The value of the estimated ages of the royal mummies at death as historical evidence. *Göttinger Miszelle* 45:63ff.

1981b   *ḥmt-nsw wrt* Meritaton. *Gottinger Miszellen* 52:75ff.

1983   A Critical Examination of the Theory that the Right to the Throne of Ancient Egypt Passed through the Female Line in the 18th Dynasty. *Göttinger Miszellen* 62:67ff.

1993   *Women In Ancient Egypt.* British Museum Press, London.

Rolfe, J., trans.

1998   *Aulus Gellius: Attic Nights.* Books VI–XIII. Loeb Classical Library Series, Harvard University Press, Cambridge, Mass.

Sauneron, S., and J. Yoyotte

1952   Le Texte Hieratique Rifaud. *Bulletin de l' Institut Français d'Archéologie Orientale* 50:102ff.

Schadel, H.

1938   Der Regierunganstritt Ramses IV. *Zeitschrift für Ägyptische Sprache und Altertumskunde* 74:36ff.

Schulman, A. R.

1964   *Military Rank, Title, and Organization in the Egyptian New Kingdom.* B. Hessling, Berlin.

Scott, N.

1976   *The Daily Life of the Ancient Egyptians.* Metropolitan Museum of Art, New York.

Seele, K. C.

1955   Some Remarks on the Family of Ramesses III. *Ägyptologische Studien Hermann Grapow zum 70. Geburtstag gewidmet,* edited by O. Firchow, pp. 296ff. Akademie-Verlag, Berlin.

1960   Ramesses VI and the Medinet Habu Procession of the Princes. *Journal of Near Eastern Studies* 19:184ff.

Seibert, I.
1974   *Women in the Ancient Near East,* translated by M. Herzfeld, revised by
        G. Shepperson. Abner Schram, New York.
Simpson, W. K.
1972   *The Literature of Ancient Egypt: An Anthology of Stories, Instructions, and
        Poetry.* With translations by R. O. Faulkner, W. K. Simpson, and E. F.
        Wente, Jr. Yale University Press, New Haven, Conn.
Smith, G. E.
1912   *The Royal Mummies.* Institut Français d'Archéologie Orientale, Cairo.
Spawls, S.
1995   *The Dangerous Snakes of Africa: Natural History, Species Directory, Ven-
        oms, and Snakebite.* Blandford, London.
Spencer, A. J.
1982   *Death in Ancient Egypt.* Penguin, Harmondsworth and New York.
Stadelmann, R.
1994   Royal Palaces of the Late New Kingdom. In *Essays in Egyptology in
        Honor of Hans Goedicke,* edited by B. Bryan and D. Lorton, pp. 309ff.
        Van Siclen, San Antonio, Tex.
Troy, L.
1986   *Patterns of Queenship in Ancient Egyptian Myth and History.* Almquist &
        Wiksell, Uppsala.
U.S. Department of the Navy
1991[1966]   *Poisonous Snakes of the World.* Reprint. Dover, New York.
Van Siclen, C.
1974   A Ramesside Ostracon of Queen Isis. *Journal of Near Eastern Studies* 33:150ff.
Vercoutter, J.
1992   *The Search for Ancient Egypt.* H. N. Abrams, New York.
Von Beckerath, J.
1962   Queen Twosre as Guardian of Siptah. *Journal of Egyptian Archaeology* 48:70ff.
Weidner, W.
1954–1956   Hof- und Harems-Erlasse assyrischer Konige aus dem 2.
        Jahrtausend v. Chr. *Archiv für Orientforschung* 70:257ff.
Wilkinson, R. H.
1992   *Reading Egyptian Art: A Hieroglyphic Guide to Ancient Egyptian Painting
        and Sculpture.* Thames and Hudson, London.
1995   *Valley of the Sun Kings: New Explorations in the Tombs of the Pharaohs.*
        University of Arizona Egyptian Expedition, Tucson.
Willems, H.
1990   Crime, Cult, and Capital Punishment (Mo'alla Inscription 8). *Journal
        of Egyptian Archaeology* 76:27ff.
Wilson, J. A.
1948   The Oath in Ancient Egypt. *Journal of Near Eastern Studies* 7:129ff.
Yoyotte, J.
1958   The Tomb of a Prince Ramesses in the Valley of the Queens (No. 53).
        Journal of Egyptian Archaeology 44:26ff.

Index

Abu Simbel, 56
Abydos, 139
Adi-ram, 19, 86
adultery, 121, 126
Aegean, xxi, 28
Ahmose, 64
Ahmose-Nefertari, 64–65, 107
Akhenaten, xiv–xv, 56, 66, 71, 136
Akhet, 147
Alalak, 29
altar, 125
Amanakhopshaf, 35, 36, 38, 40, 41, 42, 43, 44, 87, 137, 138, 140
Amanemwis, 88
Amankhau, 16, 24, 130
Amarna, xv
Amenemhet I, 68, 83
Amenhotep I, 65
Amenhotep II, 57
Amenhotep III, xiv, 54, 56, 59, 62, 65, 66, 92, 107, 108
Amenmesse, xxi
Amorite, xii
Amun(re), 21, 26, 92, 93, 99
Amun: harem of, 61; high priest of, 62, 136, 138, 140, 141; priesthood of, 92, 136; servant of, 72; temple of, xix, xx, 38
"Amun-Endowed-with-Eternity," 128
Amurru, 29
animal sacrifice, 124
Ankhsheshonq. *See Instructions of Ankhsheshonq, The*
apartments, king's, 101
Apollonia, Saint, 111
Apophis, 111
"Arabian Nights," 49

Arabs, 58
Arad-ninlil, 69
archives, 117
Arinna, xvi
armed guard, 18
Armenia, 28
army, xv, xix, 9, 17, 23, 83, 84, 85, 93, 128, 134, 135, 139
aromatics, 51
artisans, xx
Arvad, 29
Arzawa, 56
Ashhebsat, 14, 24, 127–28
Ashurbanipal, 69
Asia Minor, 28, 88
assassination, 7, 10, 22, 67–68, 88, 113
Assyria, xv, 50, 58, 69, 70, 118, 120–21, 124, 125; laws of, 124
Atef-crown, 26
Atum, 26, 98
audience hall, 101, 103
Avaris, 89
Aye, 62

Baal, 88
Babylon, xiv, xvii, 56, 57–58, 118
Baghdad, 49
bailiff, 10, 17, 120, 128, 130
balcony, 100
Balkans, 28
Banebdjed, 34
Barga, xvii
barge, royal, 91
bark: portable, 77, 122, 123; royal, 9, 21, 74, 79, 106, 109, 111
bastinado, 118, 119, 120
bathroom, 101

beating, 117–20, 124, 128
Beni Hassan, 120
Beya, xxi
bi3yt, 122
body count, 100
Bonemwese, 9, 15, 16, 21, 23, 46, 84, 85, 86, 127, 128, 129, 130, 134
branding iron, 18, 19
brazier, 124, 125, 126, 129, 130, 131
Breasted, James Henry, 34
Bubastis, 80
burial, 76
butler, 14, 16, 17, 22, 23–25, 32, 73, 75, 81, 83, 86, 112, 128, 129, 130

Cairo Calendar, 108–9
calendar, 147, 148
Canaan, 86, 118
Canaanites, xiv, xxi, 46, 77
captives, xxi
Carchemish, 29
carriages, 70
Carter, Howard, 60
castor oil plant, 110
cattle, xiii, 19, 23, 51, 74, 76, 77, 127
cataract, xxi
Censorinus, 148
children, royal, 36–37, 87–88
Christ, 125
city wall, 125
Cleopatra, 112
cobra, 112
coffin, 132
coiffure, 53
concubines, 32, 70
conspiracy, 64; harem, 3, 5, 9, 34, 71, 75, 76, 78, 81, 83, 85, 86, 93, 98, 104, 121, 125, 126, 129, 132
conspirators, 5, 35, 72, 75, 110, 113, 126, 127, 133, 138; arrest of, 128
copper, xx, 30
coronation, 92, 104
cosmetics, 52
court protocol, 71
court record, 4

creation, mound of, 100
crocodiles, 121, 130
crown prince, 9, 38, 40, 42, 43, 44, 69, 134, 136, 137, 138, 139, 140
crucifixion, 125
Cyclades, 28
Cyprus, 28, 29

dancing, 52
Darius, 70
daybooks, 9, 115
days, epogomenal, 147
decapitation, 123, 126
defense, legal, 22
Deir el-Bahri, 107, 116, 131
Deir el-Medineh, 105, 107, 109
Delta, xix, xxi, 7, 26, 30, 32, 34, 78, 80, 89, 93, 110, 125, 128, 140, 141
Diodorus, 62, 87, 117, 141
disease, 79
Djame, 94
Djehuty-rekh-nafa, 11, 15, 129
document, authorizing, 76
Drovetti, B., 5

economy, 30, 47, 72
Edfu, 124
Eighteenth Dynasty, xii, xv, xix, 92
Eleventh Dynasty, 51
"Eloquent Peasant, The," 120
embalming, 115, 126, 132
embezzlement, 141
empire, xiii, xix, 138
Esarhaddon, 69
Ese Ta-Habazillatu, 32, 34, 35, 38, 40, 41, 44, 45, 67, 87, 138
Eski Serai, 57
eunuchs, 58, 70
Euphrates, xii
execution, 23–25, 117, 125, 128, 129, 137; block, 123

faience, 52
Faiyum, 51
fan bearer, 38, 40, 42, 43, 44

fire, death by, 124, 126, 128, 129
First Dynasty, 117
folktale, 54
foreigners, xx
funeral procession, 115
funerary papyri, 126
furnace, 124, 125, 128
furniture, 52

Galen, 112
garden, 98
garrison, xiv, xix, 85
gate, of city, 125
gatekeepers, 128
Gaza, 29
Geb, 26
Gebel Silsileh, 77
general, 83, 84, 127
generation-levies, 32
god(s): abomination of, 121; statue of,
    122, 128
gold, xiii–xiv
grain, xxi, 30, 104
Great Harris Papyrus, xx, 92, 106, 107,
    109, 114, 133
Greek Islands, 27–28

Habazillatu, 32, 34
Hall of Judgment, 128, 130
Hammurabi, 118, 119, 121
hands, severed, 100
Harakhte, 26
harem, xx, 6, 7–8, 10, 13–14, 16, 17,
    19, 23–25, 34, 37, 46, 47, 59, 60, 67,
    68, 71, 76, 86, 93, 99, 110, 113,
    114, 129, 131, 133; agent of, 25, 76,
    86, 129; apartments of, 96–98; gate
    of, 86, 127, 129; overseer of, 51;
    Persian, 52; Turkish, 53–54, 69;
    wives of, 86
harper songs, 52
harpist, 52
Harsiese, 126
Hathor, prophetess of, 62
Hatshepsut, 65, 66, 116, 131

Hattusas, xvi
Hattusilis, xvi, xvii
healing, 81, 111, 112
Hebrews, 29
Heb-sed, 92
Heliopolis, xvi, 26, 44, 88, 91, 93, 111
hell, Christian, 126
herald, first, 71, 88, 128
herds, overseer of, 19
Herodotus, 64
hieratic, 5, 106
high priests, xxi
Hittite(s), xv, xvi, xvii, 28, 99; law, 119
ḫkrwt-nsw, 53
ḥmt-nsw (wrt), 54–57, 63
Hnetenamana, 16, 24, 130
ḫnr, 61
ḫnrt, 50
ḫnrt-nsw-šmsw, 70
Horemheb, xv
Hori, 11, 13, 17, 25, 80, 128, 130
horoscopes, 108
Horus, 111
House of Life, 16, 21, 82, 83, 112, 129,
    134
ḥr-ḫnw-ḫnỉ, 115
ḥsyt-nsw, 53
hunting, 70
Hurri-warriors, xii
ḥwt wr, 120
Hyksos, xi, xix, 64–65, 91

impalement, 123, 124, 125, 126
incense burner, 122
Indo-European, xii
Instructions of Ankhsheshonq, The, 125,
    126–27
interrogation, 119, 120
inundation, xxi, 147
ỉpt, 50
iron, 30
Isis, 111
Israel, 58
Istnofret, 38
It-amana, 138

Iyroy, 16, 24, 79, 81, 83, 85, 93, 129;
    tomb of, 80

Jerusalem, 125
jewelry, 52
jubilee, 56
judges, 10
Judicial Papyrus of Turin, 3, 4, 8, 9, 10,
    34, 58, 76, 80, 117

Kadashman-enlil, 57–58
Kadesh, xii, xv
Kara, 11, 13, 88, 93, 128
Karnak, 38, 125, 136, 140
Karpusa, 14, 24
Kedendenna, 11, 15, 88, 128
Khaemmalu, 14, 25
Khaemope, 14, 25
Khamwese, 35, 38, 42, 44, 45, 139
Khartum, xiii
khato land, xx
Khepri, 98, 111
Kheruef, 56, 58, 108
Khonsu, 61
Khosrau I, 69
king: children of, 70, 71, 98, 100;
    daughter of, 98; killing of, 67;
    mother of, 63, 70; nurse of, 62;
    ornament of, 59, 62; "right-hand"
    men of, 71; scribe of, xviii, 40, 42,
    43, 77, 78, 80, 87; son of, 23, 44,
    135; speeches of, 100
kiosks, 99
kitchen, palace, 74
Kiya, 56
Kode, 29
Kush, xiii, xviii, 15, 23, 35

labor, forced, 117
lake, 66
landholding, xix, xx
law, 117, 118, 129
lector priest, 81, 113, 122
legitimacy, 70
librarians, royal, 8, 25, 128, 130

library, 8, 24, 82, 83
Libyans, xxi, 15, 27, 30, 73, 99, 141
lion, 111
Lucy, Saint, 111
Luxor, 36, 94
Lycian, 73

Maadje, 22
magic, 8, 10, 18, 21, 23, 24, 74, 76,
    109, 111, 112, 113, 130; books of,
    79, 83, 113
magician, 16, 79, 81, 122
Maharbaal, 11, 15, 88, 129
Mahu, 20
Mai, 10–11, 13, 17, 25, 57–58, 88, 93,
    128, 129, 130
Maiamana, 38, 42, 44
Maiaria, 75
mandrake, 110
Mantemtowa, 11, 88, 93, 128
Mantikhopshef, 38, 42, 44, 139, 140
Mari, 50
marines, 88
marriage: diplomatic, xiv, xvii, 21;
    incestuous, 64
Mastesuria, 8, 13, 15, 23, 73, 75–76,
    77, 110, 128
Mayatas-amana, 16, 17, 88
medical books, 110
Medinet Habu, 94–95, 98, 104, 105,
    107, 114, 115, 128, 135, 138
Mediterranean, xix
Medjay, 21, 85, 119
Megiddo, xii
Memphis, xviii, 44, 74, 89, 90, 92, 134
Mendes, 34, 125
"menfat," 41, 42
merchants, xiv
Merenptah, xxi
Merenre-Antyemzaef, 64
Mereruka, 118
Merikare, 122
Meritaten, 56
Mertisiamun, 130
Meshwesh, xxi, 27

Mesopotamia, xii, 56
Messui, 8, 16, 24, 79, 83
Min, 37, 38, 100
mine land, xx
miracle, 122
mirrors, 52
misogyny, 37, 63
"mistress of the house," 62
Mitanni/Mitannians, xii, xiii, xiv, xv
Mi-wer, 51, 57, 91
monotheism, xv
Montu, 26, 61
mortality, 63
mortuary temple, 37–38, 77, 84, 90,
    93, 94, 99, 100, 101, 123, 137
murder, 119
Mushki, 28–29
musical troupe, 61
mutilation, 17, 25, 118, 119, 128, 130

Naneu, 17, 25, 130
natron, 122
necropolis, xviii, 137
Nefertari, 56
Nefertiti, 56, 67, 71
Neferura, 65
New Year's Day, 148
Nibdjatfe, 16, 24, 83, 112
nightshade, 110
Nile, 89, 91, 94, 139
Nineteenth Dynasty, xv, xxi, 35, 114
Ninurta-tukulti-ashur, 69
Nitocris, 64
nobility, xviii
Nubia, xi, 46, 65, 84, 93, 99
Nubkheshed, 138
nursery: children of, xviii; royal, 87

oasis, 27
oath, xiv, xvi 19, 119
officers, administrative, 104
Onias, 90
oracle, 19, 77, 122, 136
ordeal, 120, 126
Osiris, 9, 11, 26, 36, 139

Osorkon, chronicle of, 124, 126
ostracon, 122

Pabasa, 10, 11, 13, 17, 20, 25, 88, 128,
    129, 130
Paerswana, 11, 15, 128
Pahamnata, 84
Paibakamana, 8, 13, 14, 15, 16, 18,
    23–24, 72–73, 74, 76, 77, 81, 83, 93,
    110, 127, 128, 134, 135
Pairy, 8, 15, 17, 23, 24, 76, 77, 78, 79,
    84, 93, 94, 104, 128, 129, 130
palace, royal, 100–4, 126
palanquin, 38, 71
Palestine, 28–29, 57
Panhayboni, 8, 19, 23–24, 76, 77, 78,
    81, 122, 127, 128
Panibenkeme, 138
Panouk, 8, 13, 15, 23, 73, 76, 112, 128
Papyrus Lee, 3, 4, 5, 9, 19, 22, 76, 78,
    81, 83, 86, 98, 112, 119
Papyrus Mayer, 117, 119
Papyrus Rifaud, 3, 5, 9, 20, 21, 22, 74,
    79, 80, 83, 84, 85, 86, 106, 109,
    111, 113, 127, 134
Papyrus Rollin, 3, 4, 5, 74, 81, 112
Papyrus Varzy, 3, 4, 19, 77, 78, 128
Paramesses, xv
Parennuta, 11, 130
Pasai, 9, 10, 16, 17, 23, 46, 79, 83, 84,
    85, 86, 93, 113, 127, 129
peasantry, xxi
Pefrawa, 11, 128
Peloponnese, 28
Peluka, 14, 24, 73, 104, 127, 128
Pelusiac branch, 89, 90, 91
penima, 50
Pentau, 8, 13, 23, 73, 76, 128
Pentawere, 7, 16, 23, 24, 34, 35, 36, 37,
    40, 44, 79, 83, 84, 85, 86, 87, 88, 93,
    114, 129, 130, 131, 134, 137, 139
Pepy I, 68
Pepy II, 64
perjury, 119
Petewentamana, 13, 24

phalluses, severed, 100
Pharaoh, xviii; fields of, xx
Philistines (Peleset), 28–29
ph-nṯr, 77, 122, 128
Phrygia, 28
physician, 81, 118, 126, 129
Pi-Ramesses, xviii, 7, 89, 90, 91, 92, 93,
   106, 134
plague, 139
poison, 109–10, 113, 130
police, chief of, 10, 17, 25, 30, 130
poliomyelitis, 139
pool, 99
poppy, 110
Pre-emheb, 11, 88, 93, 130
Prehiwonmef, 35, 38, 42, 44
Prekaminef, 8, 16, 23, 79, 81, 83, 129
priests, xix, 84, 122, 123, 124
prime minister, 31, 75
princes: scenes of, 37–39, 100, 138;
   costume of, 42
princesses, 71; foreign, 56, 58
prisoners-of-war, 73, 100
prophesying, 77
Proyet, 147
Ptah, 26; high priest of, 44
punishment, 117ff, 126
purification, 122

Qantir, 80, 90
quarries, 136
queen, 25, 32, 64, 68, 69, 70, 71, 103;
   house of, xx
Quintus Curtius Rufus, 70

racism, 129
Ramesses I, xv
Ramesses II, xc, xvi, xxi, 31, 37, 38, 44,
   49, 56, 69, 75, 84, 89, 91, 136
Ramesses III, xx, xxii, 3, 7, 9, 10, 20,
   21, 22, 26, 29, 30, 34, 37, 38, 43,
   44, 49, 51, 57, 60, 67, 69, 71, 73, 80,
   85, 87, 89, 90, 91, 92, 94, 104, 105,
   107, 113, 121, 126, 132, 137; accession of, 27; age of, 107; burial of,
   114, 115; butlers of, 75; coffin of,
   107, 115; death of, 105ff, 107, 108,
   110, 112, 113, 128, 134, 140, 141;
   military campaigns of, 99; mummy
   of, 55, 106, 107, 115, 131; prayer of,
   133; as protector, 111; sarcophagus
   of, 40, 116; sons of, 35, 36, 87, 114,
   139, 141; speeches of, 32; tomb of,
   114, 115
Ramesses IV, 9, 21, 31, 38, 86, 88, 93,
   105, 106, 107, 133, 134, 135, 136,
   137, 138, 141; ill health of, 137; sarcophagus of, 137
Ramesses V, 44, 51, 137, 138, 139, 141
Ramesses VI, 32, 34, 36, 38, 40, 42, 88,
   126, 137, 138
Ramesses VII, 138, 141; sarcophagus
   of, 139
Ramesses VIII, 38, 42, 43, 139
Ramesses IX, 44, 126, 139, 140, 141
Ramesses X, 140
Ramesses XI, 140, 141
Re, xvii, 9, 18, 20, 21, 22, 26, 44, 75,
   86, 88, 91, 106, 111
rebellion, Theban, 124
regicide, 25, 64, 81, 93, 106
Rekhmire, 120
reliefs, military, 99–100
Rhinocolura, 118
Rhodes, 28
Rifaud, 5
Ruma, 77

Saqqara, 74
Sardinia, 29
Sea Peoples, xxi, 27–28, 29, 30, 99
seal, royal, 78–79
Sekhmet, 20, 79; priests of, 16, 21, 24,
   80, 81, 85, 112
Sennacherib, 69
Sesi, 98
Sesostris I, 68, 87, 124
Seth, 78
Sethnakhte, xxii, 26, 67, 87, 114
Sety I, xv, 49, 69, 87

Sety II, xxi, xxii
sexual responsibilities, 69–70
sharecroppers, xxi
Sharon, 29
Shomu, 105, 106, 107, 147
Shotmaadje, 8, 16, 24
Sicily, 29
silver, 30
Sinai, 118
singing, 52, 61, 98
Sinuhe, 69
Siptah, xxii
Sirius, 147, 148
sistrum, 61
Sit-amana, 66
slaves, 73, 100
smallpox, 134, 137, 139
Smendes, 141
snake charmer, 112
snakes, 109, 110, 111, 112, 113
Sneferu, 60
sorcery, 121
Sothic cycle, 106, 148
Sothis, 124, 147
špst wrt, 54
statue, 77
stela, 136, 137
strikes, 30
suicide, 20, 23–24
Sun-disc, xiv
sun god, xviii, 67, 98
sun temples, xv
Sutakhopshaf, 36, 38, 42, 43, 44, 87, 139, 140
Sutemhab, 18, 78
Sutempiamana, 14, 25, 86
Sutempidjehuty, 14, 25, 86

Tanis, 90
Tawosret, xxii, 67
taxes, xiii, xv, xx, xxi, 31, 117
Taynakhte, 17, 25, 130
Tell el-Yehudiyeh, 90
temple estates, xix, xx, 121
temples, xix, 125

Tenth Dynasty, 122
Teya, 7, 8, 10, 13, 16, 23, 25, 34, 36, 37, 40, 42, 44, 45, 46, 51, 58, 64, 65, 66, 67, 72, 73, 76, 79, 93, 104, 113, 114, 130, 133, 139, 141
Teya-maienese, 26
Thebes, xi, 7, 26, 27, 30, 31, 37, 44, 67, 67, 77, 78, 85, 89, 90, 91, 92, 93, 94, 104, 106, 113, 136, 140, 141; mayor of, 62; rebellion of, 125–26
Thoth, 61
throne room, 101–2
Thutmose II, 65
Thutmose III, xii, 63
tomb(s): desecration of, 118, 131; king's, 93, 95, 137, 139; robberies of, 116f, 121, 123, 141; Theban, 75; size of, 74, 137; walls of, 126
torture, 119
transcripts, court, 10, 31, 73, 77, 86, 127, 129, 132
treason, 121
treasury: scribe of, 24; overseer of, 76, 77, 78, 93; superintendent of, 15, 20, 23, 128
treaties, xiii, xvi, xvii
trial, scene of, 120
tuberculosis, 139
tubqum, 50
Turkey, 49, 56, 58
Tutankhamun, 114
Twelfth Dynasty, 117
Twentieth Dynasty, 26, 34, 35, 114
Twenty-first Dynasty, 107, 123
Twenty-second Dynasty, 123
Twenty-sixth Dynasty, 126

Ugarit, 28–29
underworld, 126
Upper Egypt, 92

Valley of the Kings, 114, 137, 138, 139, 140
Valley of the Queens, 35, 36, 37, 43, 44, 59, 60, 136, 138

viceroy, xiii, xviii
vineyards, 98
viper, 112

Wady Hammamat, 136
Wahibre-Makhy, 127
Warona, 14, 24, 73, 127, 128
Wawat, xiii
wax figures, 18, 19, 81, 112, 113
wb3, 75
weavers, 51, 57
Weny, 68, 129
West Semitic, 32
wet nurse, royal, 62
wife, 62, 63

Wilbour Papyrus, xx
window of appearance, 101, 103
windows, 96
wine, 75
women, 30, 37, 49, 70, 71, 76, 98, 99, 120, 124; as captives, 67; costume of, 51; foreign, 57; legal position of, 130; statues of, 61–63
wounds, 118
wrestling, 103

Yeniny, 15, 24, 73, 127, 128

Zimri-lim, 57